Water resources: issues and strategies

## THEMES IN RESOURCE MANAGEMENT
### Edited by Professor Bruce Mitchell, University of Waterloo

**Already published**
John Blunden: Mineral resources and their management
John Chapman: Geography and energy: Commercial energy systems and national policies
Paul Eagles: The planning and management of environmentally sensitive areas
R. L. Heathcote: Arid lands: their use and abuse
**Adrian McDonald** and **David Kay: Water resources: issues and strategies**
Francis Sandbach: Principles of pollution control
Stephen Smith: Recreation geography

**Forthcoming titles**
John Pierce: Food, land and man

ADRIAN McDONALD and DAVID KAY

# Water resources:
# issues and strategies

Longman
Scientific &
Technical

Copublished in the United States with
John Wiley & Sons, Inc., New York

**Longman Scientific & Technical**
Longman Group UK Limited,
Longman House, Burnt Mill, Harlow,
Essex CM20 2JE, England
*and Associated Companies throughout the world.*

*Copublished in the United States with*
*John Wiley & Sons, Inc., 605 Third Avenue, New York, NY 10158*

© Longman Group UK Limited 1988

First published 1988, 1993

. **British Library Cataloguing in Publication Data**
McDonald, A. (Adrian), *1946–*
    Water resources : issues and strategies.
    —— (Themes in resource management).
    1. Natural resources : Water : Management
    I. Title    II. Kay, David    III. Series
    333.91

ISBN 0-582-30121-1

**Library of Congress Cataloging-in-Publication Data**
McDonald, A. T.
    Water resources.

    (Themes in resourcé management)
    Bibliography: p.
    Includes index.
    1. Water-supply——Management.    2. Water quality.
    3. Water resources development.    I. Kay, David,
    1953      . II. Title.    III. Series.
    TD353.M49    1988        333.91            88–12948
    ISBN 0–470–21150–4 (Wiley)

Set in AM Comp/Edit 10/12 Times Roman

Printed in Malaysia by VP

# Contents

# List of plates

# List of figures

# List of tables

# Acknowledgements

Many people deserve our thanks for their help with the preparation of this book. Our families have endured the anti-social behaviour of the authors with good humour and resigned understanding. Friends have helped with light relief and sometimes welcome interruption. The figures were produced with the help of John Dixon and Tim Hadwin in Leeds and Trevor Harris in Lampeter and we are grateful for their professional advice and guidance. Tables were typed by Margaret Hodgson in Leeds.

The book would not have been started or indeed finished without the encouragement of Bruce Mitchell. He has helped to clarify and focus our thoughts in many sections. His incisive editorial comments have been a constant reminder that we were writing on a topic in which our editor is a leading international authority. His support, advice and friendship have been invaluable. Joan Mitchell was always welcoming on our visits to Canada and encouraged us by placing us on her list of potential 'finishers' in Bruce's series. We thank her for her confidence.

In a topic of the breadth which this book attempts, our friends and colleagues in the water industry have provided a useful sounding board for our thoughts and they have taught us a great deal about the constraints within which practical management decisions are taken. To Tony Edwards, John Stoner, Roger Fisher, Charlie Pattinson, Dick White and many others go our thanks.

The staff of Longmans have been invaluable. Delays do not fluster them, and they encourage with a mixture of, possibly apocryphal, tales of the author who is 'much later than you' and the occasionally firmer enquiry requesting to know 'where is the book?'.

Our wives Christina and Noreen have borne the brunt of this project. They have taught our young children to play silently when '*daddy's working*', they have cheerfully provided sustenance and encouragement and we would certainly not have completed without their help. Our long-suffering children, Magnus, Duncan, Chris, Alison and Niki, will be pleased to have their fathers back again.

Naturally, errors in fact or interpretation are the responsibility of the authors alone.

Adrian McDonald
David Kay
Yorkshire, September 1987

# Foreword

The 'Themes in Resource Management' Series has several objectives. One is to identify and to examine substantive and enduring resource management and development problems. Attention will range from local to international scales, from developed to developing nations, from the public to the private sector, and from biophysical to political considerations.

A second objective is to assess responses to these management and development problems in a variety of world regions. Several responses are of particular interest but especially *research* and *action programmes*. The former involves the different types of analysis which have been generated by natural resource problems. The series will assess the kinds of problems being defined by investigators, the nature and adequacy of evidence being assembled, the kinds of interpretations and arguments being presented, the contributions to improving theoretical understanding as well as resolving pressing problems, and the areas in which progress and frustration are being experienced. The latter response involves the policies, programmes and projects being conceived and implemented to tackle complex and difficult problems. The series is concerned with reviewing their adequacy and effectiveness.

A third objective is to explore the way in which resource analysis, management and development might be made more complementary to one another. Too often analysts and managers go their separate ways. A good part of the blame for this situation must lie with the analysts who too frequently ignore or neglect the concerns of managers, unduly emphasise method and technique, and exclude explicit consideration of the managerial implications of their research. It is hoped that this series will demonstrate that research and analysis can contribute both to the development of theory and to the resolution of important societal problems.

*Water Resources: Issues and Strategies* is the sixth book in the series. McDonald and Kay consider the 'science' associated with water resources, indicating where the science is strong and where it is tentative and inconclusive. They explicitly link the science with policy, and examine opportunities for these two spheres to complement one another.

After introducing some of the basic concepts associated with the science and management of water, McDonald and Kay provide a systematic review of the issues and opportunities associated with water supply, flooding and erosion control, water quality, and power generation. In each of these chapters they identify an array of possible strategies and consider their strengths and weaknesses. In the chapter focused upon river basin planning and management, they illustrate how these different aspects usually must be considered together. Decisions taken regarding flood control can have implications for water quality. Policies developed for water quality have ramifications for policies focused upon water supply. Trade-offs often are made as managers seek to identify a mix of activities which will satisfy the needs of many users.

McDonald and Kay draw their examples from a variety of regions and scales. The fundamental problems created by inadequate water in many Third World regions is highlighted. The magnitude of the work needed to provide potable water and sanitary disposal of wastes at a global scale is almost overwhelming. Their book and the writings of others suggest that the Water Decade (1981–1990) of the United Nations is addressing one of the most basic problems of the world.

The two authors write as individuals who conduct basic research and who complete investigations in collaboration with water managers. McDonald studied at the University of Edinburgh, completing an undergraduate degree in ecological science and a doctorate in which he studied the physical and economic effects of flooding in an agricultural area in southwestern Scotland. Kay completed his studies at the University of Leeds during which he investigated the effects of catchment management on water quality. McDonald and Kay have collaborated on studies of water quality in Britain and Canada. Their research and consulting experience provides an excellent background for preparation of a book on *Water Resources: Issues and Strategies*.

Bruce Mitchell
University of Waterloo
Waterloo, Ontario

February 1988

# CHAPTER 1

# Introduction

## 1.1 Water: the prime resource

Water is among the most essential requisites that nature provides to sustain life for plants, animals and humans. The total quantity of fresh water on earth could satisfy all the needs of the human population if it were evenly distributed and accessible.

(Stumm 1986:201)

The fact that water is not evenly distributed or accessible to large sections of the global population defines the central resource management problem addressed in this book.

Water is an important resource being used in a variety of ways at many different levels which produces social, spatial and organisational problems. Given also its potential as a source of hazard, the result is a management task of remarkable complexity. A specific water resource at one site is frequently being used in several different capacities at the same time. It is therefore subject to multiple-use management, or perhaps, to management based on compromise and conflict resolution.

Historically, nations have flourished on a basis of advanced water resource development and nations and individuals have conflicted over water rights. As early as 4500 BP, the Mesopotamian cities of Lagash and Umma were in dispute over water. The apparently civil nature of many water resource developments was, in reality, frequently more military in nature, being the expression of the desire for a more secure water supply at times of conflict. Jerusalem is a well-documented case. Initial tunnelling gave access to the Springs of Gihon, but as the city developed the supply was augmented initially by rainfall (Amivan 1975) and later by water transfer (Mazal 1975). Some works were clearly non-military: the linking of the Tigris and the Euphrates in pre-Christian times by the

1

Shatt el Hai canal, the drainage works to control sheet flows to the Agora in Athens (Thomson and Wycherley 1972) and the irrigation works of the pre-eminent 'hydraulic' civilisations of Sumeria and Egypt (Biswas 1972). The eventual failure of these civilisations has been ascribed by some writers to the failure to match water engineering to suitable social and managerial expertise, a thought that finds a clear echo in the criticisms of resource developments in the Third World today (Hart 1977; Jayaraman 1981).

The stresses produced by water resource inadequacy are not, however, solely limited to antiquity. The development of the American West is an episode of recent history strongly influenced by the water needs of individuals and groups. Such water stress is most clearly seen in the actions of the pioneers, early settlers and initial developers. Bowden (1971) argued that much of the custom of the indigenous peoples of the water-poor regions of the western United States has been developed to conserve water. In many respects the American 'West' may be unrecognised today but, in water terms, it remains an area of conflict. Conflict is now resolved through legal processes (Radosovich 1979) and conflict is likely to continue in the future because of resource shortage. In the view of the USDA (1981:120):

The energy crisis of the 1970s will take a back seat to the water crisis of the 1980s and 1990s.

Given the multi-faceted nature of this resource and its demonstrable importance in many areas through history (Falkenmark 1986a), it is perhaps surprising to note that in the resources field, water is often the poor relation, the 'stepchild' to use Barbara Ward's terminology (Ward 1977). The United Nations' Mar del Plata conference in 1977 was perhaps the most significant meeting to address water resource issues that has been held in the last century, yet it was poorly funded and poorly managed. It had a budget of about one-twentieth of that provided for the 1979 World Industrial Conference and for a long time had no organiser.

The Mar del Plata conference (United Nations 1978c) resolved to provide an adequate supply of water to everyone over the next decade. To supply the estimated 1,000 million people who do not have reasonable access to a safe water supply (I.T.D.G. 1978) would require the weekly connection of 2 million people, or the equivalent of the combined populations of the states of Montana, Idaho and Wyoming, or the combined cities of Bordeaux, Helsinki, Oslo and Calgary (population figures are taken from Paxton 1984). There is little evidence of any realistic attempt to develop water resources at the pace required to reach the objectives of the Mar del Plata conference.

It is perhaps an enigma that conflict has occurred throughout history and exists today, both in developed and developing countries, over a resource that is for many people so cheap that the market treats it as a free good. Indeed, Falkenmark (1986b:109) has stated:

It has been shown that frustrations over scarcity of water and overdependence for water upon upstream countries may develop into disputes. Indeed, water can be a strong contributing factor to armed conflict, even if this is not being recognized.

## 1.2 The creation of an issue

It is the purpose of this book to identify and elaborate on some of the major issues that will be of concern to water resource managers at the turn of the century and also to identify alternative management strategies. The origin and history of issues may well be complex and varied but can be broadly classed into two sources: professional and public.

### 1.2.1 Professional issues

At a simplistic level, it might be assumed that the division into professional and public issues is made on the basis of science and politics respectively. This cannot be so for resource management is not simply a technical operation. The resource manager must formulate sensible and practical policies from the findings of both natural science and social science and cannot avoid either science or politics. Public issues are often areas of conflict arising from the expression of public opposition, usually having a strong base at the local political level (Lowe *et al.* 1986). Once having emerged, such issues should become a matter of professional concern. These issues may have a very limited basis in natural science but may arise more as a consequence of fear of the unknown or fear of change. It is the place of the resource manager to present the tangible, factual basis of the issue and to assess and incorporate the intangible component. It should also be a concern to recognise and respond to the public assessment of the issue. Because of differences in the perception of hazard, the public perception may not correspond to that of the 'experts'.

Such a line of argument presupposes, however, that the resource manager has a wholly rational approach and is not influenced by a previously adopted viewpoint or discipline position. Such a presupposition finds little support in the literature. For example, O'Riordan (1976) suggested a continuum of environmental ideologies ranging from the 'deep environmentalists', the extreme ecocentrists, to the 'cornucopians', the extreme technocentrists. While many scientists in highly respected organisations, say the United Kingdom Atomic Energy Authority, are strongly in the latter camp, equally respected environmental scientists such as Falkenmark (1986a) are clearly 'ecocentrist'. In part this dichotomy of view stems from the discipline base of the resource manager but there is an element of conditioning by recent political policy. Thus, for example, the 'sunshine' policies of the US, policies of openness and access to information, may well be a part of the entrenched environmentalism, the response to which is one of accommodation (Mitchell 1974). European 'closed' or secretive policies may, on the other hand, have served to alienate that group who feel strongly about environmental issues and who, in the face of government rejection, opt for the more extreme reaction that has typified European responses.

Introduction

### 1.2.2 Public issues

Not all the issues that are discussed in this text are high on the media scale of interest. The media do have an interest in the more extreme, recent and emotive problems. They will have an effect in increasing environmental awareness and stimulating debate, especially in a climate where environmental issues would not otherwise reach the public consciousness. This attention may be short-lived, and Downs (1972) has termed this the 'issue attention cycle'. He defined five stages,

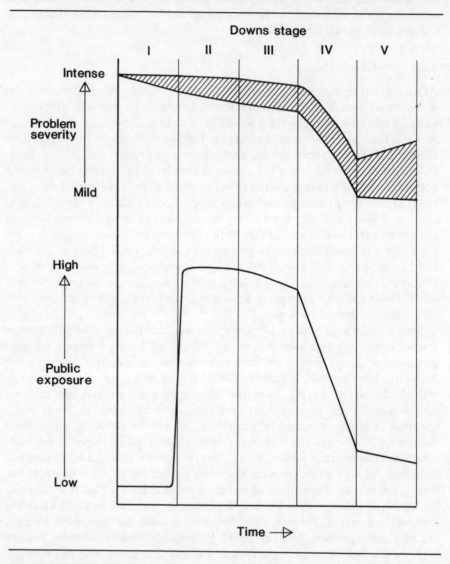

*Fig. 1.1* The issue attention cycle: the relationship between problem severity and public exposure

namely: (i) the pre-problem stage; (ii) alarmed discovery and euphoric enthusiasm; (iii) realising the cost of significant progress; (iv) gradual decline of intense public interest; (v) the post-problem stage. The development of both public attention and problem severity are shown in Fig. 1.1.

Public issues arise from many different circumstances but may be considered to stem from a combination of at least three situations:

1. Growing awareness of global and regional disparities in water resource availability engenders increased expectations and growth or change in water demand.
2. The maintenance of the existing level of water resource utilisation becomes impossible on the same resource base or pricing structure.
3. Resource utilisation, abuse or disregard by one group or nation causes or threatens to cause damage to another group or nation.

The first category is related to developing world problems. The second, on the whole, refers to the difficulties of continuing to provide cheap, relatively plentiful water in developed countries, a difficulty that has been greatly exacerbated by the growth of the environmental lobby and by the recognition that water resource development proceeds only in the face of competing resource uses. The growth in environmental awareness has caused the third group of problems, those focused on the importance of environmental quality and external diseconomies, to be more widely recognised. Such problems will be found on all scales, from the single basin (for example, the quality of the Rhine in Holland) to the global scale (for example, the potential environmental modification in the Arctic induced by river diversions).

Human expectations have changed over time. What has been an adequate, even admirable, supply at one time may today be seen as woefully inadequate. Many of the techniques applied today are little different in principle from those used in the past, but the scale is much greater. For example, in Roman times, Nimes was the second city of the Empire after Rome itself. The water supply to Nimes was taken from the Spring of Uzes and transferred by aqueduct via the Pont du Gard (Plate 1.1).

Such a water supply system using canalised transfers is no different in concept to that being used in the region today. The water is now taken from the Rhône and is distributed through a larger and more complex system. Although impressive, this system is tiny compared to the continental transfers outlined in Chapter 4. Problems and issues arise not only because of the techniques but because of the growth in scale and complexity of the projects and of the societies and environments in which they are set.

## 1.3 Structure

Two themes are central to the concept of a 'resource'. The first is that a particular facet of the natural environment is involved. This might be biotic, for example

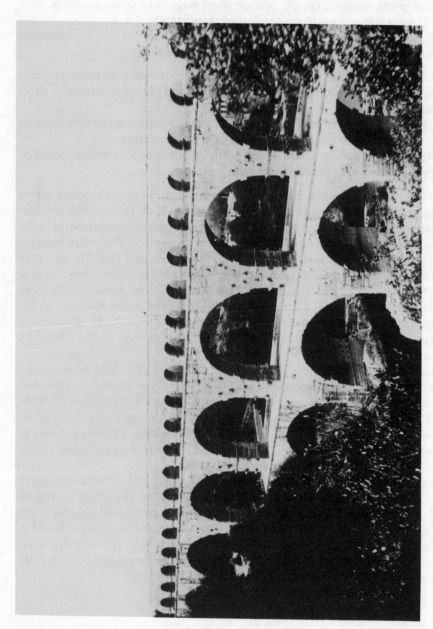

*Plate 1.1*  Pont du Gard, part of the Roman aquaduct taking water to Nimes from the  Spring of Uzes

the grasslands, or it might be abiotic, for example iron ores. The second is the need for that resource by people. Without these two themes, the resource does not exist. If a facet of the natural environment is not of any value, economic, aesthetic, real or perceived, then it is not a resource.

In Chapters 2 and 3 we examine these two themes under the heads of the physical resource and the human resource. In both of these chapters the material starts at a basic level. The reader familiar with one of these aspects may wish to omit some of this material. In Chapters 4 to 7 the subject is treated in a thematic manner. We choose to select only four major themes: water quality, water supply, flood problems and hydro-power. The selectivity is made to allow some depth to be developed.

It is a matter of convenience for writers on resources management to view the different aspects of the subject as separate entities. In reality they are inseparable topics, although this does not stop them being administered in many cases by separate organisations! However, there is a growing recognition of the need for an integrated form of management, and in many countries there are evolving plans and organisations that treat the river basin as an organic entity. There is, in these attempts, a great variety of means and degrees of success and these are examined in Chapter 8.

From the discussion of the resource base and the thematic and integration aspects of water resource management, a number of issues emerge. For some of these issues it is possible to recognise a way forward, perhaps even solutions. Certainly it is possible to recognise parallels from which lessons may be drawn. In the penultimate chapter we try to draw out these threads and to present them in a coherent structure. The stronger of these threads we present in the conclusions.

# CHAPTER 2

# The physical resource

## 2.1 Water at the macro scale

In this chapter we introduce the physical properties of water and describe the global water cycle. Water is a unique substance. Its specific and latent heat capacities make it an ideal medium for effecting energy transfers away from the equatorial regions. A knowledge of these basic physical properties is essential to understand the ways in which water affects the global energy balance which, in turn, determines distribution patterns and hence water resource availability.

### 2.1.1 Physical characteristics

The presence of the some $1.4 \times 10^9$ km$^3$ (WRI 1986; Korzoun and Sokolov 1978) of water in the global hydrological cycle has a marked effect on the earth's radiation balance, producing a narrower temperature range than would exist on a waterless planet. In this equable environment, all life forms have evolved and adapted to both the relatively small oscillations in temperature and the presence of large quantities of this useful solvent liquid. The results of this evolutionary environment are seen in a biosphere containing organisms which are composed mainly of water and which depend on the continued existence of this most basic resource.

Water can exist in all three matter states at a single location on the globe. All changes between the solid, liquid or gaseous states are controlled by energy levels which determine the availability of specific and latent heat energy in any mass of water.

Figure 2.1 shows the temperature of a given mass of water subject to constant energy input. This could represent a test tube being heated by a gas flame. Moving from the starting point at A, with a temperature of –25 °C, the water is in its solid state as ice. The energy input to the ice mass has the effect of raising the temperature of the solid but, as the temperature reaches 0 °C, the rigid crystalline structure of the ice breaks down to the more random molecular pattern of the liquid state.

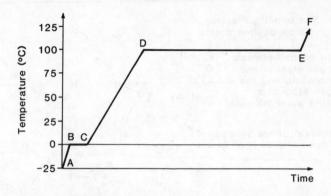

*Fig. 2.1* The effects of constant heat input to a mass of water. *Source*: Davidson (1978:1017)

In the solid state, water molecules are held in the fixed pattern by strong hydrogen bonds which are the forces of attraction between the unshared electron pairs of each oxygen atom and the adjacent hydrogen atoms. The locations of these hydrogen bonds can be seen in Fig. 2.2. Each dipolar water molecule is oriented so that its single oxygen atom is bonded with two hydrogen atoms and its two hydrogen atoms are bonded with the oxygen atoms of two adjacent molecules. The crystalline structure produced is rigid but relatively expansive, and therefore low in density when compared to the liquid state (Fig. 2.3). This

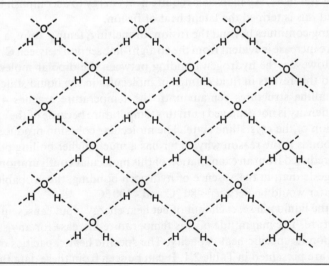

*Fig. 2.2* The crystalline structure of ice. *Source*: Russell (1976:5)

9

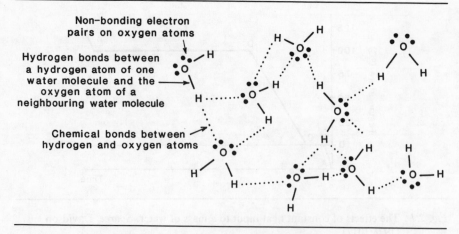

Non-bonding electron
pairs on oxygen atoms

Hydrogen bonds between
a hydrogen atom of one
water molecule and the
oxygen atom of a
neighbouring water molecule

Chemical bonds between
hydrogen and oxygen atoms

*Fig. 2.3* The molecular structure of water. *Source*: Russell (1976:5)

explains why water undergoes a volume reduction as it passes from the solid to the liquid state (Davidson 1978). It can be seen from Fig. 2.1 that this phase change requires the input of heat energy without the consequent temperature rise. This is seen in the horizontal section of the temperature curve at 0 °C between B and C (Fig. 2.1). The reason for this characteristic of the temperature curve is that energy is required to break down the strong hydrogen bonds which produce the crystalline structure of ice. While the heat energy input is being used to break down these bonds, there is no energy available to produce a temperature rise in the water mass. All materials require heat energy to accomplish the phase change, and this is termed the latent heat of fusion.

As heating continues beyond the fusion, or melting, temperature, a constant temperature increase is evident from the straight-line section between C and D on Fig. 2.1. However, the hydrogen bonding between the dipolar molecules still persists and this results in fluid clumps of molecules in the liquid state. In fact, some crystalline structures remain until the temperature reaches 4 °C, and maximum density is not achieved until this temperature because of the expansive configuration of the crystalline state. The molecular cohesion produced by the hydrogen bonds is the reason why water has a much higher boiling point than would be predicted from an examination of this molecular configuration. Russell (1976) suggests that, in the absence of hydrogen bonding, the probable boiling point of water would be between –80 °C and –100 °C.

During the liquid phase, each unit of net heat energy input causes an increase in temperature. The magnitude of this temperature increase for any substance depends upon its specific heat capacity. The specific heat capacities of several substances are presented in Table 2.1. It can be seen from these data that water has the ability to absorb large quantities of heat when compared to other compounds which make up common terrestrial surfaces.

*Table 2.1*  Specific heat capacities of common terrestrial surfaces

| Substance | Specific heat capacity $(kJ\,kg^{-1}\,K^{-1})$ | Increase in temperature of 1 kg on absorption of 4.2 kJ (K) |
|---|---|---|
| Water | 4.2 | 1.0 |
| Quartz sand | 0.8 | 5.3 |
| Kaolinite clay | 1.0 | 4.2 |
| Humus | 1.9 | 2.2 |

*Source*: Davidson (1978:93)

At the boiling point of water, a second phase change occurs as the liquid converts to the gaseous state. Latent heat of vaporization is required for this transition. In fact, 2,256.7 joules of energy are used per gram of water vaporized and this period of transition is characterised by a horizontal section on the graph between D and E, in Fig. 2.1, during which the temperature of 100 °C remains constant although energy input continues. It is not necessary to have a temperature of 100 °C before evaporation can occur, but at lower temperatures more energy is required to achieve the phase change.

In addition to this amelioration of global temperature oscillations produced by the specific and latent heat capacities of water, the presence of lateral movements of warm ocean currents and air masses produces a distribution of heat energy away from the equatorial zones. This is achieved by warm poleward flows on the oceanic western boundaries, such as the Gulf Stream, Kuroshio and Brazil Currents, which dissipate large quantities of energy in the winter hemisphere. In the region of these currents the oceans lose heat to the atmosphere which is balanced by a net heat gain in the cold upwelling zones on the eastern oceanic margins.

Gaseous water is no less significant in reducing latitudinal variations in global temperatures. In fact the atmosphere is responsible for over half the global energy transfers from areas of positive to negative net radiation. The mechanism can best be understood in terms of parcels of air moving poleward and equatorward. The net movement of air in both directions must be zero, but the mean absolute moisture content of air with, tropical source region will be higher because of the temperature difference. The resultant net poleward transport of water vapour or *moist static energy* is seen in thermally-driven monsoons and tropical cyclones in the low latitudes (Wallace and Hobbs 1977).

The temperature regulation produced by phase changes and lateral transfers of energy in the oceans and atmosphere is only one part of the total effect produced by water in the biosphere. This illustrates the interplay between the physical properties of the compound and the global environment, but the reader should be aware that water in all its phases has a marked effect on albedo (the ability of a surface to absorb or reflect energy) and the wavebands of energy absorbed and emitted from all elements of the biosphere. A detailed explanation is outside the scope of this book but can be found in Atkinson (1974) or Wallace and Hobbs (1977).

In addition to its role in global temperature regulation, the water cycle is a natural desalination system which distributes usable water resources according to the energy budget of the earth. Falkenmark and Lindh (1974:14) have suggested that this often produces a resource,

in the wrong place, at the wrong time or with the wrong quality.

- **Wrong place**   A single tropical storm in the Bay of Bengal between 12 and 13 November 1970 resulted in flooding which killed approximately 225,000 people

- **Wrong time**   The timing of water inputs to the Sahelian region of Africa has caused severe famine over the last decade (Todorov 1985)

- **Wrong quality**   Inadequate drinking water quality contributes to 27,000 deaths per day (Barabas 1986)

The extent to which this is a valid statement can only be judged on the basis of reliable data describing each component of the global water cycle. The International Hydrological Decade (1965 to 1974) was the most significant attempt to generate such a macroscale data base. This global research programme was co-ordinated by the UNESCO secretariat in Paris and the results were reported, in a series of papers, to the 1977 Mar del Plata conference. The momentum of this research effort continues still under the aegis of UNESCO and WMO which are joint sponsors of the International Hydrological Programme (Biswas 1978; United Nations 1978c; and Rodda *et al.* 1976).

### 2.1.2   The global water balance

Table 2.2 contains data based upon the calculation of Hoinkes (1968) and Meinardus (1928). These estimates of global water volumes are broadly similar to the data presented by Kalinin and Bykov (1969), Skinner (1969) and L'Vovich (1974).

These estimates vary slightly from the more recent data presented by Korzoun and Sokolov (1978) who calculate a global water volume of $1.386 \times 10^9$ km$^3$, of which approximately 97 per cent is ocean water and 3 per cent or $3.4 \times 10^7$ km$^3$, is fresh water. These authors, however, suggest an error range of $\pm$ 10 per cent on current global water balance calculations. In view of this level of error, the German and Russian investigators demonstrate remarkable agreement. The best available explanation of how the global water balance data have been derived is offered by Baumgartner and Reichel (1975). The remainder of this section utilises the notation devised by these workers and explains the calculation of the global water balance components on the basis of their methods and those of Korzoun and Sokolov (1978).

*Table 2.2* Global water volumes

|  | *Volume (km³)* | % |
|---|---|---|
| Oceans | 1,348,000,000 | 97.39 |
| Polar ice caps, icebergs, glaciers | 27,820,000 | 2.01 |
| Ground water, soil moisture | 8,062,000 | 0.58 |
| Lakes and rivers | 225,000 | 0.02 |
| Atmosphere | 13,000 | 0.001 |
| TOTAL | 1,384,120,000 | 100.00 |
| Fresh water | 36,020,000    = | 2.60 |

*Fresh water as a percent of its total*

|  | % |
|---|---|
| Polar ice caps, icebergs, glaciers | 77.23 |
| Ground water to 800 m depth | 9.86 |
| Ground water from 800 to 4,000 m depth | 12.35 |
| Soil moisture | 0.17 |
| Lakes (fresh water) | 0.35 |
| Rivers | 0.003 |
| Hydrated earth minerals | 0.001 |
| Plants, animals, humans | 0.003 |
| Atmosphere | 0.04 |
| TOTAL | 100.00 % |

*Source*: Baumgartner and Reichel (1975:14)

The global water balance is shown graphically in Fig. 2.4.

The world water balance for each areal component is defined as:

$$D_s = E_s - P_s$$

for the oceans, and:

$$D_L = P_L - E_L$$

for the land surfaces; where:

$D_s$ = oceanic evaporation transferred to the land surfaces
$E_s$ = oceanic evaporation
$P_s$ = precipitation to the oceans

$D_L$ = runoff from the land
$E_L$ = evaporation from the land
$P_L$ = precipitation onto the land surfaces

Baumgartner and Reichel (1975) have produced maps describing each of the equation components, defined above, for the whole globe and these provide the

13

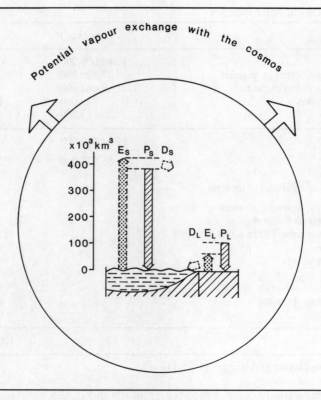

*Fig. 2.4* The global water balance. Modified after Baumgartner and Reichel (1975:16)

most definitive statement of the global water balance to date. The definition of P, E and D for each global region often involves extrapolation and estimation from similar regions with a more complete data record, and often individual components require estimation from a sounder knowledge of the remaining two parameters using the relationship:

$$P = E + D$$

where:

P = precipitation
E = evaporation
D = runoff

The three global maps formed the basis of more detailed statistical calculations describing the water balance using 50 zones of latitude for both continental and oceanic areas.

*Fig. 2.5* The global distribution of P. *Source:* Baumgartner and Reichel (1975:Map 1)

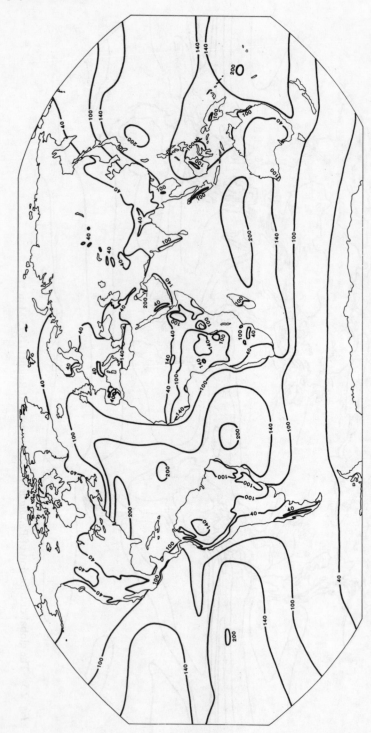

*Fig. 2.6* The global distribution of E. *Source:* Baumgartner and Reichel (1975:Map 2)

*Fig. 2.7* The global distribution of D. *Source*: Baumgartner and Reichel (1975:Map 3)

### 2.1.2.1   Estimation of P

The designation of continental isohytes was based upon mean rainfall at stations defined in the Walter–Leith atlas. The station density was, at best, between 2 and 3 per 100,000 $km^2$ and, where a less dense network of stations existed, expert extrapolation was used to draw an isohyte. The location of isohytes was then checked against the relationship:

$$P = E + D$$

where E and D were known. However, difficulties arise due to inaccuracy in estimating changes in icepack storage or indeed $D_L$ for the polar regions. In subarctic regions the available precipitation values are generally higher than would be expected from the relationship given above because of turbulent eddy effects reducing measured precipitation totals. This was evident particularly in the northern USSR where ground-level gauges are not normally employed. Further corrections of P were applied to readings from the east coast of the central Asiatic arid zone where values of $D_L$ for the Salween, Mekong, Yangtze and Hwang Ho rivers indicate a higher value for $P_L$ in this region.

The oceanic precipitation was estimated from the charts of Albrecht (1960), Knoch (1961) and Drosdov (1964). The total $P_s$ values derived from the charts of these authors are 377,000 $km^3$, 407,000 $km^3$ and 385,000 $km^3$ respectively. The mean (planimeter) value for $P_s$ from these authors is 395,000 $km^3$. However, Baumgartner and Reichel (1975) use a $P_s$ value of 381,100 $km^3$ following a consideration of available data points and their computed values for $D_L$ and $E_s$.

### 2.1.2.2   Estimation of E

Continental evaporation values can be estimated in two ways, either *hydrographically* or *meteorologically*. The former requires a knowledge of $P_L$ and $D_L$, using the relation:

$$P_L - D_L = E_L \text{ or } AE_H$$

where:
$AE_H$ = actual evaporation, calculated hydrographically

The main *meteorological* method involves the Thornthwaite formula and evaporation calculated by this means is termed $AE_T$. In general, $AE_T - AE_H$ increases with increasing latitude and this is shown in Table 2.3 which contains a small part of the data presented by Baumgartner and Reichel (1975).

### 2.1.2.3   Estimation of D

Runoff data is very sparse for polar and equatorial regions. In the former regions the central problem is to estimate $D_L$ for areas of ice storage which may undergo

*Table 2.3*  Evaporation values and latitude at Bergen, Glasgow and Valencia

| Place | | $P_L$ (mm) | $PE$ (mm) | $AE_T$ (mm) | $AE_H=E_L$ (mm) | $AE_T-AE_H$ (mm) | % |
|---|---|---|---|---|---|---|---|
| Bergen | 60° | 1,960 | 580 | 580 | 400 | 180 | 45 |
| Glasgow | 56° | 945 | 590 | 590 | 430 | 160 | 37 |
| Valencia | 52° | 1,415 | 635 | 635 | 550 | 85 | 16 |

*Source*: Baumgartner and Reichel (1975:23)

cyclic changes over many years as the $P_L/D_L$ balance alters. In the equatorial regions, rainfall totals are very high but little gauging of large rivers has been completed.

Baumgartner and Reichel (1975) attempted to alleviate these problems by using their calculated $P_L$ and $E_L$ values to calculate $D_L$ from the relation $D_L = P_L - E_L$. In this way they estimate the global $D_L$ value to be 397,000 km³.

Water vapour export from the seas to the land ($D_s$) was calculated by dividing the oceans into a series of squares each containing 76,200 km². Each $D_s$ value was calculated from the relation $D_s = P_s - E_s$ and Fig. 2.4 was constructed from this information. This global circulation system produces different recycling times for the storage locations shown in Table 2.4.

The data presented above on global water resource availability have been used by many authors (Quigg 1977; Falkenmark and Lindh 1974) to define the limits of world industrial, agricultural and population growth, and also to outline the potential problem areas of resource scarcity. It also forms the basis of the estimates of regional hydro-power potential reported in Chapter 7.

*Table 2.4*  Global storage locations and resumption periods

| Type of water | Period of resumption |
|---|---|
| World ocean | 2,500 years |
| Ground water | 1,400 years |
| Soil moisture | 1 year |
| Polar glaciers and permanent snow cover | 9,700 years |
| Glaciers in mountain areas | 1,600 years |
| Underground ice in permafrost zone | 10,000 years |
| Water storage in lakes | 17 years |
| Swamp water | 5 years |
| Water in stream channels | 16 days |
| Atmospheric moisture | 8 days |

*Source*: Korzoun and Sokolov (1978:2204)

## 2.2  Water at a micro scale

The existence of high-quality data describing the global distribution of water resources is important to international organisations deciding upon drought alleviation and food production strategies (Obeng 1980a). However, the majority of resource management decisions are taken at a national or regional level and the information required for efficient planning is not available from the global scale aggregate data described above. Of more interest to the resource manager is the effect of catchment land-use strategies on the quantity and quality of resources available. The average direct supply water gathering ground in the United Kingdom produces a runoff of some 0.01 km$^3$. In the global context, such discharges are **micro scale** and it is at this **catchment** scale that most of the detailed hydrological process information has been generated. This section will outline the background to catchment scale investigations. The resource implications will be further explored in 2.3.2 below.

The most common approach to the determination of land-use influences on water quantity and quality has been through comparative basin studies. For these studies, contiguous basins of similar geology and morphometry are selected and direct comparisons of the effects of different land uses are determined (the comparative study). The alternative approach requires a period of calibration following which the effects of a deliberate change in use are observed (the longitudinal study). In a few cases these two approaches have been combined. Examples of this type of experimental design can be seen in the Wagon Wheel Gap (US) study, reported in Bates and Henry (1928), or in the more recent Plynlimon (UK) experiments summarised by Blackie and Newson (1985).

In a wide-ranging review of basin studies, Rodda (1976) traces the birth of catchment scale research to the work of Perrault (1674), who measured the rainfall and discharge of the Seine basin above Aigney le Duc. After a three-year investigation, Perrault concluded that only one-sixth of the rainfall incident on the basin was converted to streamflow at Aigney. More recent experiments have generally been designed to investigate both the water quality effects of catchment use as well as the water quantity implications. Table 2.5 shows the major basin research programmes conducted in recent times.

It was against this background of basin studies that the International Hydrological Decade (IHD) Co-ordinating Council decided to offer encouragement and guidance for UNESCO member states wishing to establish experimental catchments as part of their contribution to the IHD. Rodda (1976) estimates that this resulted in some 3,000 catchment studies completed during the period of the IHD.

At a catchment scale, the most important physical modifications to the water resource base take place in the vegetation and in the soil. The most significant change in vegetation cover is between forest and a treeless ground cover. Such changes are currently taking place at a significant rate in many areas, for example deforestation in the Himalayas and the equatorial forests. In addition, there has been a reduction in tree cover due to fuelwood use in India and the Sahel (Centre for Science and Environment 1982).

Unfortunately, as in the case of global water budgets, the data base from which to predict the effects of catchment modification is at its weakest in the areas cited above. Some field studies exist (Norton *et al.* 1979) as do some desk

*Table 2.5*  Major basin research programmes

| Researcher | Publication Date | Location | Area |
|---|---|---|---|
| Perrault | 1694 | Seine | France |
| Engler | 1919 | Sperbelgraber | Switzerland |
| Hirata | 1929 | Ota | Japan |
| Bales & Henry | 1928 | Wagon Wheel Gap | USA |
| Wicht | 1965 | Jokershock | S. Africa |
| Dils | 1957 | Forest Coweeta | USA |
| Pereira | 1967 | Forest Aberdare | E. Africa |
| Low | 1956 | Stocks Reservoir | UK |
| Deij | 1954 | Castricum | Netherlands |
| Newson | 1979 | Plynlimon | UK |
| Rennett & Thomas | 1982 | Murray River | Australia |
| Blackie & Newson | 1985 | Balquidder | Scotland |
| Blackie & Newson | 1985 | Kershope | UK |
| Blackie & Newson | 1985 | Coalburn | UK |
| Hornung | 1985 | Beddgelert | Wales |
| Blackie & Newson | 1985 | Llanbrynmair | Wales |
| Blackie & Newson | 1985 | Nant y Moch | Wales |
| Stoner | 1986 | Llyn Brianne | Wales |

Modified from Rodda (1976:257–8)

studies (Todorov 1985; Hare 1983). Intensive studies within temperate research catchments may offer some guidelines on the important hydrological and geomorphic effects of vegetation change. However, caution should be exercised in the transfer of this information to tropical and semi-arid environments where the research information base is much weaker.

### 2.2.1  Catchment studies in Britain

At one time it was a common belief that:

> forests increase both the abundance and frequency of local precipitation over the areas they occupy, the excess of precipitation as compared with that over adjacent unforested areas, amounting in some cases to more than 25 per cent. (Zon 1927; quoted in Lee 1980:18)

By 1948, the view of American foresters had changed. They then recognised that forested catchments caused a reduction in total water yield. However, the view that forests had the beneficial effect of maintaining increased dry weather flows and therefore alleviating drought conditions still remained (Kittredge 1948).

In Britain the government report on the public access to gathering grounds (HMSO 1948) highlighted the lack of hydrological information in this area. An early hydrological process-based attempt to provide information on the effects of catchment afforestation was made by Law (1956, 1957) at Stocks Reservoir. This small, 37.5 km², catchment is in north–west England. Daily rainfall records from 1910 are available, together with 50 years of runoff data (Walsh 1987; Calder *et al.* 1982). This catchment was characteristic of many UK upland gathering grounds. Law set up a small (450 m²) lysimeter in a 25-year-old stand of Sitka Spruce (*Picea sitchensis*). For a one-year period the interception loss was 371 mm and the transpiration loss was 740 mm. This was 290 mm greater than the loss from an adjacent grassland area in a period of 984 mm of rainfall. This amounted to a 42 per cent reduction in available water resources from the forested areas. This conclusion was of immediate concern to the forest and water industries; not least because he related his hydrological finding to an economic assessment which indicated that the forest industry should pay £500 ha⁻¹ to compensate for the additional engineering structures required to make good the water loss.

Law's conclusion had the effect of shaking the previously harmonious relations between the water and forest industries, both of which were single-purpose resource agencies with a conservative and cautious approach to major policy decisions. It is possible to criticise the research on the grounds that the small experimental plot was unrepresentative of large forest stands because *edge effects* would result in exceptionally high evapotranspiration rates. This allowed both the forest and water industries to agree on a call for further research which created a breathing space for both agencies to consider their positions.

The first of the new research findings (Rutter 1963) confirmed that Sitka Spruce caused losses from intercepted water which were significantly higher than Penman estimates of evaporation from an open water surface and therefore, by implication, from grassland areas. Both Rutter *et al.* (1971, 1975) and Rutter and Morton (1977) went on to develop a number of computer models of the interception process which were calibrated for several British forest stands.

The next phase of investigation centred on the experimental catchments of the Institute of Hydrology. These catchments are shown in Fig. 2.8.

The two principal sites, Plynlimon and Coalburn, are characteristic of the traditional Welsh and Pennine water-gathering areas of the United Kingdom (Clarke and Newson 1978). However, the first data presented by the Institute of Hydrology staff came not from an experimental catchment but from an instrumented pine forest near Thetford in East Anglia (Gash and Stewart 1977). Their results indicated an interception loss of 213 mm from a rainfall input of 595 mm during 1975. The transpiration loss was calculated at 353 mm giving a total loss of 566 mm, which was *lower* than the Penman $E_t$ estimate of 643 mm. The implication of this research was that the annual water loss was lower than on an equivalent grassland area, and this conflicted directly with the work of Law and Rutter. However, in the British context, the Thetford area was not characteristic of the maritime, western margin, water-gathering areas and as a result attention swung to the Plynlimon catchments where research had been conducted since the early 1970s.

The headwater catchments of the Rivers Wye and Severn were chosen because they were of similar morphology and morphometry, draining the Plynlimon massif in, what Calder *et al.* (1982) have termed, 'reservoir country'. The

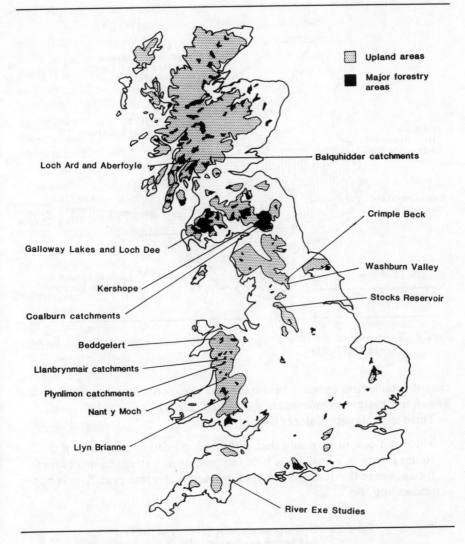

Upland areas

Major forestry areas

Balquhidder catchments

Loch Ard and Aberfoyle

Crimple Beck

Galloway Lakes and Loch Dee

Washburn Valley

Kershope

Stocks Reservoir

Coalburn catchments

Beddgelert

Llanbrynmair catchments

Plynlimon catchments

Nant y Moch

Llyn Brianne

River Exe Studies

*Fig. 2.8*   Experimental catchments in the United Kingdom. *Source*: Blackie and Newson (1985:2)

northerly Severn catchment was first afforested in 1937/8 following the state purchase of farm holdings during the 1930s economic depression. The sequence of subsequent afforestation is shown in Fig. 2.9.

Today, some 67.5 per cent of the Severn catchment is afforested and this compares with only 1.2 per cent of the Wye. Details of catchment morphometry are presented in Table 2.6.

After ten years of experimental work at Plynlimon, Newson (1979) was able to confirm the broad conclusions of Law which were that upland conifer plantation

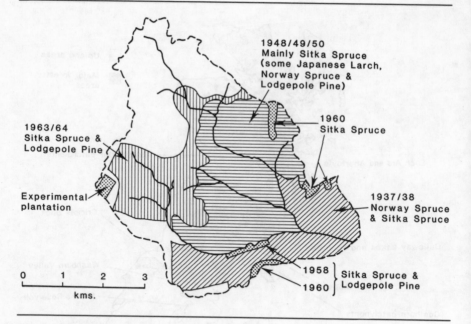

*Fig 2.9* The sequence of afforestation in the Severn experimental catchment. *Source*: Newson (1976:35)

caused a reduction in water resource yield. Newson's data for the Wye and Severn headwater catchments are shown in Table 2.7.

These data allowed Calder (1979:14) to state:

> There can now be no doubt that in the high rainfall upland areas of this country, regions which are of vital importance as water catchment areas, the answer to the question *'Do trees use more water than grass?'* must be a resounding *'Yes'*.

*Table 2.6*   Drainage basin morphometry of the Wye and Severn catchments, UK

|  | Wye | Severn |
|---|---|---|
| Area (km$^2$) | 10.55 | 8.70 |
| Afforestation (%) | 1.20 | 67.50 |
| Strahler order | 4 | 4 |
| Drainage density (km.km$^{-2}$) | 2.04 | 2.40 |
| Stream frequency | 2.88 | 3.6 |
| Main channel slope (m.km$^{-1}$) | 36.3 | 67.0 |
| Main channel length (km) | 7.32 | 4.58 |
| Bifurcation ratio | 1.54 | 1.67 |

*Source*: Newson (1976)

24

*Table 2.7* Hydrology of the Wye and Severn catchments, UK. Annual values of *P*, *Q*, and *P* – *Q*: Wye and forested area of the Severn catchment only: Years 1970–80 (units: mm)

| Year | P: Precipitation | | Q: Streamflow | | P – Q: Losses | | Difference in losses (Severn-Wye) |
|------|------|--------|------|--------|------|--------|------|
| | Wye | Severn | Wye | Severn | Wye | Severn | |
| 1970 | 2,869 | 2,485 | 2,415 | 1,636 | 454 | 849 | + 395 |
| 1971 | 1,993 | 1,762 | 1,562 | 797 | 431 | 965 | + 534 |
| 1972 | 2,131 | 2,124 | 1,804 | 1,342 | 328 | 782 | + 454 |
| 1973 | 2,606 | 2,380 | 2,164 | 1,581 | 442 | 799 | + 357 |
| 1974 | 2,794 | 2,703 | 2,320 | 1,785 | 474 | 918 | + 444 |
| 1975 | 2,099 | 2,035 | 1,643 | 1,213 | 456 | 822 | + 366 |
| 1976 | 1,736 | 1,645 | 1,404 | 921 | 332 | 724 | + 392 |
| 1977 | 2,561 | 2,573 | 2,236 | 1,638 | 325 | 935 | + 610 |
| 1978 | 2,356 | 2,367 | 2,128 | 1,668 | 228 | 699 | + 471 |
| 1979 | 2,742 | 2,683 | 2,463 | 2,016 | 279 | 667 | + 388 |
| 1980 | 2,695 | 2,517 | 2,377 | 1,914 | 318 | 603 | + 285 |
| Mean | 2,417 | 2,300 | 2,047 | 1,501 | 370 | 799 | + 429 |

*Source*: Calder *et al.* (1982:Table 2)

Calder explained the water loss in terms of the increased aerodynamic roughness and therefore eddy diffusion from afforested areas. The loss does not result from the slightly higher interception capacity which forests exhibit over comparable grassland. The fact that the main source of loss is the interception store goes some way to explaining the anomalous results for Thetford forest reported by Gash and Stewart (1977). Calder (1979) suggested that the Thetford data results from the relatively low number of rainfall hours experienced (350 at Thetford, 1,380 at Plynlimon in 1975). In dry periods, the pine transpiration rate is lower than for a grassland area, and therefore this forest causes a reduction in water losses because evaporation from the interception store is not of sufficient duration to compensate for the reduced dry period losses. These results clarify many of the processes through which forests exercise an influence on water yield. As such they are of some relevance in attempting to interpret the hydrological significance of major land-use change in a variety of regions. However, in interpreting the results in areas where there is significant artificial water storage, the strategic implications have to be tempered by an understanding of the operational requirements of the resource system.

The data presented by the Institute of Hydrology had significant implications for the British water industry. Figure 2.10 shows the three distinct management phases which characterise most temperate water supply reservoirs.

During the *winter full* condition, the reservoir spillway will operate and impounded water will be lost as runoff. This is also the period of maximum loss from the interception store. If the impoundment size is relatively small in relation to its total catchment area, then it would normally be expected to overspill early in the winter, and any loss due to increased afforestation would merely cause a

## 1. Autumnal filling of the depleted reservoir

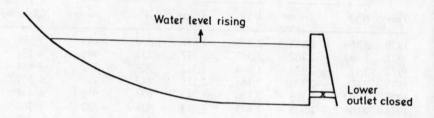

Water level rising

Lower
outlet closed

## 2. Winter full condition

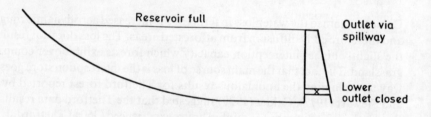

Reservoir full

Outlet via
spillway

Lower
outlet closed

## 3. Summer drawdown

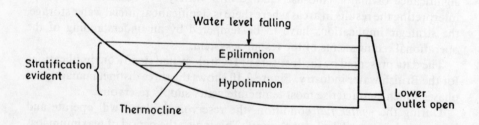

Water level falling

Epilimnion

Stratification
evident

Hypolimnion

Thermocline

Lower
outlet open

*Fig. 2.10* The three management phases of a temperate direct-supply reservoir.
*Source*: Kay and McDonald (1983a:613)

reduction in the overspill, or waste, volume rather than the available resource. In such a situation the main effect of increased catchment afforestation would be to produce a slower autumnal filling of the impoundment (Newson 1979). In areas where the relative impoundment capacity was larger, an increased loss due to afforestation could have much more serious consequences if, for example, the winter losses produced a failure to reach spillway height before the summer drawdown period. In both scenarios the effect of afforestation is to increase the susceptibility of the resource system to a given drought sequence (Clarke and Newson 1978).

Strategic estimates of the national water losses produced by an increase in catchment afforestation have been made by Calder and Newson (1979). For the catchments supplying the major upland reservoirs, they have calculated the percentage increase in loss which would be produced by an increase in afforestation to 50 per cent canopy coverage. Figure 2.11 is taken from their paper and the calculations are based on the graph depicted in Fig. 2.12.

At the same time as the hydrologists were completing their quantification of water loss from the uplands and evaluating the national resource implications for the water industry, other equally powerful interests were planning their resource management proposals for the British uplands. The strategic need for home-produced timber was highlighted by the Forestry Commission (1977) and the Centre for Agricultural Strategy (CAS 1980). The latter report suggested that the area of afforestation in Britain should be doubled to 4 million ha over the next 50 years. This would cover over one-third of the British uplands which are currently used for water-gathering grounds. The total area of potential resource conflict is shown in Fig. 2.13.

This conflict has not been resolved. Indeed, new factors in the debate are arising which indicate that afforestation can have significant *quality* effects on upland waters as well as the established *quantity* reduction (NCC 1986). These quality factors include nutrient enrichment, modification of the ionic balances and resultant acidities, and changes to the mobility of toxic chemicals (Stoner and Gee 1985; Magnuson 1982; D'itri 1982; Hutchinson and Havas 1980). These are dealt with in more detail in Chapter 6.

Afforestation does have beneficial quality effects, such as reducing enteric bacterial concentrations (Kay and McDonald 1982b; McDonald and Kay 1982), and there is evidence of reduced flooding from afforested catchments (Lloyd 1950). This shift in the emphasis of upland catchment research led Newson (1983:267) to state:

for many reasons attention in the water industry has now swung from water quantity implications of land use to those of quality.

## 2.3 Assessing the physical base

### 2.3.1 Evaluating the global water balance equations

Few other resource problems have prompted such a co-ordinated international research effort as that seen during the IHD (WMO 1974). Rodda (1976)

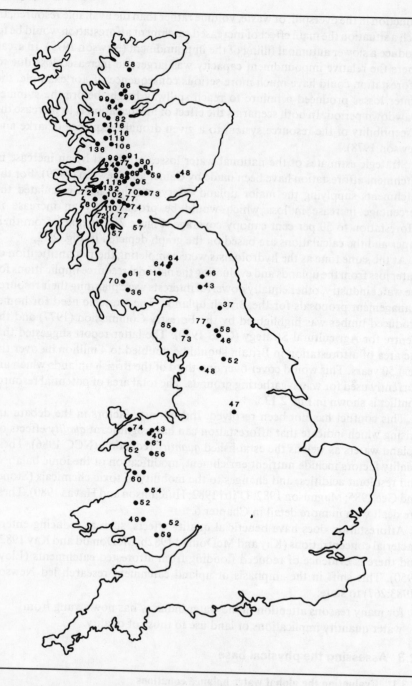

*Fig. 2.11*  Increase in water loss (%) due to conifer afforestation. A 50 per cent canopy coverage is assumed compared with a grassed catchment. *Source*: Calder and Newson (1979:1636)

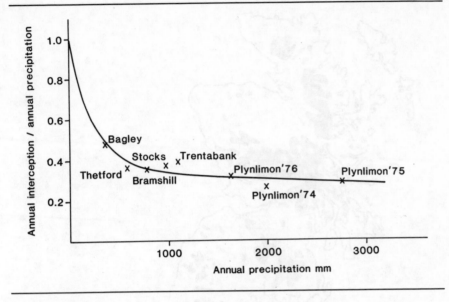

*Fig. 2.12*   Measurements of annual interception losses. *Source*: Calder and Newson (1979:1633)

suggested that over 3,000 studies of representative and experimental basins were conducted under the aegis of UNESCO. With such a commitment of international effort, one might think that an accurate picture of the total water resource base would be available. However, such an assumption would be ill-founded because the basic data used in the global calculations were not of sufficient quality or quantity to reduce the error range of the water balance estimates below ± 10 per cent (Korzoun and Sokolov 1978). Indeed, these authors suggest that we do not have sufficient information on the atmosphere/cosmos interchange of water vapour to allow valid statements on this multi-annual equilibrium of the water cycle components. They further hypothesise that a 1 per cent excess of evaporation over precipitation with cosmic loss could cause a global loss of 5,770 km$^3$ per year and a waterless planet in only 240,000 years (0.005% of the earth's age). These calculations, which were presented to the Mar del Plata conference in 1977, were purely speculative but they do illustrate our lack of fundamental understanding of the stability of the global water cycle. To understand the reasons why the error range is so high it is necessary to examine the original data base from which the global calculations were derived.

### 2.3.1.1   Errors in precipitation estimates

Probably the most often measured and yet error-prone determination is that of precipitation. The *true* rainfall is defined by Rodda *et al.* (1976) as '*the amount of*

*Fig. 2.13* The areas of resource conflict in the UK uplands. *Source*: Calder *et al.* (1982:Fig. 1)

*rain which would have reached the ground if the gauge had not been there'*. All gauges cause some atmospheric turbulence which causes a lower rainfall total than would be experienced in the absence of the gauge. Hence Rodda *et al*. (1976) suggest that all rainfall data merely describe relative, not actual, precipitation. The difference between relative and actual rainfall is greater in areas of high wind or exposure, such as mountain areas. The error is compounded by the lower instrument density and the irregularity of readings. As a result, individual instruments, which are subject to large measurement errors, are often used to extrapolate over very wide areas and this is one of the major reasons for the underestimation of precipitation over the land surface. In addition, rainfall is often higher in mountainous areas, and the absolute magnitude of any error is correspondingly greater. The error from these areas is therefore greater in magnitude than a similar percentage error from lower rainfall and less exposed lowland measurement sites.

Within national boundaries it is possible to standardise collection methods. The effects of exposure can be reduced or at least made uniform by consistent gauge designs. In the UK these include the Meteorological Office turf-wall or ground-level gauges, which reduce eddy effects and preclude splash input. However, on a global scale there is little attempt at standardisation in either gauge design or installation procedures. The indeterminate underestimates produced are further complicated because a significant proportion of the precipitation input to highland regions is in the form of snow. This input is quantifiable by snow poles or an examination of the soil's natural radioactivity which experiences attenuation on passage through a snowpack (Rodda *et al*. 1976). However, these methods require considerable labour and technological commitment, and the effects of snow input on the more ubiquitous rain gauge determinations is to exacerbate further this underestimation problem. Commenting upon the precipitation determinations available to them, Baumgartner and Reichel (1975:126) stated:

> The key to error evaluation in the water budget is precipitation.
> Investigations of the accuracy of precipitation measurement have shown
> that the amounts collected in rain gauges are usually smaller than the
> amounts striking the ground. The influence of wind on the deposition and
> transposition of solid precipitation and welling and evaporation losses vary
> with the type of instrument and with the different installation heights of the
> receivers above the ground, variable climatological conditions cause great
> differences because of variable effects of the above-named factors at
> particular latitudes and elevations. Reliable data scarcely exist.

It is possible that the problems of precipitation estimation will be overcome by a combination of ground-based radars and satellite remote survey (WMO 1974). The former technique can be used to quantify rainfall, as demonstrated by Harrold *et al*. (1973, 1974). The accuracy of radar precipitation measurements depends upon an understanding of the relationship between rainfall intensity and raindrop dimension. Since this relationship will always be subject to random influences, it is likely that some error will always occur. The magnitude of this error using current technology is ± 10 to 20 per cent of rainfall total (Doviack 1983; Hauser and Amaynec 1983).

In an attempt to correct some of the errors of underestimation, Baumgartner and Reichel (1975) adjusted their estimates of $P_L$ (precipitation onto the land) by +10 to 12 per cent at 60 °N and by 14 to 33 per cent at 70 °N. These authors estimate their errors in $P_s$ (oceanic precipitation) at ± 5 per cent and their figure is based upon the views of a number of global studies dating from 1955 to 1970 (Budyko 1970). The discrepancy between the various workers stems from the different approaches used when extrapolating from island or coastal zone data to areas of open ocean. This produces an increase or decrease in the figures used rather than a set of different isohyetal patterns on the oceans themselves. Any reduction in this error value could only stem from an extension of the sparse observational network into these open-ocean areas, stationary weather ships, or automated collectors.

### 2.3.1.2 *Errors in runoff and evaporation estimates*

A surprising level of agreement exists in defining the global runoff volume. Indeed, Baumgartner and Reichel (1975) assume an accuracy of ± 5 per cent for this parameter. However, the importance of studies such as the IHD, in defining runoff more accurately, is demonstrated by the correction in the value of $D_L$ which was required following the measurement of runoff in the Amazon and Orinoco rivers. The accuracy value calculated above must be taken, therefore, as a realistic error range of the existing measurement techniques. The extension of current technology to presently unmeasured locations could necessitate a further adjustment of the absolute runoff value. The existence of error in $P_L$ and $D_L$ determinations causes an error in $E_L$ since, by definition:

$$E_L = P_L - D_L$$

With a global $E_L$ value of $75 \times 10^3$ km$^3$ ± $4 \times 10^3$ km$^3$ the error on this parameter is about ± 5 per cent. This is 1 per cent higher than the evaporation error term for the oceans of ± 4 per cent (i.e. $E_s$ estimates range from $418 \times 10^3$ km$^3$ to $452 \times 10^3$ km$^3$). The global significance of each of these error values can only be judged against the amount of water in active circulation, which is equal to $P_Q$ or $E_Q$ (i.e. global precipitation and evaporation). This global figure is approximately $500 \times 10^3$ km$^3$ y$^{-1}$ and the error values of each component in relation to global circulation are set out in Table 2.8.

### 2.3.2 Basin hydrological studies: accuracy and applications

There are many potential errors in basin hydrological studies (Edwards and Rodda 1972). The extent to which each of these sources of error causes a bias in the overall result is largely a function of instrument design and installation.

Table 2.8  Errors in the global water balance estimates

| Component | Component error | Global error (%) |
|---|---|---|
| $P_L$ | $= \pm\ 5 \times 10^3\,km^3$ | : 1.0 |
| $D_L$ | $= \pm\ 2 \times 10^3\,km^3$ | : 0.4 |
| $E_L$ | $= \pm\ 4 \times 10^3\,km^3$ | : 0.8 |
| $E_S$ | $= \pm 17 \times 10^3\,km^3$ | : 3.4 |
| $P_S$ | $= \pm 17 \times 10^3\,km^3$ | : 3.4 |
| $P_G = E_G$ | $= \pm 22 \times 10^3\,km^3$ | : 4.4 |

*Source*: Baumgartner and Reichel (1975:129)

Indeed, a major goal of the IHD representative basin programme was to provide an improved set of guidelines on the correct design and use of the available instrumentation. The main criticism of experimental basin research has not hinged on the potential for cumulative errors in the measurement techniques employed, but instead on the cost and duration of this type of study (Rodda 1976).

Writers such as Renne (1967) and Ackerman (1966) have stressed the problems of transferring results from basins which may not be representative. This same criticism was levelled at the early research of Law (1956). Newson (1982) suggested that the necessary political motivation required to implement British catchment scale studies stemmed from disenchantment with Law's research design. These studies have been further criticised by Kay and McDonald (1982b) because of the spurious air of holistic research claimed by the practitioners who have often adopted a narrow research focus and merely attempted to answer single, fashionable questions reflecting single-purpose resource agency perceived problems, rather than attempting any comprehensive evaluation of the range of potential resource management options. This narrow focus has been attributed to the power of single-purpose resource agencies in British upland land use and the lack of any co-ordinated land-use planning policy in upland Britain (Lowe *et al.* 1986; Newson 1982, 1983). There is evidence of recent improvements and a broadening of the questions asked if not the answers available. Newson (1982) cited the examples of increased activity among conservationists, recreationists and upland farmers as reasons for the broadening of the research question into areas of land use/water quality interaction and the resultant effects on recreational fisheries. In a very optimistic assessment of the future research implications, Newson (1982:10) suggested:

> Over the next five years the results of what may be termed the second phase of hydrological research will be available to all interests and will hopefully permit a much more sophisticated prediction than that by Calder and Newson (1979), including water quality as well as quantity. This will free water interests to take a more flexible approach to afforestation.

In the British context, there are many questions remaining on the effects of land use on catchment hydrology. Of particular relevance is the estimation of interception losses from plants of intermediate height such as bracken (*Pteridium aquilinum*) or heather (*Calluna vulgaris*) and the calculation of losses from areas of snowpack.

Research on the microscale processes that underpin the water resource base is incomplete, even in the UK. If a small relatively densely instrumented country, that has seen two decades of commitment to hydrologic research at the micro scale, still operates with imperfect knowledge, how much more complicated is the task of the water manager in understanding the physical resource base in the areas identified earlier as *globally* significant.

Microscale studies to date have established:

1. Trees use more water than grass.
2. Refined techniques exist to identify process rates.
3. The process rates themselves do not appear transferable.
4. For individual, mainly temperate, basins, comprehensive nutrient balances have been established but this information is not transferable.

To date, this does not provide the sound scientific basis for integrated land and water management which is essential for river basin planning in both the developed and developing worlds (WRI 1986; Falkenmark 1985).

# CHAPTER 3

# The human resource

In recent years there has been an emphasis on the examination and definition of the administrative structures of resource management agencies. This has occurred for two reasons. First, because academics, managers and the public wish to understand how resource policies are generated and how these policies are implemented. Second, because engineering, or technocentric, solutions to environmental management have increasingly lost credibility with the public and environmental agencies (Sandbach 1980; O'Riordan 1976). Administrative structures comprise legal, economic and institutional approaches to problems for which an engineering solution has typically been sought (Grima 1981).

Research in the field has been extensive, although the work has usually been descriptive or, at best, comparative in nature. England and Wales are well represented in such literature, having experienced four major changes in water administration in 40 years and the loss in 1983 of the National Water Council (Sewell *et al.* 1985; Kromm 1985; HMSO 1983; Sewell and Barr 1978; Okun 1977; Smith 1972; Mitchell 1970; Craine 1969; Proudman 1962). The aim of all the changes in water administration is to promote a more effective and efficient use of water resources. In this respect, these adaptations are no different from the historic water legislation provided for various areas in the Middle East (Hirsch 1959).

## 3.1 Structures for management at a national level

### 3.1.1 Natural or artificial units

Most writers on water management have considered the form and size of the basic management unit. However, in many respects *water management* and *water resources* are very broad terms embracing both supply and disposal. The efficiency with which the major functions proceed is not necessarily optimised by the choice of the same areal management unit or institutional structure. This can

35

be illustrated by considering water supply and water quality control (Fig. 3.1).

Water quality control is an act of dispersion involving both the removal and dilution of pollutants from urban and industrial waste flows. Water supply, on the other hand, is an act of concentration. Waters of a catchment which are naturally well dispersed, both temporally and spatially, are concentrated to provide a supply for urban or industrial sites.

### 3.1.1.1 *Links to other resource agencies*

The management of water resources cannot proceed in isolation from the other planning and management agencies whose field of interest impinges upon that of the water manager. For example, the river records from which a scientific assessment of river regime and flood hazard may be derived might well be collected by a water management agency. However, many of the adjustments to flooding, particularly non-structural methods such as floodplain zoning and flood proofing, lie within the jurisdiction of land planning and building regulation and control agencies. The need for effective co-ordination between agencies in such a situation is self-evident. However, there is ample proof that this coordination often does not take place. Platt (1982), discussing the 1979 flood in Jackson, Mississippi, found that the coordination between different agencies was complex and imperfect, and that flood control completed in 1978 by the Corps of Engineers was not matched by comparable non-structural measures.

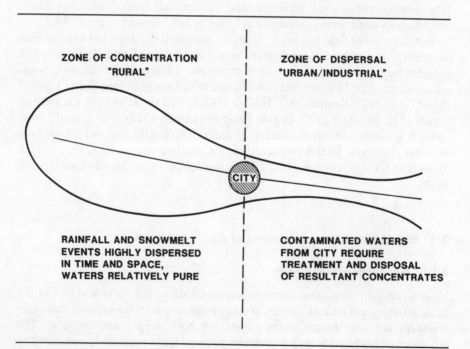

**ZONE OF CONCENTRATION**
**"RURAL"**

**ZONE OF DISPERSAL**
**"URBAN/INDUSTRIAL"**

CITY

**RAINFALL AND SNOWMELT**
**EVENTS HIGHLY DISPERSED**
**IN TIME AND SPACE,**
**WATERS RELATIVELY PURE**

**CONTAMINATED WATERS**
**FROM CITY REQUIRE**
**TREATMENT AND DISPOSAL**
**OF RESULTANT CONCENTRATES**

*Fig. 3.1* Zones of concentration and dispersal within a catchment

Some water management decisions lie outside the field of public agencies altogether. To continue the flood example, Parker and Harding (1979), in their analysis of the flood hazard in Shrewsbury, UK, highlight the floodplain control maintained by the building societies through the differential granting of mortgages to potential property purchasers in the flood-prone areas. One of the most important issues is the maintenance of effective communications both within and between private and public groups which have an interest in water management. At no time should this communication be compromised simply through the mismatch of administrative boundaries. Catchment-based units may provide hydrologically neat areas from a water industry perspective, but these may be of little relevance to other private and public agencies.

### 3.1.1.2 Geographical setting

The choice of an institutional structure for water resource management is governed, in part, by geographical setting. At least three factors are important:

1. The presence of international boundaries;
2. The size of the basin;
3. The location of the state or region within the basin.

In general terms, the greater the proportion of international boundaries that a nation has, the more complex its internal water management becomes. This is perhaps most clearly seen in the case of Atlantic Europe where all the nations are at a broadly similar level of economic development, are within the same economic community and have broadly similar political philosophies. The United Kingdom is a small island and thus has no international boundaries and has relatively short rivers. This permits the creation of simple administrative units based on a catchment or group of adjacent catchments. (However, even here, internal politics cause Wales to be considered as a single water authority when its physical structure might suggest otherwise, and Scotland to have an entirely separate and different institutional structure for water management.)

In France the planning of water resources lies in the six basin agencies of which four are wholly within France and are based on catchment units (Adour–Garomne, Seine–Normandie, Loire–Bretagne and Rhône–Mediterranée). Two are international: the first forms part of the Rhine system (Agence Financière de bassin Rhin–Meuse) and the second represents what is essentially the rump of small rivers in the north-west of the country flowing into the English Channel (Artois–Picardie). This simple structure is shown in Fig. 3.2.

Holland is a small country occupying the deltaic region of a major international basin (see Fig. 3.3). It is dependent upon external water supply and is an importer of pollution. Therefore Holland needs to resolve many water resource conflicts in the international rather than the domestic arena. To do this effectively requires that power for water management lies with the national and provincial governments. Water in Holland is supplied by water boards which have recently been enlarged to cover two or three provinces but, despite this

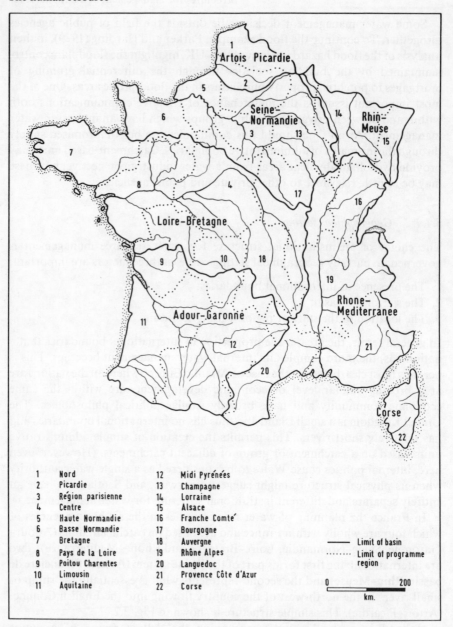

| 1 | Nord | 12 | Midi Pyrénées |
| 2 | Picardie | 13 | Champagne |
| 3 | Région parisienne | 14 | Lorraine |
| 4 | Centre | 15 | Alsace |
| 5 | Haute Normandie | 16 | Franche Comté |
| 6 | Basse Normandie | 17 | Bourgogne |
| 7 | Bretagne | 18 | Auvergne |
| 8 | Pays de la Loire | 19 | Rhône Alpes |
| 9 | Poitou Charentes | 20 | Languedoc |
| 10 | Limousin | 21 | Provence Côte d'Azur |
| 11 | Aquitaine | 22 | Corse |

— Limit of basin
······ Limit of programme region

0 _____ 200
km.

*Fig. 3.2* The administrative regions for water resource management in France

expansion, ultimate power for water management has been retained with the governments which are able to operate at the international level, essential in the context of Dutch water management (Johnston and Brown 1976).

While it must be recognised that a consideration of institutional structures is a

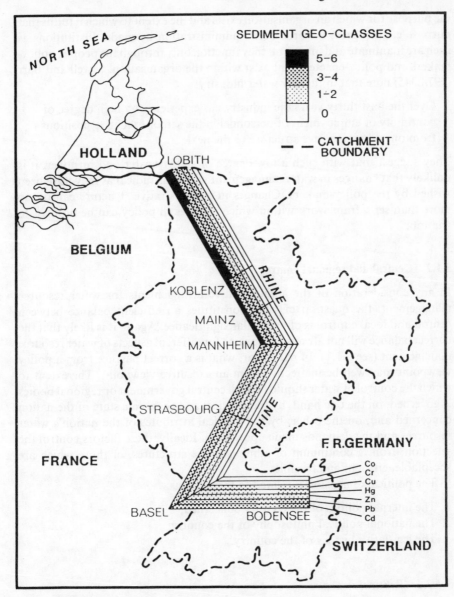

*Fig. 3.3* The place of Holland within the catchment of the Rhine showing increase in pollutant load downstream

valuable contribution to water management research, the next 20 years are likely to see a change in emphasis from the assessment of structure *per se* to the evaluation of the effectiveness of the organisation. To do this will require a definition of objectives or a definition of what constitutes failure. In both cases the criteria must be explicit, agreed and measurable. Only by a consideration of

39

the purpose for which an organisation exists and the extent to which it fulfils that purpose can progress towards better administration be made. Institutions as such are inanimate and impotent; they function only through the people, policy-makers and policy-enacters that exist within the organisation. Sewell and Barr (1978:345) note that in the UK water industry:

> Over the past thirty years the industry has experienced a high degree of continuity of employment of personnel in the senior executive positions from one administrative structure to the next.

They suggest that with such a low degree of staff transfer and turnover, it is unlikely that changes in water management will be as radical as may have been wished by the policy-makers. Changes in administrative structure can do no more than set a framework within which changes in policy can be brought to fruition.

### 3.1.2   Central and regional control

In any consideration of the administrative arrangements for water resource management, the question of what constitutes an efficient balance between central and local control is of particular significance. Again, it is likely that the correct balance will not always be the same for different aspects of water resource management (see 3.1.1). In particular, what is a correct balance from a policy viewpoint may well be ineffective from an executive viewpoint. The extent to which the control of water should lie with central government or regional bodies is governed, on the one hand, by the political and economic state of the nation concerned and, on the other, by the physical attributes of the nation's water resources and the demands made upon them. Ideally, these factors control the selection, from a continuum of administrative structures, of those which are acceptable, efficient and feasible.

The political dimension is related to three things:

1. The internal politics of the country concerned;
2. The national political philosophy of the country;
3. The legislative history of the country.

#### 3.1.2.1   Political structure

Many nations have an internal political structure which gives considerable regional autonomy. This is particularly clear in the case of the United States and Canada where the federal governments fulfil a national policy role and the provinces and states exercise strong planning control. Water resource systems internal to a region are usually within the jurisdiction of that regional government. However, when the resource is interprovincial or international, the difficulties of determining the correct role of central and regional legislature become more serious.

A strong federal structure is not the hallmark of the political organisation of the countries of Western Europe (although the cantonal system of Switzerland and the landes of West Germany are obvious exceptions). In Europe, old-established nationalist tendencies exist – Occitaine, the Basque regions, Scotland, Wales and Ireland are very clear examples. These have a modifying effect on regional political structure and thus on water resource regionalisation. In Wales, for example, a single water resource management agency has been created which covers an area where the major centres of demand are at the northern and southern extremes of the region. Logically, the south might have been an independent water authority and the north have been included under adjacent water authorities.

In France, no deviation from the basic structure of six basin agencies mentioned earlier has been permitted, except in the case of Occitaine where the aspirations of the people have been recognised by the creation of the Companie Nationale d'Aménagement du Bas Rhône et Languedoc. This water management agency was created in 1964 and, although it could be readily argued that it was conceived from a social standpoint to aid in the redistribution of development effort from the prosperous north to the poorer south, it still has a significant effect in reducing central control and giving regional power in an area of strong regional political feelings.

In the Third World the regional political structures are often more diffuse. Control of water is strongly tied to social organisation at a local, often village, level. An example of the social organisation for water resource control has been provided by Fleuret (1985) for the Taita hills in Kenya. Peters (1984) has discussed the importance of water management within the agricultural sector in Botswana. Jamaica presents a less extreme example of a Third World nation: here, water management utilities are being developed which have similarities with those found in Western nations. The problems encountered in developing such utilities have been reviewed in McBain (1985). Specific problems of village-scale water supply systems are addressed in Chapter 4 and river basin management in Third World nations is discussed in Chapter 8.

### 3.1.2.2 Political philosophy

National political philosophy also influences the extent of regional autonomy deemed acceptable. This is especially evident in the controlled economy countries. In the USSR, the overall control of water resource development lies in Moscow with the Minvodkhoz (the All Union Ministry of Land Reclamation and Water Resources; Thynne 1977). The Council for the Study of Productive Forces (Yegorov 1983) identifies the place of water resources in the overall long-term planning of the national economy. As a result, major water management projects, such as irrigation developments and river diversions, proceed with few legislative problems (McDonald 1982). In a similar manner, the dominance of President Nkrumah permitted the Volta development in Ghana to proceed in the face of dubious economic benefits and significant social costs (Chapter 8).

The human resource

In such a political climate, specific water resources may be seen as subjects of national prestige and, as is the case with the serious water-quality deterioration of Lake Baikal, may be given state protection (Nijhoff 1979). Such protection is not, however, unique to controlled economies as a consideration of the restoration of the tidal Thames in the UK would indicate (Wood 1982). Nevertheless, strong central control does much to facilitate the solution of complex water problems.

### 3.1.2.3  Legislative history

The final political factor influencing local or national control of water is the political and legislative history of the nation concerned. In the UK, for example, the separate legislation relating to Scotland, derived from its historical claim to separate nationality, produces a system of water resource management entirely different from that in England and Wales (Sewell *et al.* 1985). The difference is so marked that the majority of texts on water management in the UK in fact relate only to England and Wales (Smith 1972; Porter 1978).

### 3.1.2.4  Economic philosophy

Economic philosophy and consideration of economic efficiency are a major influence on regional and national organisations. In the US the private sector has an important role in water supply provision. Much of the supply is through small and medium-size utilities in which a considerable legacy of competitive spirit remains. With such inter-agency rivalry, the development of larger integrated utilities capable of developing water resources in a more socially and economically efficient manner is difficult. This is well demonstrated in a case study of Northern Newcastle County, Delaware (Hurd 1979). Here, four utilities had an interest in co-operation to develop the resources of the area to meet increasing demand. In their attempt to regionalise, they experienced not only engineering and economic difficulties but major political, social and legal problems. Bumstead (1979:708) suggested a possible mix of factors which influence the development of regional utilities:

The creation of regional or area wide utilities is based upon 70% politics, 20% engineering knowhow and 10% luck.

Several arguments can be advanced to support the case for larger and integrated regional utilities:

1. Small systems generate insufficient revenues. This weak financial base constrains possible expansion and improvement.
2. Reduction of competition among utilities encourages a socially equitable allocation of resources within the region as a whole.
3. Amalgamation of utilities encourages economies of scale and allows the provision of specialist facilities and staff that could not be justified within each smaller authority.

42

4. Larger management units facilitate basin-wide integration of functions and encourage long-term planning.
5. Water resource fluctuations, which can be severe over a small area, are generally moderated in a regional context. Differences in the regional severity of drought are well illustrated in the 1976 drought in the UK (see Table 3.1).

However, growth in utility size is not without penalties, the most important of which are:

1. The excessive concentration of power within one organisation.
2. The dilemma which results from the requirement of the same organisation to both operate a resource system and enforce controls on that operation.
3. The growth in administrative bureaucracy that may slow decision-making and which separates decision-makers from the community which they serve.

While there may be substantial benefits to be gained from regionalisation, significant central control still remains necessary. Boundaries continue to exist and some policies, for example internalisation of supply (that is, supply from sources within the same administrative area), may not even be directed towards the optimum benefit to the nation as a whole. Furthermore, without central control there may arise problematic divisions of responsibility between functional agencies in the same region. This may operate to the detriment of efficient resource development and conservation within the region.

*Table 3.1*  Regional variations in drought severity during the 1976 UK drought. Administrative units used are shown in Fig. 8.9

| WA | Apr | May | Jun | Jul | Aug | % LTAV | Apr – Aug Return period (Years) |
|---|---|---|---|---|---|---|---|
| North West | 23 | 37 | 88 | 33 | 58 | 47 | 300 |
| Northumbria | 25 | 41 | 92 | 42 | 56 | 50 | 180 |
| Severn–Trent | 15 | 92 | 79 | 31 | 83 | 62 | 20–50 |
| Yorkshire | 23 | 74 | 78 | 27 | 67 | 52 | 100–200 |
| Anglia | 33 | 149 | 92 | 39 | 73 | 72 | 5–10 |
| Thames | 11 | 145 | 69 | 32 | 56 | 65 | 10–20 |
| Southern | 10 | 142 | 54 | 63 | 37 | 61 | 20–50 |
| Wessex | 6 | 115 | 52 | 39 | 56 | 56 | 20–50 |
| South West | 13 | 77 | 31 | 50 | 66 | 49 | 100 |
| Welsh | 14 | 59 | 55 | 32 | 62 | 44 | 200–500 |

The return period estimates are based upon tables provided by the Meteorological Office.
Return periods refer to 5- or 7-month deficiencies starting in any month.
Adapted from the *Drought Atlas* (1977).

### 3.1.3  Regional/federal conflicts

There are many instances of conflict between central and local government which are entirely understandable since each does not necessarily have identical

43

interests. It might be reasonable to expect that conflict should not arise when both local and federal agencies have the same interests. However, when both have an executive function, inter-agency rivalry and conflict in priorities can occur.

### 3.1.3.1  Water management conflicts in California

California is a major user of water, consuming some 26 per cent of US water resources, and is also an area of seasonal aridity, possessing only 3 per cent of the nation's total available water resources. The major centre of demand lies in the south of the state, while the principal water resource is in the north. Both state and federal agencies have sought to alleviate potential water deficits by water transfer schemes. The characteristics of these projects are well summarised by Robie (1980:70), who commented:

> The Federal Central Valley Project and the California State Water Project operate side by side delivering water to customers in many of the same areas of the state. Both projects secure their basic water supplies in Northern California and use the Sacramento River as a natural conveyance system to the Sacramento–San Joaquin delta .... This situation is fraught with potential conflicts.

Figure 3.4 illustrates the main elements of the federal and state water plans. Three main areas of conflict can be identified in this resource development.

*(i) The limited availability of dam sites* Unrestricted development, particularly in the 1950s, had led to competition between agencies for the right to develop prime dam sites. By the 1970s it was clear that the optimum sites had already been exploited. The Federal Army Corps of Engineers wished to develop the Dos Rios dam site. However, this site was required by the state water project. California quickly enacted legislation which restricted development by defining the area as a wild and scenic river location.

*(ii) Failure to recognise and comply with State legislation* Federal agencies claimed that Congressional authorisation takes precedence over the requirements of state law (Gilbert 1978). State law in California requires releases of water to maintain water quality which would otherwise deteriorate because of degraded irrigation return flows (Radosovich 1979). However, Robie (1980:71) noted that:

> During the 1976/7 drought the Bureau of Reclamation refused to make all the releases from Federal reservoirs needed to meet State water quality requirements, thus requiring the State to make additional releases from its project on several occasions to make up for Federal releases.

This conflict led to the State of California challenging, in the US Supreme Court, the right of the federal agency to refuse to respond to state law. The court

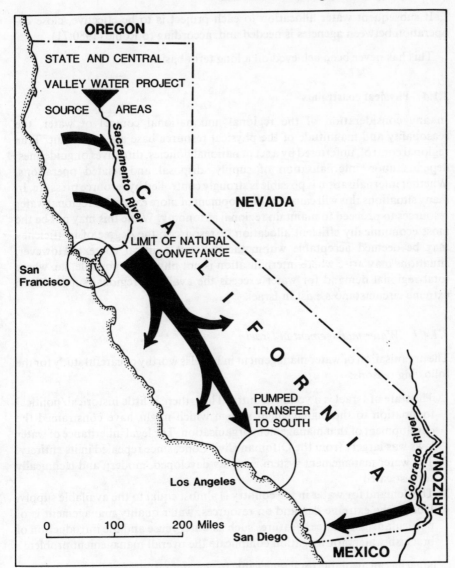

*Fig. 3.4* The main elements of the federal and state water plans

held that the federal agency must accede to state law unless by doing so it would contravene clear Congressional directives.

*(iii) Operational conflict* Releases from both federal and state reservoirs use the Sacramento River to reach the demand areas. The specific management and operation of these mixed waters can never be established and it is recognised that:

> The major water projects in California must be operated as a single system under one set of legislative and administrative policies. (Gilbert 1978:81)

If subsequent water allocation to each project is to be effective, close co-operation between agencies is needed and, according to Robie (1980:71):

This has never been achieved on a long term basis.

### 3.1.4 Physical constraints

In any consideration of the regional and national control of water, the seasonality and magnitude of the physical resource base are important. True regional control, unfettered by a set of national policies, directives or guidelines, depends upon internalisation of supply, disposal and related operations. Whether internalisation is possible is strongly controlled by resource pressure. In many situations this will cause the development of more expensive regional water resources to proceed to maintain regional autonomy. While this may not be the most economically efficient allocation of resources, the degree of inefficiency may be deemed acceptable within the regional political context. However, situations may arise where internalisation is not physically possible, i.e. where total regional demand for water exceeds the available regional supply. Such extreme circumstances exist in Israel.

#### 3.1.4.1 Water management in Israel

The organisation of water management in Israel is worthy of careful study for the following reasons:

1. The state of Israel is a young country. Thus, there is little historical/political foundation to the management system which might have constrained the development of that management organisation. The legal inheritance of water laws was largely from the Ottoman Civil Code, since repealed in its entirety.
2. The water management system is highly developed, modern and technically sophisticated.
3. The demand for water in the country is almost equal to the available supply.
4. Due to the extreme demand on resources, water quality management is of particular significance. Features such as water reuse and the introduction of brackish waters for irrigation complicate the overall management problem.

Israel has an available total renewable freshwater resource of 1.5 km$^3$ per year. This consists of 0.57 km$^3$ from the Jordan river, 0.85 km$^3$ from groundwater and 0.08 km$^3$ from storm water interception. In addition, 0.30 km$^3$ of renovated waters from sewage are available, giving a grand total of 1.8 km$^3$. Demand in 1979 was 1.7 km$^3$. Thus, demand threatens to exceed available supply and to induce a grave water crisis. Severe variations in rainfall totals from year to year exacerbate this problem. The three main water storage facilities are:

1. Lake Kinneret;
2. Yarkon–Tanninim aquifer;
3. The sand/sandstone coastal aquifer.

Together these provide only half the volume needed to protect against inter-annual fluctuations in supply. Groundwater is crucial in providing supply and in creating an element of strategic reserve. Lake Kinneret (the Sea of Galilee) has marked salinity and algal problems which constrain its use for agriculture and potable water supply. Both groundwater systems are subject to nitrate leachates and local infiltration by wastes. The coastal aquifer has limited drawdown possibilities because of saline intrusion.

Water resources are ill-distributed. The bulk of the rainfall is to the north of Tel Aviv and the Dead Sea. The National Water Carrier was built in the 1960s to connect the three main water sources and to redistribute the water on a more controlled and equitable basis (Fig. 3.5).

Water is pumped from Lake Kinneret, at first in open canal and then through closed conduit, both for local consumption and to allow recharge and exploitation of the aquifers.

The water affairs of the state of Israel are managed by the Water Commissioner through an office within the Ministry of Agriculture. The Commissioner's main function is regulation. The Commission issues operating rules, regulations and permissions in relation to water use and can demand execution of plans or can take violators to court. The Commissioner's office has no planning or policy function. However, the Commissioner is the Vice-Chairman of the Water Board – a policy agency – and is an appointed member of the National Water Planning Committee. The main long-term planning task lies with Tahal (Water Planning for Israel Ltd), a semi-independent government agency (Shamir 1977). There appears to be some dispute (Galnoor 1978) concerning the extent of government control of Tahal, but what control exists appears to come from the Ministry of Agriculture. The real power, however, is retained by Mekorot, an agency that constructs, maintains and operates many of the nation's water projects.

The fact that friction occurs between the policies of the Ministry of Agriculture, the plans of Tahal and their execution by Mekorot has led to criticism of the existing, highly centralised, water management institutions. Galnoor (1978) argued that the institutions are ageing, that agriculture is over-represented and that the policy under which the institutions operate is geared to providing 'access' in an era when genuine resource shortage threatens. He argued that the Commission should be replaced by a Water Policy Centre dissociated from the Ministry of Agriculture; that the Centre be given long-range planning powers; and that both Tahal and Mekorot be made responsible to the Water Policy Centre, the former for specific project planning and the latter for execution. In this case it is the functional co-ordination of existing national scale agencies, rather than the formation of a new administrative structure, that is required.

### 3.1.5 Accountability

The potential for political control of water resource management is at its strongest at a national level. In the UK there is little effective voter control at the

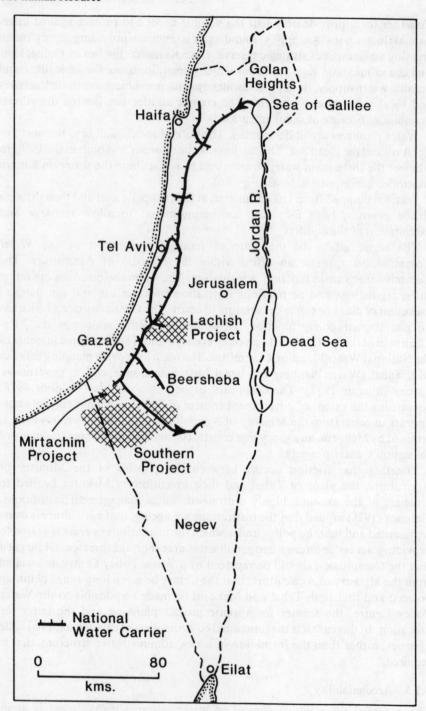

*Fig. 3.5* The national water distribution system in Israel

regional level (this is further explained in 8.5.1). As water authorities become large, multifunctional and corporate in character, it might be argued that their role as a public body may be subordinate to corporate self-continuation and expansion. Regional autonomy for such bodies, in the absence of effective regional political control, can only be seen as a force that may accentuate moves towards a strengthened corporate image rather than public service. Evidence that might support such a view within a UK context is:

1. The spread of direct billing for revenue purposes in place of the previous system in which a proportion of the local authority budget was allocated to the water management agency.
2. Societal acceptance of policing by the water authority when the authority itself is the most frequent transgressor against legislation through the unsatisfactory nature of the discharges made from the sewage treatment works under its control. In effect, the public is asked to accept self-policing.
3. The creation of policy on a regional basis by the same group of decision-makers who are then responsible for the enactment of that policy.

### 3.1.6 An effective central control

There have been no studies which have effectively evaluated the success of the relatively weak organisations that exist to provide co-ordination of water management at the national level. To be effective, such a national water agency has to possess authority based upon legislation. This is necessary because large authorities, with a substantial local financial base, may not be responsive to aspects of national policy that might not be to the corporate advantage of a particular authority. In this respect, the UK's National Water Council was failed by the government which did not provide adequate legislative authority.

Efficient central control must be through one body. Control through various ministries that might have a legitimate claim to an interest in water resource management (e.g. Environment, Health, Energy, Agriculture) would simply lead to additional problems of central co-ordination. In France, for example, the central control of regional water agencies has required the creation of an Interministerial Coordination Committee (McDonald 1974), a body which itself requires support from several minor co-ordination groups.

In the United States, the federal government established a National Water Commission (since terminated by President Reagan) with the purpose of making judgements on major resource problems. It was also required that this body furnish guidelines for the formulation of responses to the problems identified (Sewell et al. 1985). In Canada, Environment Canada fulfils a broadly similar role in providing an overview of national problems and responses. A comprehensive review of the nation's water resources and water management, including the role of Environment Canada, was completed by Pearse et al. (1985). This represents the best available assessment of total system efficiency and provides a model for other countries. However, this review does not, in itself, provide a strong central agency.

## 3.2 Management at the international level

The need for water management at an international level has been succinctly stated by a United Nations spokesperson:

> Since rivers, lakes and aquifers – and the hydrologic cycle as a whole – cross national frontiers, water policy making and planning must, to some extent at least, be carried out within an international framework. (United Nations 1979:473)

Writers such as Hardin (1969) have outlined the 'tragedy of the commons'. This concept can be applied to the management of any natural resource that is communally exploited. The global water resource system is a common good and is subject to the potential degradation explained by Hardin. Until recently, water resources could be exploited by individuals or nations, but:

> The era when water resources could be developed in comparative isolation, with little regard for the effect on other elements of the environment, is finally coming to an end, both on a national plane and on an international plane. (Teclaff 1976:808)

International organisation of water resources aims to:

**Smallest scale**

1. Resolve and avoid international conflicts.
2. Agree on the allocation of benefits from the resource project.
3. Maximise the total net benefits from the project.
4. Promote communication, education and social well-being.

**Largest global scale**

Some framework is required to enable a structured discussion of international water resources to proceed. In this section, *scale* is used to provide this structure. At the simplest level, co-operation between two governments, often relating to a specific problem, results in bilateral agreements. At a regional scale, agreements between several countries are often *problem*-oriented. At the global scale, there is little evidence of agreements to facilitate true management, but several initiatives can be identified in the areas of training, data collection and *ad hoc* efforts at problem solving.

### 3.2.1 Bilateral studies: the development of conflict

The roots of all bilateral studies and agreements lie in conflict. The use of boundary or transboundary resources by a single nation will always impact on a neighbouring state. Initial agreements seek to avoid conflict. At a later stage, attention may shift to the maximisation of the total project benefits. Conflict will re-emerge when these increased benefits are to be allocated.

### 3.2.1.1 The International Joint Commission (IJC)

The IJC was established under the 1909 Boundary Waters Treaty to regulate water resource conflict between the US and Canada. This structure arose from a number of disputes concerning water rights, particularly in the Mid-West. The political boundary between Canada and the US follows an artificial line which crosses natural structures such as drainage basins. Conflict follows directly from this geography.

The IJC has six commissioners, three from each country. One chairperson is appointed by each side and meetings are held alternately in Canada and the US. Problems may only be investigated by the IJC after a referral by either or both governments. This is a major drawback since the IJC cannot monitor, give advice or initiate *pre-emptive* investigations. In effect, an issue has to become severe enough to merit federal government concern before any IJC action can commence. The investigations of the IJC can only result in recommendations: it has no executive power. However, if *both* governments formally consent to a reference *for decision*, they are bound to implement any IJC recommendations. Such a reference *for decision* has never taken place although acceptance by the governments of IJC recommendations is extremely high. This may well derive from the fact that the IJC commissioners are all political appointees. It is unlikely, therefore, that board members would agree to measures which directly conflict with the national interests of either nation.

Consent is needed from the IJC for any operation that would modify river flow or lake levels in the other country. If the operation is approved, a control board is created to supervise the project and to ensure compliance with an IJC *Order of Approval*. Enabling powers also exist to create two other types of boards. The first, an *Investigative Board*, has a short-term technical role, to provide information concerning problems referred. The second, *Surveillance Boards*, are established following international agreement and monitor progress towards the conditions laid out in the agreement (Kay and McDonald 1982a; Pentland and Long 1978).

The IJC terms of reference specifically exclude it from the role of a resource management agency. Any such role would inevitably reduce the sovereignty of the nations concerned and has limited the activities of the IJC to conflict resolution. The IJC, therefore, is a *reactive* agency. Many resource managers have advocated a more *pro-active* role. In this mode, the IJC would be able to identify emerging problems and perhaps initiate preventative environmental strategies.

### 3.2.1.2 International aquifer management

In contrast to the boundary management between the US and Canada, that which exists between the US and Mexico is less well developed. An examination of some aspects of this southern boundary provides interesting insights to management in the absence of a well-established treaty framework and to the problems of managing groundwater resources under conditions of stress.

The Hueco Bolson aquifer underlies the Rio Grande river where it forms the international boundary between the US and Mexico. The aquifer and overlying alluvium vary between 200 m and 400 m in depth and are shown in Fig. 3.6.

In both Mexico and the US, groundwater mining to provide water for supply and irrigation has increased greatly in recent years. In total, over the last 30 years, the irrigated area has increased by some 60 per cent, and about 1,500 irrigation wells have been established to support this expansion. The result was a reduction in water level between 1903 and 1976 of as much as 25 m (Day 1978). The decline in water levels is predicted to continue through the foreseeable future (Meyer

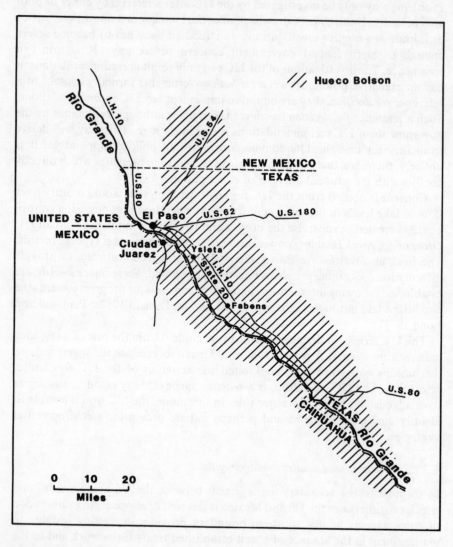

*Fig. 3.6* Location and extent of the Hueco Bolson aquifer. *Source*: Meyer (1976)

1976). Annual recharge is largely from mountains in Mexico and comprises only 5 per cent of the annual withdrawal. At current pumping rates, Gates (1975) suggested that the reserve is being depleted by 1 per cent per year.

This extreme pressure on groundwater resources results in three major problems:

1. The loss of resource and the associated increases in pumping costs;
2. Contamination by increased flows of saline and polluted waters into the freshwater aquifer;
3. Subsidence induced by groundwater depletions where compressible clays exist.

Day (1978) suggested several strategies to ameliorate the problems. These include:

1. The development of alternative water sources to replace existing aquifer supplies;
2. The promotion of water-saving strategies involving sewage reuse, water conservation technologies or pricing controls;
3. The blending of mildly saline waters with the aquifer waters to increase reserves.

To effect any of these strategies requires data on the exact nature of the aquifer and the demands made upon it. It also requires that the strategies be adopted by those who currently exploit groundwater. Both requirements have resulted in considerable opposition. To understand the basis of the opposition requires an appreciation of the water rights of the individual in both the US and Mexico. In Mexico, groundwater is a national resource; in Texas, it belongs to individual property owners who may, if they so choose, deplete it without limit.

The International Boundary and Water Commission (IBWC) was authorised to evaluate the groundwater exploitation problem on the Rio Grande following intensive water resource investigations of the Hueco Bolson and adjacent aquifers by the Texas Water Development Board and the United States Geological Survey. The IBWC examined the need to develop a comprehensive groundwater agreement. This initiative was met with anger by many politicians in Texas who argued:

That IBWC ... does not have Congressional authorisation to enter into negotiations of a potential groundwater treaty; that investigations ... are illegal; ... have been secretive in not revealing ... that investigations would be considered for the El Paso area ... and that rural and urban Texans would be negatively affected by such an agreement. (Day 1978:176)

This review shows the importance of individual state legislation in international negotiation. It also reveals the difficulties inherent in examining an international environmental problem in the absence of a strong treaty base.

53

The human resource

*Table 3.2*  UN agencies with water-related activities

| Organisation | Water-related activities |
| --- | --- |
| *UN headquarters* | |
| Department of International Economic and Social Affairs | Water policy and planning issues as well as co-ordination of water-related activities within the UN organisations |
| Department of Technical Cooperation for Development | Execution of projects entailing water management of ground and surface water management in developing countries, including the strengthening of national water legislation and administration |
| Economic Commission for Africa | Water policy and planning issues for each respective region |
| Economic Commission for Europe | |
| Economic Commission for Latin America | |
| Economic Commission for Western Asia | |
| Economic and Social Commission for Asia and the Pacific | |
| Office of the United Nations Disaster Relief Coordinator | Forecasting of and relief for effects of floods and other disasters |
| United Nations Children's Fund | Control of water-borne diseases, water supply and sanitation schemes |
| United Nations Development Programme | Financing of most of the water-related technical co-operation projects executed by one or more of these organisations |
| United Nations Environment Programme | Environmental impact of water-related activities |
| United Nations Industrial Development Organisation | Industrial water resources needs and pollution control |
| World Food Programme | Projects undertaken on a food for world basis |
| *Specialised agencies* | |
| Food and Agriculture Organisation of the United Nations | Integrated land and water development for agricultural purposes |
| International Bank for Reconstruction and Development | Investment in water development and use projects |
| United Nations Educational, Scientific and Cultural Organisation | Assessment of water resources and training, research and education programmes |
| World Health Organization | Control of water-borne diseases, water supply and sanitation schemes |
| World Meteorological Organisation | Hydrologic surveys |
| *Other organisations* | |
| International Atomic Energy Agency | Nuclear and isotope technology in hydrologic studies |

Adapted from Miller and Flanders (1985:394)

## 3.2.2 International agreements: multinational scale

When several countries have an interest in a particular water resource, agreements concerning the exploitation of that resource are essential. In principle, these multilateral agreements are no different from those of a bilateral nature discussed above although they will typically be more complex. Examples of such multilateral agreements exist for Lake Geneva and for Lake Constance (OECD 1972).

These multilateral agreements are problem-oriented, but since 1970 agreements have been formulated to tackle areas of concern that do not focus on a specific geographical location. In the EEC, for example, directives have been established which seek to specify minimum levels of environmental quality applicable within member states. These standards are uniformly applied across international boundaries within an economically and politically bound group of nations. Implementation problems associated with the EEC salmonid, drinking and bathing waters directives are discussed in Chapter 6 (EEC 1978, 1976, 1975). The application of a directive does not imply any environmental management role for the EEC. The responsibility for implementation rests with the management agencies of individual states. The current pattern of implementation reflects the political will of individual states to accept this trans-national legislation.

## 3.2.3 International agreements: global scale

At the global scale, management agencies do not exist. The UN agencies with water-related activities operating at this scale are outlined in Table 3.2.

The level of 'agreement' involved is little more than a club membership which facilitates the work of aid agencies in the limited redistribution of resources involved in current programmes. No global management is involved and, indeed, the UN general assembly resolved that:

Each nation has the sovereign right to formulate its own environmental policies, provided in the exercise of such right and in the implementation of such policies due account must be taken of the need to avoid producing harmful effects on other countries. (d'Arge and Kneese 1980:430)

The crucial role of global agencies centres on the provision and promotion of education and appropriate technology transfer (Miller and Flanders 1985). Global environmental degradation of the type envisaged by Hardin can be both insidious and cumulative. For example, the marine dumping of nuclear waste in corrodable containers typifies the present-day problem of 'commons' degradation. It is not a problem that is being adequately addressed by either global or national agencies. UN policy cited above would do little to control these potentially catastrophic environmental degradations. A major issue, therefore, must be the provision of effective management control over resource degradation and depletion at sites without specific national sovereignty.

# CHAPTER 4

# Water supply

## 4.1 Scale of the problem

Water supply is the provision of water for drinking, domestic use and irrigation. The availability of this resource is controlled by the global distribution of water as outlined in section 2.1.2 and Figs 2.5 to 2.7. The student of water supply must also consider the human population distributions which are contained within political boundaries often bearing little relation to the patterns of resource availability. At the simplest level, the hydrological and population data can be combined to estimate the per capita river runoff, as shown in Fig. 4.1.

This type of presentation provides little more than a rough guide to water resource availability for the following reasons:

1. Streamflow is variable and the timing of the high flows, when water is plentiful, may not coincide with the periods of maximum demand.
2. In many developing nations the distribution of rainfall, not stream-flow, determines the water resource availability to farmers and consumers.
3. In the water-deficient nations, the available water supplies may come from catchment areas in climatic zones outside their borders. Rivers such as the Nile, Indus and Volga all transport water to deficient regions, thus supporting agro-economic systems in the recipient nations. This factor is of increasing importance in view of the plans for large-scale interregional water transfers discussed in 4.2 below.
4. Water supply is available from fossil and active groundwater, as well as riverine abstractions. The estimates of water availability implied by Fig. 4.1 will therefore be an underestimate. To a much lesser extent, options exist for increasing supply in the deficient regions by artificially short-circuiting the hydrological cycle through desalination systems or iceberg farming (section 4.4).

To the resource analyst, a more useful concept than the total runoff of an area is that of *stable* runoff which is defined by L'Vovich as the base flow plus the stable

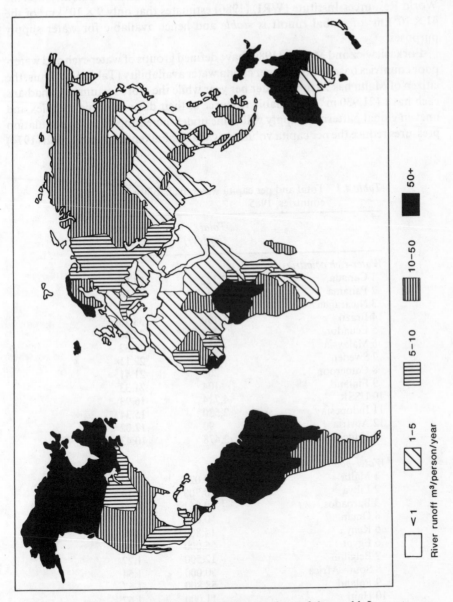

*Fig. 4.1* Total river runoff per capita in different regions of the world. In most cases
these regions are national, but some provincial units are used.
*Source*: L'Vovich (1977)

surface runoff components of river flow (WRI 1986). This *stable* portion of the river flow from the continents is a better estimate of resource availability, and the World Resources Institute (WRI) (1986) estimates that only $9 \times 10^3$ km$^3$ of the $41 \times 10^3$ km$^3$ of global runoff is *stable* and hence available for water supply purposes.

Forkasiewicz and Margat (1980) have defined groups of water-rich and water-poor countries based upon the per capita water availability (Table 4.1). Thus, the citizen of Malta has 70 m$^3$ of water per year while the more fortunate Canadians each have 121,930 m$^3$ of available resource at their disposal. This complex and uneven global pattern of supply will come under increasing stress as population pressures reduce the per capita volumes available. Falkenmark and Lindh (1974)

*Table 4.1* Total and per capita water availability in selected countries, 1985

|  | Total $(km^3/yr)^{-1}$ | Per capita $m^3 Ho^3 yr^{-1}$ |
|---|---|---|
| *Water-rich countries* | | |
| 1 Canada | 3,122 | 121.93 |
| 2 Panama | 144 | 66.06 |
| 3 Nicaragua | 175 | 53.48 |
| 4 Brazil | 5,190 | 38.28 |
| 5 Ecuador | 314 | 33.48 |
| 6 Malaysia | 456 | 29.32 |
| 7 Sweden | 183 | 22.11 |
| 8 Cameroon | 208 | 21.41 |
| 9 Finland | 104 | 21.33 |
| 10 USSR | 4,714 | 16.93 |
| 11 Indonesia | 2,530 | 15.34 |
| 12 Austria | 90 | 12.02 |
| 13 United States | 2,478 | 10.43 |
| *Water-poor countries* | | |
| 1 Malta | 0.025 | 0.07 |
| 2 Libya | 0.700 | 0.19 |
| 3 Barbados | 0.053 | 0.20 |
| 4 Oman | 0.660 | 0.54 |
| 5 Kenya | 14.800 | 0.72 |
| 6 Egypt | 56.000 | 1.20 |
| 7 Belgium | 12.500 | 1.27 |
| 8 South Africa | 50.000 | 1.54 |
| 9 Poland | 58.800 | 1.57 |
| 10 Haiti | 11.000 | 1.67 |
| 11 Peru | 40.000 | 2.03 |
| 12 India | 1,850 | 2.43 |
| 13 China | 2,680 | 2.52 |

*Sources*: WRI (1986:123) and Forkasiewicz and Margat (1980)

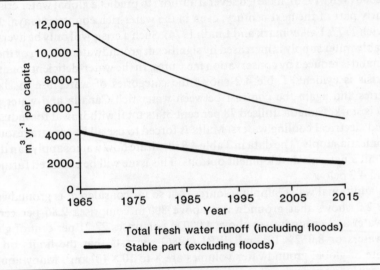

Fig. 4.2   Total freshwater runoff and stable runoff per capita to the year 2015.
         Source: Falkenmark and Lindh (1974:116)

predicted the decline in stable and total per capita water availability shown in Fig. 4.2.

The historical trends in total and per capita global water use are outlined in Figs 4.3a and 4.3b. Per capita use has doubled in this 40-year period and the total water use in 1980 was 44 per cent of the available $9 \times 10^3$ km³ stable runoff. These data, together with global water demand projections of $15 \times 10^3$ km³yr⁻¹ by the

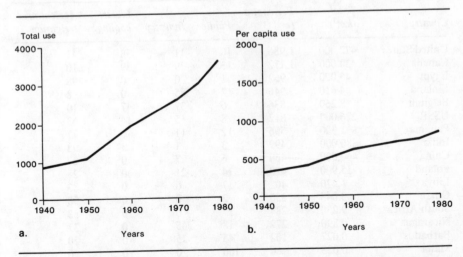

Fig. 4.3   Total (a) and per capita (b) global water use, 1940 to 1980. Source: WRI (1986:129)

year 2000 (WRI 1986), have led several authors to predict a global water crisis by the early part of the next century, even in the water-rich countries (Jayal 1985; L'vovich 1977; Falkenmark and Lindh 1974). Such a crisis will only be averted if the stable water supply is increased by significant groundwater mining or the rise in demand is reduced by conservation measures. In the water-deficient countries, the crisis is evident. Table 4.2 shows the categories of water use in sixteen countries and again the contrast between water-rich Canada and water-poor Malta is stark. Canada utilised 78 per cent of its total withdrawal for industrial use and electrical cooling waters. Malta is forced to use all its meagre resources for domestic supply. The data in Table 4.2 illustrate how water supply can direct and limit a nation's development options. This issue will be explored further in 4.2 and 4.3 below.

An additional water supply resource, not so far considered, is groundwater. Table 2.2 shows that groundwater above 800 m comprises 9.86 per cent of freshwater and groundwater above 4,000 m comprises 22.21 per cent of global freshwaters or $8.062 \times 10^6 \, km^3$. WRI (1986) suggests that the limits on this estimate of global groundwater volumes are 8 to $10 \times 10^6 \, km^3$. Many aquifers have very long resumption (recycling) periods of the order of thousands, or even millions, of years. The pumping of water from these strata is a form of mining rather than tapping a renewable resource. Problems of groundwater depletion are already evident after historically and geologically very short periods of withdrawal. The initial problem is increased aquifer depth and consequent pumping cost increases. These have been experienced in the Tamil Nadu State of

Table 4.2  Water use by sector in sixteen countries

| Country | Water withdrawal | | Share withdrawn by sector (%) | | | |
|---|---|---|---|---|---|---|
| | Total (km³) | Per capita (m³) | Public | Industry | Electric cooling | Agriculture/ irrigation |
| United States | 472.000 | 1,986 | 10 | 11 | 38 | 41 |
| Canada | 30.000 | 1,172 | 13 | 39 | 39 | 10 |
| Egypt | 45.000 | 962 | 1 | 0 | 0 | 98 |
| Finland | 4.610 | 946 | 7 | 85 | 0 | 8 |
| Belgium | 8.260 | 836 | 6 | 37 | 47 | 10 |
| USSR | 226.000 | 812 | 8 | 15 | 14 | 63 |
| Panama | 1.300 | 596 | 12 | 11 | 0 | 77 |
| India | 380.000 | 499 | 3 | 1 | 3 | 93 |
| China | 460.000 | 460 | 6 | 7 | 0 | 87 |
| Poland | 15.900 | 423 | 14 | 21 | 40 | 25 |
| Libya | 1.470 | 408 | 17 | 0 | 0 | 83 |
| Oman | 0.043 | 350 | 2 | 0 | 0 | 98 |
| South Africa | 9.200 | 284 | 17 | 0 | 0 | 83 |
| Nicaragua | 0.890 | 272 | 18 | 45 | 0 | 37 |
| Barbados | 0.027 | 102 | 45 | 35 | 0 | 20 |
| Malta | 0.023 | 60 | 100 | 0 | 0 | 0 |

Source: WRI (1986)

India, Northern Africa and in the High Plains of Texas (Beaumont 1985; Postel 1985; Margat and Saad 1984). Consequent environmental problems of coastal salt incursion have been experienced in Israel and the Gulf coast of the US and subsidence caused by the compaction of drained aquifer strata has been experienced in Mexico City, Beijing (China), Houston (Texas) and the central valley of California (WRI 1986). Significant deteriorations in groundwater quality have been experienced in many developed nations due to leaching of fertilizer salts from agricultural land (Royal Society 1983; El Ashray 1980) or contamination from sanitary landfill sites as well as marine incursions.

The pattern of abundance and scarcity is more complex than the data in Table 4.2 indicate. Even within nations, great regional disparities exist and the *quantity* data alone do not indicate the total available resource which can only be determined in relation to the required quality for a specified use category. The *quality* problem is a significant consideration for surface waters which are used to transport and dilute pollution. Reduction in quality effectively reduces the stable supply of water resources available. In a novel review of water supply options, L'Vovich (1977) presented two scenarios to illustrate the importance of water quality in future planning of water supplies. He suggested that, at 150 km$^3$ (i.e. 4% of the stable resource), global abstractions for water supply were relatively minor. However, wastewater loading to the world's rivers is some 450 km$^3$. This requires 6,000 km$^3$ of dilution and transport water, amounting to some 67 per cent of the world's stable runoff. The first scenario illustrates that all the global river flow will be required for pollutant transport by 2000 AD (Fig. 4.4b). The second scenario assumes closed cycling of thermal and industrial effluents together with improved water conservation and groundwater recharge to produce a modest increase in stable runoff resources (Fig. 4.4c). The 1977 pattern, together with both projections, is shown in Fig. 4.4.

Ten years after these projections were made, there is some evidence to suggest that, in the developed world, efforts are being made to reduce pollution loadings by the installation of wastewater treatment plants (Fig. 4.5). This effort has resulted in marked improvements in dissolved oxygen levels in 42 rivers in the developed Western nations monitored by the OECD (1985). However, there is little evidence that developed nations are moving towards closed systems for industrial effluents and thermal power station cooling waters, as recommended by L'Vovich (1977) (see Fig. 4.4c), and pollution of rivers in the USSR, China and the developing world is increasing. WRI (1986:135) have commented on the situation in India as follows:

Out of India's 3,119 towns only 217 have partial (209) or full (8) sewage treatment facilities. The result is severely contaminated waters. A 48 km stretch of the Yamuna river, which flows through New Delhi, contains 7,500 coliform organisms 100 ml$^{-1}$ of water before entering the capital, but after receiving an estimated 200 million litres of untreated sewage every day, it leaves New Delhi carrying an incredible 24 million coliform organisms 100 ml$^{-1}$. Industry is no better. The same stretch of the Yamuna

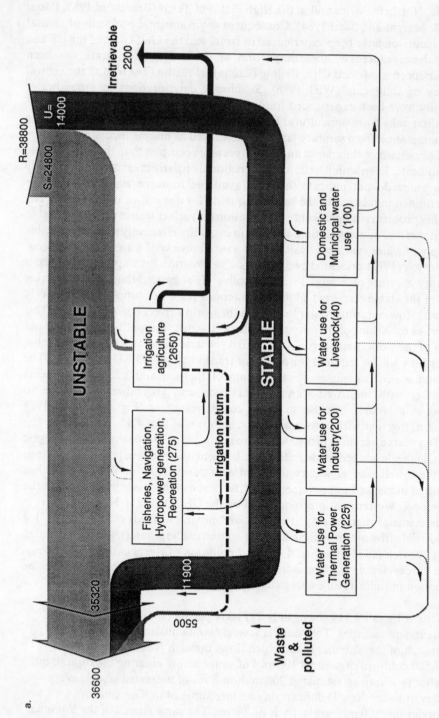

*Fig. 4.4* Three scenarios of global water resource use. (a) The present water balance of the land areas of the world showing the economic arc of the hydrological cycle.

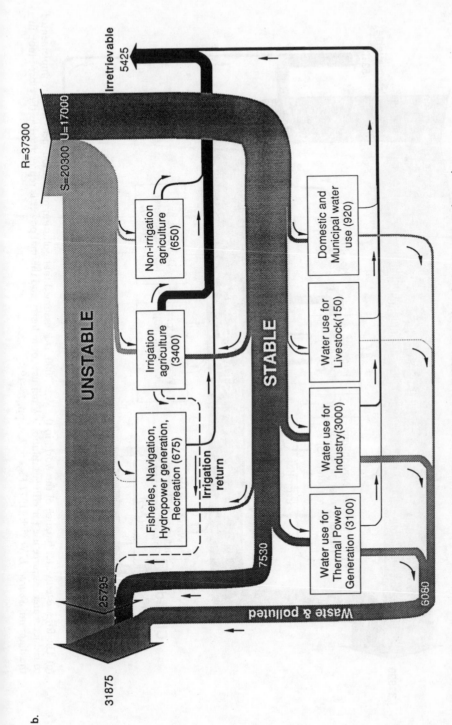

*Fig. 4.4* (b) The forecasted water balance of the world in the year 2000 assuming that present trends continue.

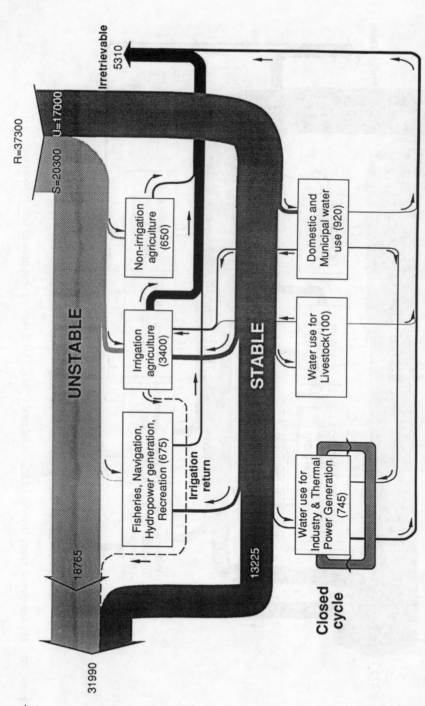

*Fig. 4.4* (c) The forecasted water balance of the world in the year 2000. It is assumed that pollution prevention measures are implemented to reduce water resource use for effluent dilution. Water use for industry and thermal power is represented as the closed loop in the diagram. *Source:* L'Vovich (1977:Figs 6, 7, 8, pp. 18–19)

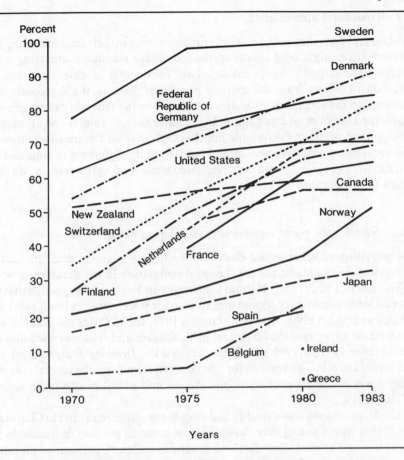

Percent

Sweden

Denmark

Federal
Republic of
Germany

United States

Canada

New Zealand

Norway

Switzerland

Netherlands

France

Japan

Finland

Spain

Belgium • Ireland

• Greece

1970    1975    1980    1983

Years

*Fig. 4.5* Trends in the percentage of population served by wastewater treatment plants for selected countries. *Source*: OECD (1985) and WRI (1986)

river picks up 20 million litres of industrial effluents, including about 500,000 litres of 'D.D.T. wastes' every day.

In developing nations, the urgent need for economic growth has reduced the priority of pollution abatement on the political agenda. In the developed world, some improvement in the *traditional* pollution of rivers by sewage effluents can be identified, but the presence of more recent pollutants and the pollution of groundwater resources are causes for serious concern. The result of this continued pollution is to reduce the availability of stable water resources and bring a possible global water crisis closer. Major water-quality issues are defined and addressed further in Chapter 6. The remainder of this chapter will examine the options for increasing and maintaining water supply in both the developing and developed nations.

## 4.2 Structural approaches

Structural approaches to water supply provision vary in their scale and aims. The smallest scale might be a simple spring-fed village standpipe supplying a few families. The largest projects envisaged are continental in scale, involving the diversion of waters from the sparsely populated areas to the dry continental interiors. In the former case the aim is to improve the reliability of supply and health for a small rural community. In the latter case, the aim is one of regional development where the economic impetus derives from the transformation of arid areas into productive agricultural land. Both the difference in aims and the vast disparity in scales should be remembered while reading this section. We shall return to this point in 4.4 below.

### 4.2.1 Small scale: water supplies in the developing world

The provision of reliable and clean water supplies is an essential element in improving the quality of life for the rural population in the developing world (WHO 1986). The 1976 UN Habitat Conference in Vancouver suggested that the international community should aim to provide water services to all rural and urban dwellers by 1990. Two years later in 1978, the UN Mar del Plata 'Water Conference' supported the targets set in Vancouver and recommended that the period from 1981 to 1990 should be declared the *Drinking Water Supply and Sanitation Decade*. The reasons for this concern stem from the central role that water plays in the areas of economic growth and public health improvement (WHO 1981).

The links between water quality and disease are explored further in Chapters 6 and 9. It is worth noting here, however, that some 80 per cent of disease in the world is water related. The developing nations suffer 96 per cent of all infant mortality (less than 5 years of age) and the majority of this is connected with inadequate water supplies (Bourne 1980). Barabas (1986) has estimated that 10 million deaths result from the 250 million new cases of water-related disease reported annually and that half the world's population suffers from infections caused by polluted waters. In addition to these '*direct health*' effects of inadequate water supply provision, there is an additional cost in time and energy expended in carrying water from the supply to the family dwelling. In a survey of East African water use, the time spent each day in transporting water was estimated by White *et al.* (1972) to average 46 minutes and could be as high as 4 hours. The mainly female water carriers could manage only 14–16 litres on each journey. Thus there is little water surplus available for the hygienically desirable processes of washing and effluent transport.

Akintola *et al.* (1980) studied water transportation in the Ibarapa area of the Oyo state of Nigeria. They calculated an average daily per capita water consumption of 21 litres for those families transporting water compared with a per capita consumption of 82.1 litres in four towns having a piped water supply. The importance of seasonal factors in the choice of available sources within this semi-arid region is stressed. Again, the women provide the labour input to transport water with the 'youngest wife' bearing the major responsibility. The majority (92%) of all households were 1.5–3.0 km from their main source of water supply. The Intermediate Technology Development Group (ITDG) (1978), reporting a study in the Lowveld region of Swaziland, noted per capita usage rates of only 5 litres a day for most households. This rose to 13 litres a day for the better-off families who were able to afford water deliveries. It was suggested that such usage rates could be expected when water is available within about 1.6 km. Thereafter usage does not significantly increase until a tap is provided within each house when per capita consumption can rise to 30–100 litres a day (ITDG 1978).

The health benefits do not solely derive from the improved quality drinking water. Feachem (1978:352) has proposed the taxonomy of water-related diseases presented below:

### The Taxonomy of water-related diseases
### 1. Faecal–oral diseases
(e.g. cholera, typhoid, diarrhoea, dysenteries, hepatitis, ascariasis). These are all infections transmitted by the faecal–oral (faeco–oral, ano–oral, and also faecal-nasal and faeco-ocular) route. They may be water-borne or water-washed.

### 2. Water-washed diseases
(e.g. infections of the skin and infections of the eyes). These are all infections related to poor hygiene (therefore water-washed) but which are not faecal–oral and not water-borne.

### 3. Water-based diseases
(e.g. guinea worm, schistosomiasis, clonorchiasis). These are all the helminths which have an aquatic intermediate host.

### 4. Water-related insect vector
(e.g. malaria, filariasis, yellow fever, trypanosomiasis). These are all infections transmitted by insects which either breed in water or bite near water.

Diseases in category 2 are significantly influenced by the *quantity* of water available for washing rather than the quality of water supplied for direct consumption. It is important therefore to tailor any water-supply strategy to the needs of the society for which it is intended. This may involve sub-optimal solutions where desirable quality conditions become secondary to essential quantity improvements. For example, the village faced with high rates of category 2 diseases would require a large *quantity* from its supply system and considerations of *quality* might be of secondary importance. It should be the aim in all water supply schemes to provide a resource *appropriate* to the needs of the population being served.

This concept of appropriateness has gained considerable ground since the mid-1960s when writers such as Schumacher and McRobie (1969) demonstrated the failure of Western technology to solve the problems of the Third World. This failure was confirmed by the 1973 WHO estimate that 86 per cent of the rural population in developing nations was without access to reasonable supplies of safe water. ITDG (1978) have blamed the importation of Western technology which produced a drift of population to the towns and used scarce capital. Schumacher (1973) suggested *intermediate technology* as one means of creating better living standards in the developing nations. In the water resource field, this concept of intermediate or appropriate technology has taken firm root and can be seen in many projects in developing nations. In essence, such projects are designed to use local resources of labour and technology with low capital inputs. Local-level control over project design and maintenance produces a climate in which the sharing of benefits within the local community follows naturally. The external initiating body, be it a national government or an international agency, is not faced with the difficult moral, social and political problems involved in allocating the benefits of a technologically simple scheme. Often the most difficult problems in implementing a scheme are the socio-political aspects of benefit sharing. Where no adequate system for the distribution of benefits exists, any imported technology is likely to fail irrespective of scale. ITDG (1978:1107) comment on this point as follows:

> Neither the high technology of the west nor intermediate technology is an entity in itself. Each is an expression of human organisation and culture, and of the goals and objectives of human society. Neither is capable of realizing its full promise if used in circumstances where the organization needed to operate it is lacking ... or where goals and objectives are ill-defined. So technology by itself promises nothing; there is no purely technological solution to the problems of poverty and underdevelopment. Technology only yields its full benefits when used within a framework of social development and strengthened organization.

The logical conclusion of this concept of appropriateness is that a project should be designed not merely to pass the test of technical appropriateness, but also to pass the tests of social, political, environmental and economic appropriateness. Table 4.3 illustrates this concept of appropriateness and defines the criteria on which a project should be judged. The same authors suggest a set of goals and objectives for water supply systems in less developed nations (Table 4.4).

The concepts of technology transfer and appropriateness are just as relevant to large-scale river basin planning projects. The projects, outlined in Chapter 8, should be measured against the criteria set out in Tables 4.3 and 4.4. The concept of appropriateness has been introduced at this time to allow the reader to measure the examples cited below against the appropriateness concepts outlined in Table 4.3. Even intermediate technology might not always be appropriate and this is well illustrated in the first example presented in 4.2.1.1.

*Table 4.3*  Criteria of appropriateness against which a water supply project should be
judged

| Criteria derived from immediate objectives | Criteria derived from stage I goals | Criteria derived from stage II goals |
| --- | --- | --- |

1.  Criteria of *technical appropriateness*:

| | | |
| --- | --- | --- |
| Functional appropriateness [fitness for purpose] | Health and sanitary appropriateness [water-borne disease data and water quality] | Health and sanitary appropriateness [water-washed disease data and water quantity and availability] |
| Environmental appropriateness, fitness for hydrological conditions, avoidance of environmental damage | | |

2.  Criteria of *social appropriateness*:

| | | |
| --- | --- | --- |
| Community appropriateness [felt needs and stated preferences in the community; scale in relation to community size and organisation] | Consumer appropriateness [changes in water carrying and in water use patterns] | Maintenance appropriateness [organisation, administration, village/government responsibilities, spare parts supply training, record-keeping] |
| Work appropriateness [organisation of labour force] | Educational appropriateness [degree of interest created in health, hygiene and other development] | |

3.  Criteria of *economic appropriateness*:

| | | |
| --- | --- | --- |
| Resource utilization appropriateness | | Production appropriateness |
| [capital and labour intensity, import bill, fuel consumption; scale economies] | | [amount of time/energy saving and volume of water available for productive purposes] |

*Source*: ITDG (1978:1111, Table 2)

Table 4.4 Goals and objectives for water supply improvements in rural areas of developing countries

| Immediate objectives | Further goals – stage I (these follow as consequences when the immediate objectives have been met) | Further goals – stage II (these follow from previous stages if complementary inputs are provided) | Further goals – stage III (these are consequences of reaching the previous goals which follow if there are also inputs on many other fronts) |
|---|---|---|---|
| *Functional:*<br>to improve the quality, quantity, availability and reliability of the supply | *Health:*<br>to reduce incidence of water-borne and water-based disease | *Health:*<br>to reduce incidence of water-washed infections (inputs required: improved hygiene, health education improved sanitation) | to achieve the greater well-being of the people through: |
| | *Energy/time (economic):*<br>to save time and energy expended in carrying water | *Social/technical:*<br>to ensure good long-term maintenance of water supply and sanitation facilities (inputs required: training, clear allocation of responsibility, build-up of local maintenance organisation) | (a) social change – greater self-reliance in the community, better organisation, better deal for the poor, women, etc. |
| *Other:*<br>to carry out this improvement in a manner which (a) secures the support of users; (b) conserves scarce resources (e.g. capital); (c) avoids adverse environmental consequences (e.g. lowering water tables, encouraging mosquitoes) | *Social:*<br>to arouse interest in the further health and economic benefits which may arise from the water supply | | (b) improved standard of living – health, nutrition, income, leisure |
| | *Economic:*<br>to provide more water for livestock and garden irrigation (water may be used for this even if it is intended solely for domestic supply) | *Economic:*<br>to use energy/time savings and increased water availability to achieve better agricultural output (inputs required: extension work, fertilizer supply, etc.) | |

*Source:* ITDG (1978:1110, Table 1)

### 4.2.1.1 The bamboo tubewell

The bamboo tubewell provides an excellent example of *appropriate* technology. This simple but effective system for lining small-bore wells was developed in the Kosi region of India (Fig. 4.6). The invention and installation of the first well has been reported by Appu (1974) and Dommen (1975). The inventor, Ram Prasad Chaudary Jaiswal, was a farmer with medium land holdings (some 6 ha) near Saharsa.

This area in the Kosi region of northern Bihar is ideal for the exploitation of groundwater (Fig. 4.6). The aquifers are of alluvial sands and silts and recharge takes place from the 1,500+ mm of rainfall together with seepage from the Kosi canal system. The groundwater table is found between 5 and 20 m depth. Well construction takes only a few hours in the soft alluvial deposits. Prior to 1969, irrigation waters came either from the Kosi project or metal tubewells. The Kosi project takes water from the Kosi river, the main Himalayan tributary of the Ganges in Bihar, and distributes it to the Purnea and Saharsa districts.

The 100 mm metal tubewells consisted of a brass strainer beneath an iron pipe

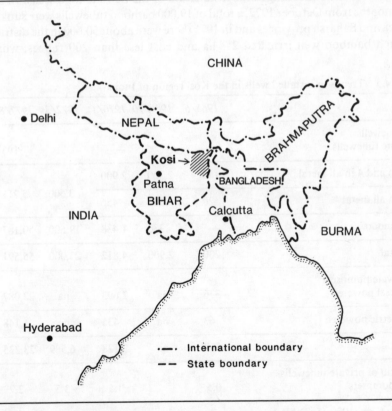

*Fig. 4.6* The Kosi region of India. *Source*: Clay (1982:190, Fig. 1)

and were sunk to a depth of 50 m. The total cost of well installation was some 8,000 rupees, which included the cost of a diesel pump to lift the water. This cost was beyond the means of small or medium farmers and only 1,580 wells were installed in Purnea and Saharsa in the period 1970–4 (Appu 1974). Farmers in neighbouring West Bengal attempted to reduce tubewell costs. They fabricated a cylinder by welding vertical steel rod to horizontal iron rings around which they wrapped rough string to produce a strainer. This reduced the cost of well lining from 4,000 to 900 rupees. The cost remained too expensive for smaller farmers and access to welding technology was not always available. It was against this background of scarce resources and limited innovation that the first bamboo tubewell was invented in December 1968.

The bamboo tubewell replaced the vertical steel rod with strips of bamboo which were secured with rough string to produce a strainer. The upper parts of the well liner were sealed with coal tar and fabric. The bamboo tubewell proved a great success, providing a plentiful and reliable source of water. Neither the locally fabricated welded steel or bamboo structures were backed by the Indian government's tubewell department which favoured the more expensive steel and brass structure. However, energetic local officials of the Purnea and Saharsa state governments encouraged the installation of the new bamboo wells. In the four months from October 1972, a total of 19,000 bamboo tubewells were sunk in Purnea and Saharsa provinces and in 1975 there were about 50,000 in the district.

Each bamboo well irrigated 2–4 ha and cost less than 200 rupees, which

*Table 4.5*  Trends in installed wells in the Kosi region of India

| | 1965/6 | 1969/70 | 1970/1 | 1972/3 | 1977/8 |
|---|---|---|---|---|---|
| 1. Tubewells: | | | | | |
| State tubewells | — | — | — | — | 193 |
| 6 in and 4 in all metal | 180 | 2,300 | 2,900 | 3,500 | 5,211 |
| 3 in all metal | 20 | 340 | 456 | | |
| Bamboo | — | 330 | 1,438 | 19,500 | 50,187 |
| Total | 200 | 2,900 | 4,812 | 23,000 | 55,591 |
| 2. Private pumpsets: | | | | | |
| Diesel powered | 336 | na | 2,693 | na | 22,087 |
| Electric powered | 63 | na | 435 | na | 1,148 |
| Total | 399 | na | 3,128 | 6,589 | 23,235 |
| 3. Ratio of private tubewells to pumpsets | 0.5 | | 1.5 | 3.5 | 2.2 |

*Source*: Clay (1980:45, Table 1)

brings the technology within the range of even the small farmer. Partial loans of up to 50 rupees for the installation of the bamboo tubewells were available from the state government, and farmers were encouraged to purchase or hire mobile diesel pumps for water lifting. Generally one pump is needed for five wells.

The Kosi region illustrates three distinct levels of project:

1. The Kosi project;
2. Metal tubewells;
3. Bamboo tubewells.

The high-cost, high-technology Kosi project, initiated in 1954 and opened in 1964, was designed to reduce flooding, yield a little hydro-electricity and provide reliable irrigation for 1.4 million ha via a network of canals. By 1966, following the Intensive Agricultural Areas Programme (IAAP) and the High Yielding Varieties Programme (HYVP), the Kosi region was well placed to provide a testbed for the aims of the *Green Revolution*. The early promise of the Kosi project has not come to fruition because of silting within the irrigation canals and insufficient sharing of project benefits throughout the community (Clay 1982). Indeed, the siltation problem often results in the closing of the canal system for up to three months, which can have very serious effects on cropping schedules (Dommen 1975). The major contribution of the Kosi project for the smaller farmer was the introduction of high-yielding wheat strains. This made irrigation very profitable but the land-holding pattern, comprising many small farmers, was not suited to the purchase of expensive items of fixed capital equipment by individual farmers.

The high-cost steel and brass well system was not economically available to many farmers. Mortgage payments for the purchase of an 8,000-rupee well would require at least 3.2 ha of land per farmer (Clay 1980). The government steel and brass wells therefore failed the test of social and economic appropriateness. This failure generated the pressure for innovation and directed it to the needs of the smaller farmer who perceived the benefits of the HYVP but to whom the available irrigation methods were not available.

The bamboo well was socially and economically appropriate and, when combined with portable pumpsets, allowed access to the technology for all farmers in the region. The reasons for the success of this simple and cheap technology probably derive from its local design and manufacture. These factors reduce the transferability of the technology which is designed for use in coarse sandy alluvium with shallow groundwaters. In other regions where the aquifer characteristics differ, such simple indigenous technology might not be appropriate. For example, where aquifers are deeper, the high costs and technology involved in hydrogeological surveys and deep drilling would warrant a more durable well structure.

### 4.2.1.2 Village-scale drinking water supplies

The concept of appropriate technology is no less applicable in the context of village water supplies than in the case of the Kosi tubewells outlined above. In many respects, the *best* solution, as seen from a Western perspective, may not always be appropriate to a given situation. As ITDG (1978:109) have stated:

> when Western engineers have worked on water supplies for low income countries, they have not usually had any clearer objective in mind than to have 'safe' water flowing out of the end of a pipe. However, for the great majority of the world's population who live in rural communities or urban slums, with grossly inadequate access to safe water, there is no possibility that available financial and human resources will give them the same high level of water provision as enjoyed by people in North America and Europe .... The danger in water supplies is that one may be distracted from good and useful improvements by the vision of what may be best, but not really attainable.

ITDG (1978) criticised the World Health Organization (WHO) water-quality standards for small-scale community water supplies which state that water should contain less than one *Escherichia coli* or 10 total coliforms 100 ml$^{-1}$. If implemented, this standard would condemn most rural water supplies in the developing world and hence fewer people would receive any form of supply. In fact the extent to which a supply fulfils the criteria of *health and sanitary appropriateness* should be judged on the basis of the disease-prevalence rates in the particular community. Feachem (1977) has suggested the design criteria in Table 4.6 to ensure health and sanitary appropriateness in rural water supply.

Simple design criteria can be applied to improve the quality of existing

*Table 4.6*   Four water supply options for rural water supplies

---

I.   Supply without treatment:
   (a)   if the water is less polluted than a specified limit and if there is no schistosomiasis or guinea-worm in the community;

   (b)   or where water is more polluted than the specified limit, only if a treatment plant cannot be maintained or afforded, if there is no schistosomiasis in the community, if water-borne infections are not prevalent, and if risks due to large numbers using the source are within specified limits.

II.  Supply without any treatment apart from 48 hours' storage:
   when there is schistosomiasis in the community, but if conditions I(a) or I(b) are otherwise fulfilled.

III. Supply with treatment:
   if the water is more polluted than a specified limit and if a treatment plant can be afforded and maintained.

IV.  Abandon the proposed water source and seek an alternative:
   if the water is more polluted than the specified limit;
   if water-borne infections are prevalent, and risks are enhanced by large numbers of users, and if a treatment plant cannot be afforded or maintained.

---

*Sources*: Feachem (1977) and ITDG (1978:1118)

supplies in rural areas. Most of these are designed to exclude human and animal faeces from the supply. For example, the hand-dug well, economically and socially appropriate in developing nations, can develop into a sink for foul surface drainage as well as a breeding ground for pathogens and disease vectors. Simple sanitary engineering techniques, such as the use of concrete well liners, can prevent faecal contamination and effect a marked improvement in the quality of supply (Fig. 4.7).

Even this type of low-technology engineering may not be appropriate where the skills and parts are not available for regular pump maintenance. It has been estimated that of the 150,000 village hand pumps in operation in India, as many as 90,000 may be inoperable at any one time due to breakdowns (*New Internationalist*, Feb. 1975, quoted in ITDG 1978). In Indonesia, hand pumps have been installed to effect the targets set under the International Drinking Water Supply and Sanitation Decade which suggest that 60 per cent of the rural population should have access to a safe water supply and 40 per cent to adequate sanitation by 1990. Mathur (1986) has observed that, in the province of South Sulawesi (Indonesia), where 17,452 shallow well hand pumps and 1992 deep well hand pumps have been installed, 8,740 (55%) of the shallow pumps and 467 (25%) of the deep pumps were inoperable due to breakdowns in 1986. The reasons for breakdown were similar to the Indian experience and included improper operation and maintenance, poor quality of the locally made pumps, pump designs inappropriate for local maintenance, and the lack of spare parts. On a more positive note, Mathur (1986) reported that the Indonesian Ministry of Health had learned quickly from its experience and had instigated measures to renovate existing pumps and to improve inadequate pump designs. Problems of pump design and maintenance are still widespread and a major aim of future water supply schemes should be to perfect this nineteenth-century technology (Arlosoroff *et al*. 1984).

In semi-arid areas the water supply is extremely variable and the main problem in developing nations lies in storing water using small reservoirs or catchment tank systems. ITDG (1978) suggest several simple and practical designs for catchment tanks. The *beehive* tank is constructed using polythene tubes filled with a weak concrete mixture which sets after the tubes have taken up the desired shape in the ground (Fig. 4.8a). Surface water entering the reservoir passes through a sand fill which acts as a filter. The principles of source protection illustrated in Fig. 4.7 should be adopted for the beehive supply. Figures 4.8b and 4.8c show two further small-scale storage systems suggested for small rural supplies by ITDG (1978).

Where surface waters of dubious quality must be used, simple treatment can be adopted to decrease both bacterial concentration and turbidity. The type of slow sand filter, shown in Fig. 4.9, is housed within an oil drum. It can treat around 750 litres of water a day and 100-fold reductions in enteric bacteria could be expected. The rapid gravity filter produces a higher flow rate of 3,000 litres a day but it does not produce such an efficient biological filter and bacterial removal is less effective.

### Unlined hand dug well

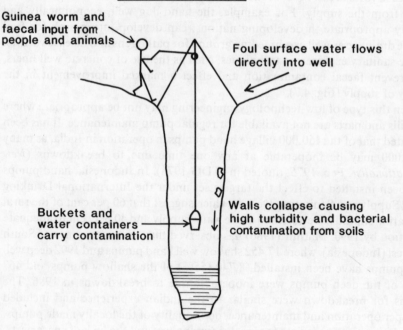

Guinea worm and faecal input from people and animals →

Foul surface water flows directly into well

Buckets and water containers carry contamination →

Walls collapse causing high turbidity and bacterial contamination from soils

### Concrete lined hand dug well

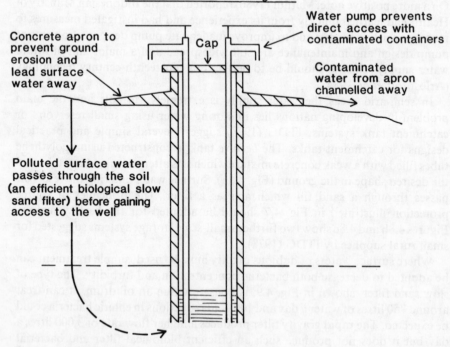

Water pump prevents direct access with contaminated containers

Concrete apron to prevent ground erosion and lead surface water away

Cap

Contaminated water from apron channelled away →

Polluted surface water passes through the soil (an efficient biological slow sand filter) before gaining access to the well

*Fig 4.7* Sources of contamination for hand-dug wells

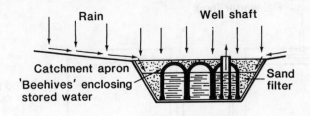

Rain      Well shaft

Catchment apron
'Beehives' enclosing
stored water

Sand
filter

a.

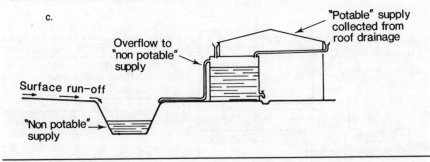

Run-off

Underground
storage tanks

b.

c.

"Potable" supply
collected from
roof drainage

Overflow to
"non potable"
supply

Surface run-off

"Non potable"
supply

*Fig. 4.8* Three simple storage systems for small rural water supplies: a: beehive tanks;
b: impervious surface catchments; c: roof water collector. *Source*: ITDG
(1978:1136–7, Figs 12, 13, 14)

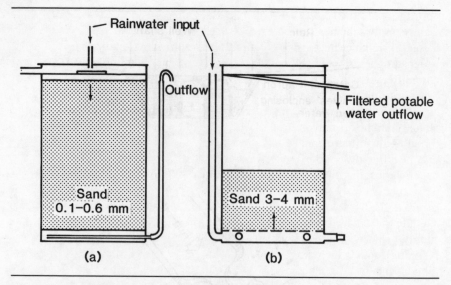

Fig. 4.9 Two simple filter designs: slow sand (a) and rapid gravity (b). *Source*: ITDG (1978:1120)

One system suggested for semi-arid regions combines storage with filtration. The sand fill dam (Fig. 4.10) consists of a low embankment and is built in stages. This allows flood waters carrying fine suspended sediment to run over the dam, trapping coarser gravels and sands. After 4–5 years the full operating depth of the aquifer (6–12 m) can be achieved and the sand fill acts as an efficient filtration system.

Even these small-scale systems require social and economic co-operation as well as rudimentary technical expertise. The success or failure of such intermediate technology is therefore dependent on the degree to which it is

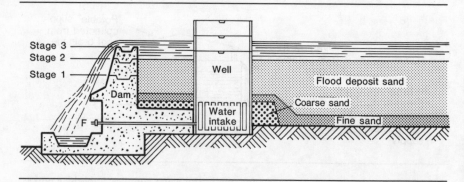

Fig. 4.10 A sand fill dam, providing water storage and filtration. The dam is built in stages to allow sediment accretion, over a period of several years, to deposit an efficient slow sand filter. *Source*: ITDG (1978:1132)

appropriate to the society for which it is intended. To some extent, small-scale water supply schemes can be used to strengthen village social structures and foster self-reliance in the rural community. The introduction of spring-fed piped water supplies into Lesotho villages provides one example where a village committee structure is a pre-requisite for government aid. This form of organisation offered a mechanism for reinforcing the development benefits of clean water which include improved hygiene and irrigation. In addition, the village committees perceive the project as village owned and take responsibility for subsequent maintenance and repair. Obviously the response of each village may be different, but the devolution of responsibility for a supply scheme to the beneficiaries presents a useful model. Parallels can be seen with the successful Kosi tubewells which were the responsibility of the individual farmers. In contrast, the Kosi canal project was a relative failure under government control. To date there have been very few post-audit evaluations of village-scale water supply projects. Cairncross *et al.* (1980:2) have set out a clear and practical planning model, including an 'evaluation' stage. They note that evaluation remains the 'neglected activity' in rural water supply planning.

### 4.2.1.3  The International Drinking Water Supply and Sanitation Decade: experience to 1986

Water supply improvements of the type outlined above, together with better sanitation, have formed the central goal of the Drinking Water Supply and Sanitation Decade (1981–90). The World Health Organisation has evaluated the success of the decade until 1986, measured in terms of urban and rural populations served by water supply and sanitation (WHO 1986). Table 4.7 presents selected statistics from the WHO data, although the survey years of 1970 and 1983 do not allow the effects of the UN initiative to be isolated from the general trend.

Historical evidence from the developed world points to the importance of water supply and sanitation in producing significant health benefits (see Chapter 6). However, good-quality epidemiological data is scarce because diseases may have multiple causes related to both water supply and general hygiene which are related to the socio-economic pattern in the community (Esrey 1985; Herbert 1985; Waxler 1985; Briscoe 1984a, b; Saunders and Warford 1976). Cvjetanovic (1986) has suggested the scheme outlined in Fig. 4.11 to represent these multiple confounding factors.

Where a successful water supply scheme is in operation, the initiating authority is often interested in facilitating modest social and economic benefits which will, in themselves, produce some improvement in public health through education and better living standards. It is probably irrelevant, therefore, to attempt to isolate the strictly *water-related* health benefits of any scheme (Feachem 1984; Blum and Feachem 1983). Describing a water supply scheme at Bara Banki, near Lucknow (India), Cvjetanovic (1986:114) has commented:

Table 4.7 Recent trends and targets for water supply (a) and sanitation (b) in the developing world

(a)

| WHO region and subsector | 1970 Population (000) Total | Service coverage | 1980 Population (000) Total | Service coverage | 1983 Population (000) Total | Service coverage | 1990 (targets) Population (000) Total | Service coverage |
|---|---|---|---|---|---|---|---|---|
| *Africa* | | | | | | | | |
| Urban | 28,732 | 70 | 44,508 | 62 | 63,662 | 61 | 54,797 | 83 |
| House connections | 28,732 | 39 | 43,297 | 30 | 63,662 | 33 | 47,999 | 41 |
| Standposts | 28,732 | 30 | 43,297 | 32 | 63,662 | 27 | 47,999 | 40 |
| Rural | 121,223 | 10 | 168,551 | 24 | 202,190 | 26 | 120,473 | 60 |
| TOTAL | 141,404 | 18 | 211,630 | 32 | 265,307 | 34 | 173,945 | 67 |
| *Americas* | | | | | | | | |
| Urban | 156,298 | 76 | 219,757 | 77 | 213,172 | 85 | 277,513 | 88 |
| House connections | 156,292 | 61 | 219,757 | 71 | 213,172 | 73 | 276,621 | 84 |
| Standposts | 156,292 | 15 | 219,757 | 6 | 213,172 | 12 | 276,621 | 4 |
| Rural | 117,939 | 24 | 119,510 | 41 | 112,026 | 40 | 81,678 | 54 |
| TOTAL | 274,237 | 54 | 339,267 | 54 | 318,602 | 70 | 245,423 | 76 |
| *Eastern Mediterranean* | | | | | | | | |
| Urban | 63,786 | 80 | 71,661 | 83 | 44,234 | 86 | 60,368 | 99 |
| House connections | 63,786 | 58 | 71,661 | 53 | 18,834 | 68 | 26,168 | 86 |

| | | | | | | | | |
|---|---|---|---|---|---|---|---|---|
| Standposts | 63,786 | 23 | 71,661 | 31 | 18,834 | 28 | 26,168 | 12 |
| Rural | 140,546 | 22 | 133,941 | 30 | 91,800 | 26 | 138,740 | 72 |
| TOTAL | 204,332 | 40 | 205,602 | 48 | 132,327 | 44 | 173,732 | 79 |
| *South-east Asia* | | | | | | | | |
| Urban | 149,418 | 51 | 232,601 | 64 | 252,999 | 66 | 309,156 | 89 |
| House connections | 149,418 | 35 | 232,601 | — | 20,592 | 22 | 1,771 | 48 |
| Standposts | 149,418 | 16 | 232,601 | — | 20,592 | 13 | 1,771 | 46 |
| Rural | 668,684 | 9 | 787,360 | 31 | 822,889 | 43 | 921,659 | 90 |
| TOTAL | 817,530 | 17 | 1,019,961 | 38 | 1,074,769 | 49 | 1,230,815 | 89 |
| *Western Pacific* | | | | | | | | |
| Urban | 31,839 | 80 | 56,403 | 81 | 34,250 | 70 | 50,117 | 87 |
| House connections | 31,839 | 70 | 56,381 | 77 | 34,186 | 54 | 44,382 | 67 |
| Standposts | 31,389 | 10 | 56,381 | 4 | 34,186 | 16 | 44,382 | 18 |
| Rural | 62,354 | 27 | 101,788 | 40 | 108,713 | 45 | 121,030 | 91 |
| TOTAL | 94,193 | 45 | 115,789 | 62 | 83,189 | 60 | 146,216 | 88 |
| *Total* | | | | | | | | |
| Urban | 430,073 | 68 | 624,930 | 72 | 608,317 | 74 | 751,951 | 89 |
| House connections | 430,073 | 51 | 389,885 | 64 | 350,446 | 61 | 396,941 | 77 |
| Standposts | 430,073 | 17 | 389,885 | 13 | 350,446 | 16 | 396,941 | 11 |
| Rural | 1,110,746 | 14 | 1,311,150 | 31 | 1,337,618 | 39 | 1,383,580 | 83 |
| TOTAL | 1,531,696 | 29 | 1,892,249 | 45 | 1,874,194 | 50 | 1,970,131 | 85 |

Water supply

(b)

| WHO region and subsector | 1970 | | 1980 | | 1983 | | 1990 (targets) | |
|---|---|---|---|---|---|---|---|---|
| | Population (000) Total | Service coverage | Population (000) Total | Service coverage | Population (000) Total | Service coverage | Population (000) Total | Service coverage |
| *Africa* | | | | | | | | |
| Urban | 25,588 | 40 | 24,182 | 59 | 23,184 | 68 | 32,904 | 82 |
| Sewer connections | 25,588 | 8 | 23,081 | 16 | 23,184 | 18 | 30,934 | 12 |
| Other | 25,588 | 32 | 23,081 | 44 | 23,184 | 50 | 30,934 | 58 |
| Rural | 111,593 | 19 | 85,042 | 21 | 108,544 | 25 | 86,939 | 57 |
| TOTAL | 135,962 | 22 | 107,504 | 30 | 97,265 | 38 | 116,772 | 63 |
| *Americas* | | | | | | | | |
| Urban | 115,054 | 76 | 137,649 | 71 | 136,713 | 80 | 135,061 | 79 |
| Sewer connections | 114,698 | 35 | 137,649 | 47 | 136,713 | 48 | 135,061 | 67 |
| Other | 114,698 | 41 | 137,649 | 23 | 136,713 | 32 | 135,061 | 12 |
| Rural | 118,768 | 23 | 70,260 | 21 | 73,444 | 20 | 94,171 | 37 |
| TOTAL | 196,488 | 54 | 187,013 | 51 | 191,152 | 61 | 189,850 | 63 |
| *Eastern Mediterranean* | | | | | | | | |
| Urban | 40,823 | 61 | 49,666 | 62 | 39,990 | 64 | 59,353 | 75 |
| Sewer connections | 40,823 | 7 | 25,966 | 31 | 14,590 | 37 | 25,153 | 70 |

| | | | | | | | | |
|---|---|---|---|---|---|---|---|---|
| Other | 40,823 | 54 | 25,966 | 49 | 14,590 | 47 | 25,153 | 19 |
| Rural | 107,389 | 13 | 109,975 | 6 | 70,977 | 7 | 115,556 | 25 |
| TOTAL | 148,179 | 26 | 132,601 | 24 | 105,704 | 26 | 174,909 | 42 |
| *South-east Asia* | | | | | | | | |
| Urban | 148,846 | 78 | 232,541 | 30 | 249,649 | 31 | 309,156 | 68 |
| Sewer connections | 148,846 | 28 | — | | 20,592 | 4 | — | |
| Other | 148,846 | 49 | | | 20,592 | 22 | | |
| Rural | 668,684 | 4 | 786,220 | 6 | 809,570 | 7 | 907,859 | 30 |
| TOTAL | 817,530 | 17 | 1,018,761 | 12 | 1,059,219 | 13 | 1,213,215 | 34 |
| *Western Pacific* | | | | | | | | |
| Urban | 31,359 | 80 | 56,294 | 92 | 29,018 | 80 | 50,855 | 73 |
| Sewer connections | 31,359 | 20 | 56,294 | 17 | 28,997 | 13 | 44,128 | 20 |
| Other | 31,359 | 60 | 56,294 | 76 | 28,997 | 67 | 44,128 | 49 |
| Rural | 59,745 | 23 | 101,351 | 62 | 93,488 | 57 | 95,038 | 85 |
| TOTAL | 91,104 | 43 | 110,526 | 78 | 77,106 | 58 | 138,736 | 80 |
| *Total* | | | | | | | | |
| Urban | 361,670 | 73 | 500,332 | 53 | 478,554 | 53 | 587,329 | 72 |
| Sewer connections | 361,314 | 26 | 242,990 | 36 | 224,076 | 36 | 235,276 | 51 |
| Other | 361,314 | 47 | 242,990 | 40 | 224,076 | 36 | 235,276 | 26 |
| Rural | 1,066,179 | 9 | 1,152,848 | 13 | 1,156,023 | 14 | 1,299,563 | 36 |
| TOTAL | 1,389,263 | 26 | 1,556,405 | 23 | 1,530,446 | 24 | 1,833,482 | 43 |

*Source:* WHO (1986:10–11, Tables 2 and 3)

83

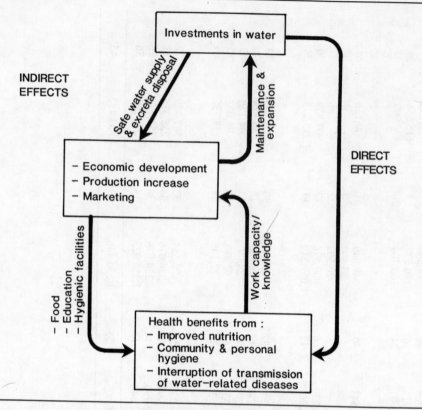

*Fig. 4.11* Direct and indirect effects of water supply and sanitation on health: a conceptual framework. *Source*: Cvjetanovic (1986:109)

The initial effects of water supply and sanitation in Bara Banki, besides being beneficial to health, also triggered economic development, transforming poor villages with a subsistence economy into marketing areas. This led to economic prosperity and wellbeing.

and on water supply improvements at Mraclin (Yugoslavia):

Even the second world war did not stop the progress initiated in 1926 in Mraclin, a village that continued to lead in health and wellbeing in the area for decades. The elimination of enteric infections resulted in a ten fold decrease in infant mortality rate and brought about changes in the appearance of the village and the lifestyle of the population, with the advent of prosperity and good health. The provision of safe water supply and sanitation undoubtedly played a role in this process of development although their exact contribution cannot readily be measured.

This anecdotal evidence for the health benefits of water supply provision is

supported by historical analyses of disease-incidence trends as shown in Fig.
4.12. These trends imply, but do not prove, a causal link. The problems of
quantifying health benefits make any detailed mid-term audit of the International Drinking Water and Sanitation Decade difficult. Some improvements
can be identified in the proportions of people connected to 'safe' water supplies

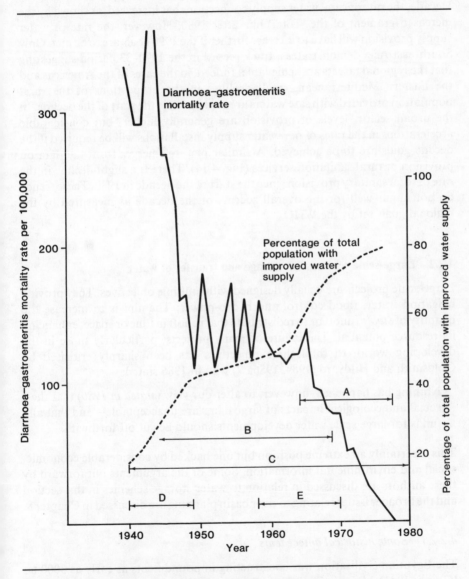

*Fig. 4.12*  Trends in diarrhoea–gastroenteritis mortality rates and population
percentage with access to improved water supply in Costa Rica.
*Source*: McJunkin (1982) cited in Cvjetanovic (1986:112)

(Table 4.7). However, at the end of 1983, less than 40 per cent of the rural population and 75 per cent of the urban population in developing countries had access to safe water supplies (Deck 1986). Figure 4.13 shows the trends in rural water supply provision for the survey years of 1970, 1980 and 1983, together with the 1990 targets.

During the period of the International Drinking Water Supply and Sanitation Decade, the rate of rural water supply connections has increased, as shown by the increased gradient of the 'Total' line after 1980. However, the rate of water supply provision will have to increase further if the 1990 goals are to be met. Only South-east Asia demonstrates a track record in the 1970–83 period suggesting that the regional targets are achievable. Indeed, in the cases of the Americas and the Eastern Mediterranean, small declines in the proportions of the rural population provided with safe waters are evident since the start of the decade. In the urban sector, levels of provision are generally higher, but considerable accelerations in the rates of new water supply installations will be required if the decade goals are to be achieved. A similar picture emerges from the data on provision of rural sanitation services (Fig. 4.14). There is a slight decline in the rate of total sanitary provision since the start of the decade in 1980. These trends do not augur well for the overall success of the decade as measured by the regional goals set by the WHO.

## 4.2.2 Large-scale schemes for storage and transfer of water

Large-scale projects are usually designed with multiple objectives. They provide irrigation water, flood control and hydro-power. The aim is to increase the quantity of *stable* runoff or to redistribute that runoff in time or space, enhancing its resource potential. The failure of many projects, particularly those in the developing world, to fulfil these objectives has been sharply criticised by Goldsmith and Hildyard (1984, 1986a:7) who in 1986 stated:

> Nothing has happened, however, to alter our view (*stated in 1980*) that the social and ecological impacts of large dams are unacceptable – and that all funds for large scale water developments should be cut off forthwith.

This is certainly an extreme position but one backed by considerable economic, social and environmental information. Some of the arguments put forward by these authors are discussed in relation to water storage schemes in this section and the broader issues relating to river basin planning are discussed in Chapter 8.

### 4.2.2.1 Some historical antecedents

The Egyptian civilisation was constructing impoundments as early as 3000 BC (Goudie 1981). Major irrigation and flood control structures were constructed in the Szechwan province of China in 250 BC (Jones 1954).

The Tukiangyen irrigation system in Szechwan was born out of the necessity

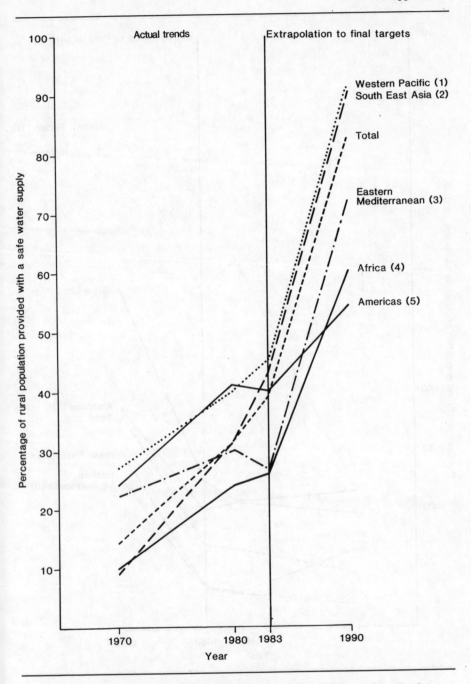

*Fig. 4.13*  Trends in water supply provision for the rural population of developing countries. *Source*: WHO (1986: data from Table 2)

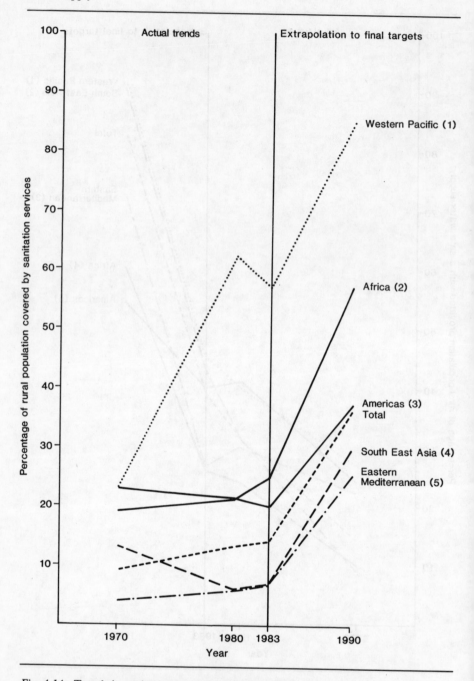

*Fig. 4.14* Trends in sanitation provision for the rural population of developing countries. *Source*: WHO (1986: data from Table 3)

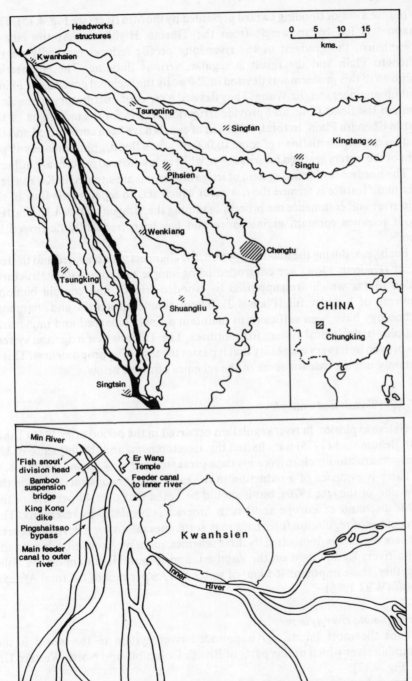

*Fig. 4.15*   The Tukiangyien irrigation system based on the Min river diversion.
*Source*: Jones (1954:544, Fig. 1)

to reduce a major flooding hazard presented by the Min river (see Fig. 4.15). This channel is fed by snowmelt from the Tibetan Highlands. At the city of Kwanhsien, the gradient of the river-long profile reduces markedly on the Chengtu Plain and the result is regular, serious flooding. The engineering solution to this problem was devised in 250 BC by the regional governor, Li Ping, and his engineer son, Er Wang. They devised a series of distributory channels to contain the flood flows and provide irrigation waters for 0.2 million ha of the fertile Chengtu Plain. In total, 1,171 km of canals have been constructed and the system can cope with flows of some 10,000 $m^3$ $s^{-1}$. In flood, approximately 40 per cent of the waters are used for irrigation, while at low flow 60 per cent are utilised.

The headworks for this system of irrigation canals are situated in Kwanhsien. The main feature is termed the *fish snout* which acts to separate the flow of the Min river and commence the process of taming the 'dragon' (Plate 4.1). The fish snout requires constant maintenance and has been frequently destroyed by floods.

Each year, during the low-flow period, the channels are excavated and the fish snout repaired. Flows are controlled using simple temporary dam structures called Matza which are supported by wooden tripods and contain bamboo sausages of boulder fill (Plate 4.2). These simple structures and 'bamboo' technology have been sufficient to maintain a finely balanced and immensely complex hydrological system for centuries. The Tukiangyien irrigation system has proven by its very durability that it passes the tests of appropriateness. This is certainly not the case for some of the schemes outlined below.

### 4.2.2.2    Trends and examples

A relative explosion in river regulation occurred in the period after 1945 (Table 4.8). Beaumount (1978) has charted this development, and the influence of US dam construction is clear from his data presented in Fig. 4.16 and Table 4.8.

There is evidence of a reduction in the rates of dam construction since the recession of the late 1970s, but it should be noted that over 40 per cent of the stable discharge of Europe and North America is regulated by reservoirs. The percentage of regulation for Africa may seem anomalous for a developing area but here the data is dominated by three schemes, namely: Akosombo dam on the Volta river, Kariba dam on the Zambesi, and Aswan High dam on the Nile. Together, these impound 465 $km^3$ of water or 13.6 per cent of the total African runoff (WRI 1986).

### The Columbia river system

Perhaps the most intensively impounded river system in the world is the Columbia river which drains parts of British Columbia and North Western US (see Fig. 4.17).

The exploitation of the Columbia system offers several lessons for those who assume that the logic of engineering design or the quick technical fix can solve complex political, social and environmental issues.

*Plate 4.1*  The main diversion of the Min river at Kwanhsien looking upstream. The channel on the left is the main irrigation feeder canal.
*Source*: Jones (1954:Fig. 4)

*Plate 4.2*  Temporary dam, or Matza, construction. *Source*: Jones (1954)

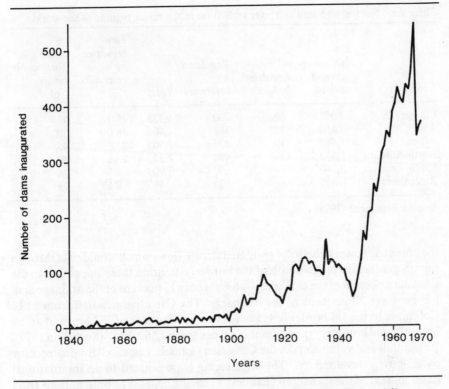

*Fig. 4.16*  Trends in dam inauguration. *Source*: Beaumont (1978:Figs 1 and 2)

The US portion of the Columbia system was exploited in the early years of this century for extensive irrigation development. Over 11,200 km of irrigation feeder canals were dug and 28 major projects were commenced under the Theodore Roosevelt administration. These impoundment projects had severe effects on the valuable Columbia salmon fisheries. The full hydro-electric and irrigation potential of the US Columbia system was developed later by both the US Army Corps of Engineers and the Bureau of Reclamation which formulated plans for 30 dams in the 1930s (Netboy 1986).

These structures have also reduced flooding in the lower Columbia around Dalles where major floods in 1894 and 1948 caused severe property damage and loss of life. The estimated discharges of these flood events were 35,118 $m^3 s^{-1}$ and 28,604 $m^3 s^{-1}$ respectively. The 'manageable' flood level at Dalles is 22,656 $m^3 s^{-1}$. By 1959, US storage of some 9.9 $km^3$ had been constructed. An additional 13.6 $km^3$ of storage would be required to reduce a flood of 1894 proportions to manageable levels. This extra storage was not available to US engineers because by 1959, 238 m of the available 537 m headfall south of the border had already been utilised and schemes to use all the remainder were under construction.

The flood reduction benefits of additional Canadian storage are paralleled by

*Table 4.8*  Natural and artificial river regulation in the major regions of the world

| Continent | Of under-ground origin | Regulated by lakes | Regulated by reservoirs | Total | Flow regulated by reservoirs (%) | Total stable runoff (%) |
|---|---|---|---|---|---|---|
| Europe | 1,065 | 60 | 200 | 1,325 | 15.1 | 43 |
| Asia | 3,410 | 35 | 560 | 4,005 | 14.0 | 30 |
| Africa | 1,465 | 40 | 400 | 1,905 | 21.0 | 45 |
| North America | 1,740 | 150 | 490 | 2,380 | 20.6 | 40 |
| South America | 3,740 | — | 160 | 3,900 | 4.1 | 38 |
| Australasia | 465 | — | 30 | 495 | 6.1 | 25 |

*Source*: Beaumont (1978)

the potential power benefits of regulated stream flows which would pass through the US generation plants south of the border. Attention therefore swung to the Canadian portion of the catchment which is only 13 per cent of the drainage area but provides 30 per cent of the discharge. The Canadian headfall from Lake Columbia to the US border is 415 m over a river distance of 772 km, and at the international boundary the Columbia carries some 2,662 m$^3$ s$^{-1}$ (Swainson 1979). Its headfall and volume make the Canadian Columbia an excellent prospect for hydro-power development. The engineering logic pointed to an international development of the Canadian channel to provide benefits to both nations (Kay and McDonald 1982a). In spite of this engineering logic and the close economic, political and cultural relationships of the Canadian and US peoples, it took some 20 years of acrimonious discussion, through the mechanism of the International Joint Commission (IJC), before an agreement on the development of Canadian storage was ratified in 1964 (Krutilla 1967; Sewell 1966). Swainson (1979) has reviewed the political processes within Canada which led to the agreement. His account of the manner in which decisions have been taken offers considerable insight into the political considerations which control project implementation. In the case of the Columbia agreement, one Canadian province, British Columbia, was able to steer the federal-level negotiations. Swainson's account uncovers a process of decision by political conflict rather than the rational process of maximising net benefits that one might expect from this model example of integrated transboundary resource management.

The problems of international river basins are receiving increasing attention (United Nations 1980). The 1977 Mar del Plata conference called for an international code of conduct to regulate the use of international river systems. There is some evidence that this call has been translated into action in the form of long-range integrated river basin planning in the Nile Basin, the Tisza valley and the del Plata Basin (WRI 1986; Cano 1985; David 1985; Mageed 1985; Falkenmark and Lundqvist 1984). However, there is little evidence of the strong trans-national basin authorities which would be required for a fully integrated

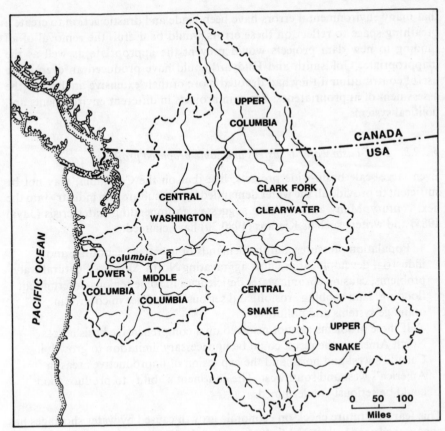

*Fig. 4.17* The Columbia river system. *Source*: Netboy (1986)

approach to river basin management. In the Columbia negotiations, the IJC was available to oil the wheels, but it does not offer a model for a control and management agency. The contention by WRI (1986) that models for such agencies can be found in the UK regional water authorities is optimistic in the extreme since they differ in both scale and political structure from the international organisations required.

Many other examples could be cited of river impoundment. Goldsmith and Hildyard (1986a) have compiled a critical evaluation of 31 schemes. They estimate that 365 large dams were constructed in the twelve months to 1986. They suggest that the majority of projects are technical and economic failures which have enslaved many developing nations with a huge debt burden. The total debt burden of the developing nations was some $700 billion in 1986, a considerable proportion of which is attributed to dam projects. This burden threatens not only the debtor nations but also the Western economic system which is vulnerable to the threat of default by the developing nations. This analysis led directly to the position set out in the statement quoted in 4.2.2 above. While it is certainly true that many environmental errors have been made and drastic action to create a breathing space to reflect on these errors would be useful, the removal of all funding to new dam projects would prevent the appropriate as well as the inappropriate. Goldsmith and Hildyard could have produced an even more useful contribution if they had devoted more of their extensive analysis to the assessment of appropriateness for dam projects in different environments and political systems.

### 4.2.2.3 Inter-basin water transfers and some proposed projects

Even large-scale basin-wide projects, like that on the Columbia, may not be sufficient to provide all the water demanded by agriculture and industry into the next century. Many authors have suggested an impending water crisis (Jayal 1985) and writers such as Kierans (1980:30) have claimed:

> Population pressures and the demands of urban, agricultural, and industrial development are now aggravating North America's natural water problems, causing chronic water deficiencies in some regions, intermittent flooding, land robbing erosion, and serious difficulties in controlling drainage systems and pollution.
>
> If these problems are not resolved on a comprehensive basis across North America, the result could be unnecessary limitation to growth in Canada's west and north and the expansion of unproductive areas in America's west and southwest. The continent's ability to produce food could be seriously undermined.

This fear of a future check on economic growth caused by water shortages has encouraged proposals in North America and the USSR for major continent-wide inter-basin transfers of water. These mega-projects have focused on the diversion of river systems which drain the poorly developed arctic regions to provide irrigation and hydro-power for the more populous, but arid, areas in the continental interiors. Projects of similar scale have been suggested for the diversion of the Chang Jiang (Yangtze) river to provide irrigation waters for the drought-stricken North China Plain (Stone 1986).

### NAWAPA

The main North American proposal was suggested by the construction engineers R. A. Parsons and Co. in 1964 (Parsons 1975). This scheme, called the North American Water and Power Alliance (NAWAPA), is probably the most widely known and some might say 'infamous' water transfer proposal (see Fig. 4.18). The plan involves the transfer of some 136–308 km³ of water mainly from the Columbia, Kootenay, Fraser, Yukon, Laird, Peace and Skeena rivers in Canada and the Copper, Susitna and Tanana rivers in Alaska. About 17 per cent of total runoff would be diverted to the southern water-deficient areas in central Canada, south-western United States and northern Mexico. In addition, 59 km³ would be diverted from the eastern flanks of the Rocky Mountains and arctic Canada into

Lake Superior. This would provide hydro-power generation and increase lake levels, diluting the heavy pollution loading of the Great Lakes (Kay and McDonald 1985).

The NAWAPA plan involves the building of 369 facilities comprising 240 reservoirs, 112 irrigation systems and 17 navigable channels. It would take an estimated 30 years to complete and, in 1976, the costs were estimated at $12,000 million. One proposed impoundment (the Alaskan Tanana reservoir) would have a design capacity of 3,500 km³, or 39 per cent of present global stable runoff. Canada would be the main water donor and the US would be the chief recipient nation. Assuming implementation of the 136 km³ plan, the US would receive 83 km³, Canada 27 km³ and Mexico 26 km³. The additional areas of irrigated land show a similar pattern with 16.1 million ha in the US, 3.4 million ha in Canada and 2.9 million ha in Mexico. The plan would result in net power benefits of some 70,000 MW for sale in the US and Canada as well as providing navigable waterways linking Alberta with the Great Lakes system and central US. Parsons have suggested that the plan would benefit 33 American states, 7 Canadian provinces and 2 territories, as well as the 8 northern states of Mexico (Micklin 1977).

Many environmental problems have been raised to set against these potential benefits. Seismic activity would be likely, given the envisaged weight of water in the Rocky Mountain trench (Williams 1986; Goudie 1981). This, together with the existing active fault zones beneath the huge proposed Alaskan dams, is a cause for concern. The effects on trans-Canadian transport links and migration of economically important andronomous fish species have also been cited as relevant considerations (Micklin 1977). More significant than these environmental issues are the political problems which NAWAPA would create both between the US and Canada and indeed between the federal, provincial and state levels of government within each nation. The Columbia River Treaty was perceived by some as a federal sell-out of provincial interests in British Columbia (see 4.2.2.2 above). The NAWAPA project, with such environmental costs to Canada, and benefits distributed largely to the US, would generate powerful political opposition. The growing Canadian confidence and desire to demonstrate economic independence from their southern neighbour suggests that the NAWAPA plan has little prospect of implementation (Golubev and Biswas 1979).

*Soviet river diversions*
Micklin (1986:91) has commented that:

> compared with some large scale diversion projects proposed for North America, most notably NAWAPA, the Soviet projects appear economically favourable, technically feasible, and politically simple.

Partial implementation of the Soviet transfer plans is underway and two major schemes are involved (Table 4.9).

The Siberian scheme will provide water from the Ob, Irtysh and Yenisei rivers

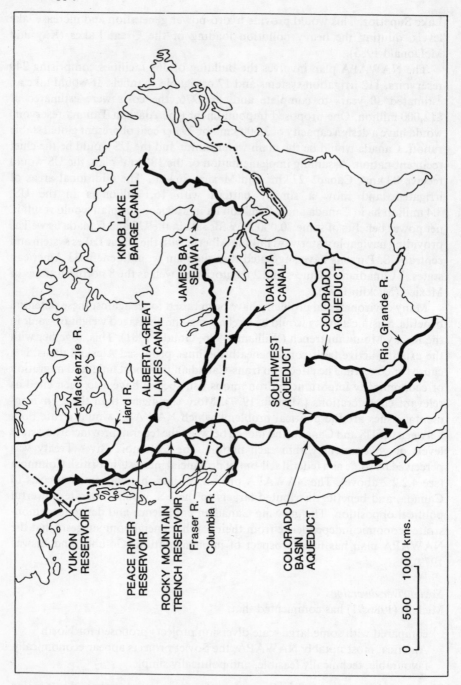

*Fig. 4.18* The North American Water and Power Alliance proposal. *Sources*: Micklin (1977); Parsons (1975)

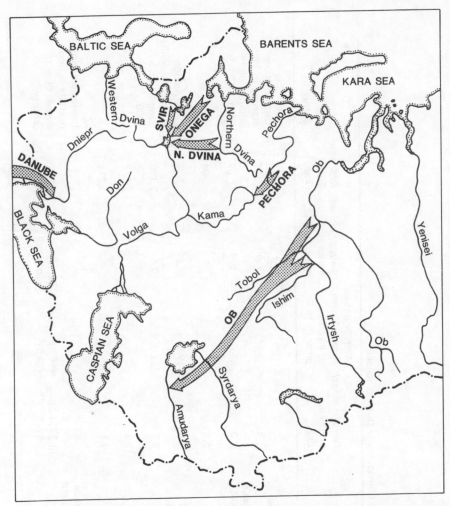

*Fig. 4.19* The diversion scheme for Soviet rivers. *Source*: Micklin (1986:94) and (1981:490)

which flow northwards, discharging some 397 km³ of water into the Arctic Ocean via the Kara Sea (Fig. 4.19). The full scheme will divert 60 km³ of flow into the Syrdarya and Amudarya rivers, in Central Asia, which drain into the Aral Sea. This transfer could be effected by reversing the flow of the Irtysh, using a series of small dams, to the city of Tobol'sk where a reservoir would feed the main diversion canal. This structure would carry water 2,200 km over the continental divide between Western Siberia and Central Asia. The unlined waterway would be over 12 m deep and 108–212 m wide throughout its course. Most of the flow would be powered by gravity, but 2,200 MW of electrical power would be required to lift water over the continental divide which is 113 m above the

Table 4.9 Characteristics of the proposed Soviet water transfer schemes

| Project | Source of diversion | Average annual diversion (km³) | Average annual flow reduction at diversion point (%) | Average annual mouth flow reduction (%) | Reservoir area (km²) | Status |
|---|---|---|---|---|---|---|
| European schemes | | | | | | |
| First stage of first phase | (a) Lakes Lacha & Vozhe | 1.8 | 52.9[a] | 11.5[a] | 27 | Construction starting in 1986; completion by 1990 |
| | (b) Lake Kubena & upper Sukhona R. | 4.0 | 42.6 | 3.6[b] | 67 | |
| First stage total | | 5.8 | | | 94 | |
| Second stage of first phase | (a) Lake Onega | 3.5 | 19.9[c] | 4.5[d] | 7 | Construction starting in 1990s; completion by 2000 |
| | (b) upper Pechora river | 9.8 | 51.0 | 7.5 | 2,170 | |
| Second stage total | | 13.3 | | | 2,177 | |
| First phase total | | 19.1 | | | 2,271 | |
| Second phase | (a) Lower Sukhona & Malaya Northern Dvina rivers | 10.2 (14.2)[e] | (59.2)[e] | (13.0)[e] | 230 | Implementation possible in first decade of next century |
| | (b) Lake Onega | 3.6 ( 7.1)[e] | ( 9.0)[e] | ( 9.0)[e] | None | |
| Second phase total | | 13.8 | | | 230 | |

| | | | | |
|---|---|---|---|---|
| First and second phase total | | 32.9 | 2,501 | Implementation possible in first half of next century |
| Onega Bay Reservoir | Rivers influent to Onega Bay | 27.6 | 69.0 | Unknown |
| European diversions total | | 60.5 | 2,501 | Unknown |
| | | | | Final designs to be ready in 1986; construction could start in 1988 and be completed by 2000 |
| *Siberian schemes* | | | | |
| First phase | (a) Irtysh river at Tobol'sk | 17.0 | 25.4 | 69.0 |
| | (b) Ob' river at Belogor'ye | 10.2 | 8.5 | 7.1 |
| First phase total | | 27.2 | | |
| Second phase | Mainly Ob' river at Belogor'ye (with possible compensation from Yenisey river) | 32.8 | | Possible implementation during the first half of the next century |
| Siberian diversions total | | 60.0 | 18.8[f] | 15.7[f] |
| | | | | Unknown |

*Notes:*

[a] Onega river.
[b] Northern Dvina river.
[c] Svir' river.
[d] Neva river.
[e] Includes earlier stages and phases of diversion.
[f] Excludes effect of compensation from Yenisey river.

*Source:* Micklin (1986:Table 1).

Ob–Irtysh confluence. Approval for detailed engineering designs for the first stage of the Siberian diversions, involving 27.2 km$^3$ of transfers from the Ob and Irtysh, was given by the Council of Ministers in January 1984 and engineering works could commence in 1988 if the plans are ratified by the Council of Ministers.

The main use of the diverted water will be for irrigation in Kazakhstan and Central Asia, where the irrigated area could be expanded sixfold to 50 million ha. The additional waters would not allow for any reversal in the fall in water levels evident in the Aral Sea. This saline lake has experienced an 8 m drop in its water surface since 1960 and a 28 per cent reduction in area, caused by irrigation waters abstracted from the main tributaries, the Amudarya and Syrdarya rivers. If these trends continue, the supplies of new irrigation waters would be exhausted by the year 2000. The first stage of the Siberian scheme would cost $41 billion (1983 base) including the provision of irrigation facilities in the Aral basin (Micklin 1977, 1984, 1986).

Engineering work for the European scheme of water transfers has commenced. The first stage may be complete by 1990, involving a transfer of 5.5 km$^3$ into the Volga system from the upper Sukhona river and Lakes Kubena, Lacha and Vozhe. Some 19.1 km$^3$ of flow will be diverted into the Volga, from Lake Onega and the upper Pechora river. The second phase will involve diversions from the lower Sukhona, Malaya and Northern Dvina rivers. The third phase would include a barrage scheme, the Onega Bay Reservoir, to create a freshwater reservoir in the White Sea. From this reservoir, water could be pumped through the installed structures into the Volga system. The form of the scheme, beyond phase one, is still open to speculation. The diverted water will be used for increased irrigation on some 4 million ha to improve navigation on the Volga and Kama rivers and to generate an additional 3.5 billion kWh of electricity in the Kama–Volga hydro-power plants (i.e. 2 billion kWh net after pumping requirements). In addition, the first-phase water will have some effect on the declining levels of the Caspian Sea. The proposed input is adequate until the year 2000, but additional resources (up to 98 km$^3$) may be required in the next century to reverse the Caspian level reductions. The costs of phase-one construction will be $3 billion (i.e. $0.16 billion·km$^{-3}$ of transferred water). This makes the European scheme a much more cost-effective project than the parallel Siberian proposal which delivers water at a cost of $0.67 billion·km$^{-3}$.

Environmental concerns have surrounded the Soviet river diversions since the first schemes were proposed by Davidov in the late 1940s. The early proposals suggested diversions of 315 km$^3$ of flow from the Ob and Yenisei rivers, producing 75 km$^3$ of flow into the Aral and Caspian Seas, 45 million ha of irrigation and 13,000 MW of power benefits (Mikhalov et al. 1977).

Moiseev et al. (1980) suggest that the diversion of 31 per cent of the Ob and Yenisei could trigger significant environmental changes in the thermal and salinity balance of the Arctic Ocean, resulting in drastic alterations in the Arctic ice regime. This could have significant implications for global weather patterns.

The Kara Sea and Northern Greenland are major zones of ice export to the

Arctic basin and it is thought that a major change in the thermal and salinity regimes of either of these areas could trigger significant effects in the remainder of the Arctic Ocean (Micklin 1981; Zakharov 1976). The resultant effects are unknown but significant climatic implications could be expected because of the effects of an ice mass on albedo and atmosphere interchange of water vapour, as well as the sensible and latent heat transfers between the atmosphere and oceans (Lamb and Morth 1978).

At this stage there is no agreement even on the direction of any effects on Arctic ice regimes, let alone the magnitude of those effects. Some workers have argued that the freshwaters from the Ob and Yenisei form a buoyant cold layer preventing upward movement of saline and warmer waters from depth. This could have the effect of enhancing ice formation in the Kara Sea area. Any reduction in the buoyant plume of freshwater could trigger less ice formation and a warmer Arctic Ocean. The alternative school of thought suggests that a reduction in the freshwater inputs to the Kara Sea would cause a diminution of surface gradient currents which presently encourage warm deep Atlantic water to enter the Arctic basin. The reduction in this heat flux would result in heavier ice conditions in the Arctic and a delayed spring breakup of ice in the Ob and Yenisei Gulfs (Micklin 1981; Ivanov and Nikiforov 1976; Aagaard and Coachman 1975).

Even the huge Davidov plan would only deprive the Arctic of 8.8 per cent of its annual freshwater input of 3,508 km³. All projections regarding the direction and magnitude of any effects are dependent on very sensitive trigger mechanisms related to the Kara Sea. The data are not available for comprehensive numerical modelling in this area and, as such, these projections remain little more than educated guesses (Micklin 1981).

While these large-scale projects catch the imagination, they may not pass the test of political, technical, economic or environmental appropriateness. However, interregional water transfers have been implemented on a smaller scale where the demand of the recipient region can justify the overall project costs. Golubev and Biswas (1979) cite examples from Mexico and India which appear to suggest that, even in these developing nations, large-scale water transfer projects can result in significant net benefits. This counters to some extent the contentions of Goldsmith and Hildyard (1986a) which might imply the failure of all capital-intensive water projects in the developing world.

## 4.3  Non-structural approaches

Szesztay (1976) has formulated the model of water resources development outlined in Fig. 4.20. So far only the first two stages of the Szesztay model have been considered. These are devoted to the principle of providing sufficient quantity of water to meet increases in water demand. The third stage is concerned with the management and control of demand by water conservation technology and pricing mechanisms. As the third stage is reached, Szesztay

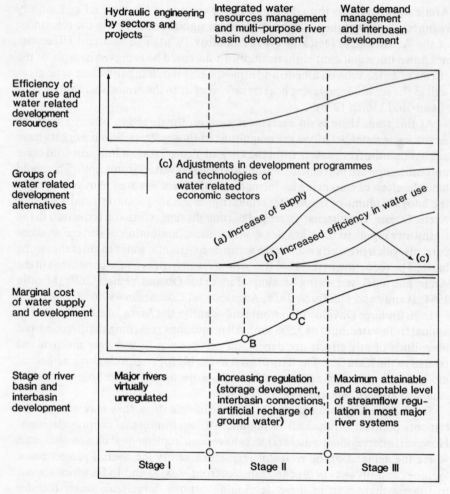

Fig. 4.20 Szesztay's model of stages in water resource development. *Source*: Szesztay (1976:492, Fig. 1)

(1976:493) suggested that the impacts of reduced water availability begin to impinge on socio-economic development:

> Under such conditions virtually all fields of knowledge having a bearing on economic and social affairs of human life become water-related in one way or another ... the task of solving water problems can hardly be separated from solving social and economic problems in their broader context.

Szesztay was promoting the integrated approach to water demand management and this echoes the calls of Falkenmark (1985) and ITDG (1980) who advocated recognition and integration of water supply provision within large-scale projects.

### 4.3.1 Demand forecasts

Good demand forecasts are of central importance in project design and resource planning. Gardiner and Herrington (1986) suggest three main types of forecast:

1. Judgemental forecasts;
2. Causal forecasts;
3. Extrapolative forecasts.

The judgemental forecast is based on personal or group knowledge: it may be purely subjective or merely an adjustment of a more formal forecast. The causal forecast is based on an examination of the causal relationships which influence water demand. The extrapolative forecast is based on the extension of past trends into the future. It centres only on past levels of water demand and may involve some form of time series analysis (Sterling and Antcliffe 1977).

Each type of forecast has been used in water demand studies. The extrapolative method is the most common in the water industry. However, it has been severely criticised because of the simplistic assumption that past rates of change in the factors influencing water demand will continue into the future (Parker and Penning-Rowsell 1980). In addition, extrapolative forecasting takes no account of either technical change or ownership patterns of water consumptive appliances.

Causal forecasting attempts to unravel these relationships. It involves the definition of different water-use categories (i.e. industrial and domestic) and the definition of the determinants of water demand in each use category. Because of this extra disaggregation, the method is often referred to as the 'component' or 'analytical' technique. Both approaches suffer from a reliance on demographic and economic projections. However, the application of the more rigorous component methods has led the British water industry to adjust downwards many of its extrapolative water demand forecasts made in the 1970s following a period of rapid economic growth (Parker and Penning-Rowsell 1980). The data requirements for the component method are still a major drawback. Limited information exists on patterns of household water use and often this is generated for small socio-economically atypical areas such as in the Malvern and Mansfield comparative studies conducted by the Severn Trent Water Authority (Thackray et al. 1978).

Both component and extrapolative methods can provide adequate demand estimates if used with relevant data over short forecast periods, but they must be applied with caution when long-range planning projections are required. The data demanding causal forecasting is more costly than the extrapolative method. However, forecast errors can be very expensive when the forecasts result in unnecessary commitment of capital resources. The case of Kielder reservoir (UK) has been noted by Gardiner (1986) and Pearce (1982) to illustrate the problems associated with a project built too early because of incorrect demand estimates produced by simplistic extrapolative forecasts.

The three modes of forecasting defined above are common to all resource areas. However, water demand forecasting must also take into account peak loads on the system. This is important from the viewpoint of either large-scale systems, where peak loadings might spread over a full season for, say, irrigation or lawn watering (Bland 1985), or the very small-scale system, such as a block of flats, where the definition of instantaneous peak loads is important for hydraulic design considerations (Courtney 1976). In addition, the effects of projected losses due to leakage and the potential for unexpected disruptive events must figure in any planning strategy (Gardiner and Herrington 1986).

The potential rewards for successful demand prediction are great. The aim should be to delay the commitment of capital resources until they are essential. In Britain, the water industry has more often been criticised because it has committed capital resources, for example the Kielder impoundment, well before demand levels could have justified the investment. This safety margin is understandable and allows the resource management agencies to claim a prudent approach to future supply provision. It is likely that the voices claiming financial profligacy for early implementation of large projects would be drowned by the protests which would follow from water shortages in a developed nation.

In the rural areas of developing nations, the infrastructure does not exist to either assess demand or fully satisfy it. The exact definition and prediction of demand is therefore of limited relevance. However, demand peaks in standpipe use and the consequent waiting times are important considerations (Cairncross et al. 1980; ITDG 1978).

The growing proportion of urban dwellers in the developing world has a major impact on water demand projections because of the associated industrial development and the higher proportion of dwelling taps in the urban area. Mowli (1980) has suggested that the proportion of India's population living in the urban centres will almost double by the year 2011 (to 39% or 450 million in total). The projected effect on water demand is a sixteen-fold increase by the year 2011.

This explosive growth in the urban population is particularly evident in South American cities. Mendoza (1979) has outlined the problems of meeting demand growth in Mexico where the government aims to provide potable supplies to 2,300 new users each day. A trebling of the present water system is required if the goals of 70 per cent rural provision are to be met by the year 2000. The investment involved amounts to some $14 billion. Mexican cities, such as Monterrey, demonstrate very rapid growth of around 7 per cent annually, equivalent to one new suburb every week, caused by immigration from the rural areas.

This population growth makes demand planning difficult in many developing nations where large debt burdens are accruing merely to keep pace with increasing water demand (Goldsmith and Hildyard 1986a; Martinez 1979). Samuels and Kerr (1980) have outlined a model for predicting water demand in rapidly growing urban centres which they have calibrated for the city of Blantyre in Malawi. Their model uses three predictors: income, population and water use; and three sectors: domestic, industrial and public. It is not yet possible to evaluate the utility of such a model. Any detailed model requires extensive small-area information and Samuels and Kerr (1980) stress the importance of metering in providing sectoral demand information.

### 4.3.2 Managing demand

Like all commodities, water demand is partly determined by cost (Renshaw 1982). In the UK, where industries are metered but domestic consumers, on the whole, are not, there is a significant difference in the rates of demand growth. Figure 4.21 shows the UK demand growth for three regional water authorities.

The unmetered supply shows considerable growth in a time of almost stable population numbers. This suggests a profligate use of water by UK consumers which might imply the need for a programme of metering (Lucas 1980; Smith 1974). However, it would be extremely difficult for the UK water industry to argue for domestic metering on the basis of these data unless it addressed the greater waste caused by leakage from the supply system which accounts for some 30 per cent of the resource supplied (HMSO 1983).

In addition to pricing, the water industry has some degree of legislative control over consumption rates when use restrictions are imposed during drought periods. One example of this form of legislative conservation was seen during the 1976 drought when the UK government passed the Drought Act in August 1976. This extended previous legislation and empowered the water industry to ban car washing and lawn sprinkling, and to instigate water rationing. Other physical means of reducing water consumption have focused on the redesign of domestic appliances such as showers, toilet cisterns and washing machines to effect household savings on domestic consumption of over 50 per cent (Stone 1978). However, the implementation of these physical conservation measures is unlikely unless a domestic metering system encourages the individual consumer to invest in reducing consumption.

### 4.4. Lessons and conclusions

This chapter has examined the options for water supply and conservation at a number of scales. There is a dichotomy between those who favour a technical fix to the problems of water supply and those who suggest that the technical solution will never solve this resource problem. The words of Goldsmith and Hildyard (quoted on p 86) illustrate the latter position. Keirans (quoted on p 96) exemplifies the former. Such a rigid stance on this issue is unwise. To suggest that large-scale projects are not relevant to the needs of developing nations, where the water supply problems are huge, is clearly nonsense. Indeed, the Chinese irrigation project on the Min river or the Indian Western Jamuna canal, built in Mughal times to carry water from the Himalayas to Uttar Pradesh and Punjab (Murthy 1979), provide ample evidence that developing nations can benefit from large-scale projects. It is not the scale of Western technology imported to developing nations that causes problems but the nature of the projects themselves. In the developed world, where the *engineering approach* (Williams 1986:11) to planning dominates, the infrastructure exists to utilise the power or irrigation benefits that flow from the project. This is not always true of large-scale schemes in the developing world. Too often the benefits are simplistically

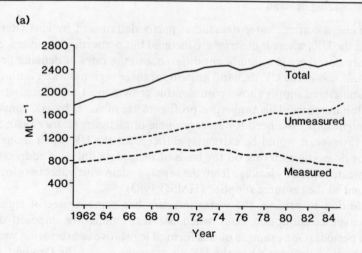

(a)

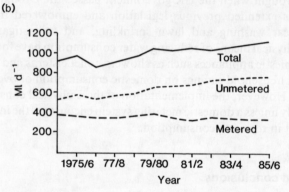

(b)

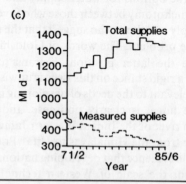

(c)

*Fig. 4.21* Trends in metered and unmetered supplies for three UK regional water authorities. *Sources*: Anglian (1986:7); NWWA (1986:24, Fig. 7B); Yorkshire (1986:16 LTT)

evaluated from the perspective of the developed world. The criteria of 'appropriateness' suggested by ITDG (1978) offer the best yardstick against which to evaluate projects of any scale.

In this context, the Min river diversions are seen to be technically, economically and hydrologically appropriate. In contrast, the huge NAWAPA plan fails on almost any appropriateness yardstick chosen. In both the developed and developing nations, the projects envisaged have grown in scale and cost. As a result, the potential for large-scale social and environmental impacts has never been greater. It is important, therefore, to consider these aspects in all new large-scale water supply projects at an early stage in project design. Falkenmark (1985) has stressed this point in calling for greater 'integration' between land and water in all large-scale water projects. This integration is central to the concept of river basin planning which is addressed in Chapter 8 where several large-scale projects are examined and the main elements of this integration are defined. It is this more holistic and flexible approach to project design and management that offers the best hope for overcoming some of the problems associated with the types of large-scale project examined in 4.2.2 above.

The major consumptive use of water is for irrigation. By the year 2000, both the total and consumed irrigation waters will have shown a tenfold increase during the present century (Fig. 4.22). The storage and transfer schemes outlined above all aim to direct and increase the stable component of global runoff to allow for increases in irrigation. Even the huge Soviet inter-basin transfer plans which may involve some $120 \text{ km}^3$ in the next century will provide only small (3.5%) increases to the present supplies of irrigation waters (Golubev 1984).

Several exotic water supply sources, such as iceberg farming, were examined in the early 1970s (Cooper 1973). Weeks and Campbell (1973) presented a detailed desk study which indicated the financial feasibility of towing icebergs from the Amery and Ross ice shelves in Antarctica to Australia and Atacama in South America, respectively. Approximately half the freshwater volume is lost in transit, but huge quantities can be delivered (over $10 \text{ km}^3$ in a single trip). The economic projections of such schemes appear promising with delivered costs of only $0.002 per $m^3$ for iceberg waters compared with large desalination plant costs of $0.19 $m^3$ (1973 base). However, the use of icebergs has not progressed beyond these interesting and promising desk studies.

Desalting of waters has also been proposed for water supply in arid areas. Rapid growth of global desalting capacity has been evident in recent years. In the period 1971–9, capacity grew from 0.93 to $4.49 \times 10^6 \text{ m}^3 \text{ day}^{-1}$ (i.e. 0.02% of global stable runoff). The process of desalting has a great deal to contribute in relatively small-scale plants providing high-cost water for domestic consumption in water-deficient regions. However, its contribution on a global scale to total resource availability is very small. It is unlikely that the imported technology of desalination would ever be appropriate for use in the developing world. Western writers advocating such a strategy might benefit from an examination of failures in lower-level technology such as the Indonesian hand-pump example cited by Mathur (1986).

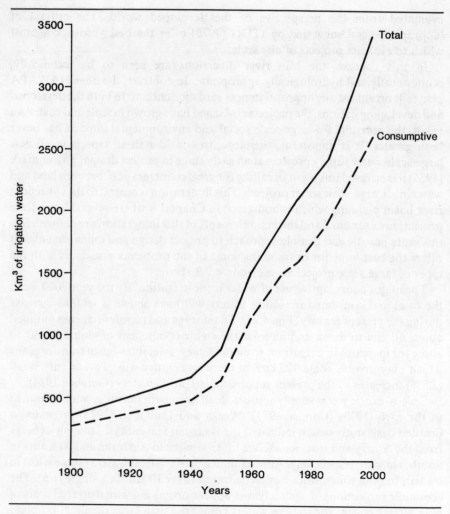

*Fig. 4.22* Total and consumptive waters used for irrigation. *Source*: Golubev (1984:61)

The main lesson of this chapter is that the total quantity of water flow is adequate for industrial growth and agricultural development into the foreseeable future but that there are problems in matching supplies to demands at different places and times. Furthermore, the use of water courses for effluent transport requires large volumes of water and effectively reduces the potential water supply. As the scenarios of L'Vovich (1977) presented in Fig. 4.4 demonstrate, the issue of water quality is impossible to separate from that of water supply. Specific parameters of water quality are examined in Chapter 6 and the impacts of water quality considerations within the context of river basin planning are addressed in Chapter 8.

# CHAPTER 5

# Flooding control and management

## 5.1 Introduction

For most of the time that people have existed on earth, hazards have been a normal part of the natural environment. Flooding is the most significant of all natural hazards, being responsible for approximately 40 per cent of fatalities from natural disasters (Table 5.1). These disasters are the cause of some 4 per cent of deaths globally each year.

The effects of flooding on health are well established. In the UK, Bennet (1970) identified a 50 per cent increase in the number of deaths from homes that had been flooded. Cancer formed a significant element in this mortality increase. A similar increase in surgery attendances and hospital admissions was evident. Morbidity and mortality increases predominated in the male population, a phenomenon also observed in floods in Lismore, Australia (Handmer and Smith

Table 5.1 Estimates of global fatalities caused by different types of natural disaster

| Type of hazard | Frequency (%) |
| --- | --- |
| Floods | 40 |
| Tropical cyclones | 20 |
| Earthquakes | 15 |
| Drought | 15 |
| Other | 10 |

| | Fatality distribution (%) | Cost distribution (%) |
| --- | --- | --- |
| Developed countries | 5 | 75 |
| Developing countries | 95 | 25 |

111

1983). Significant effects on mental health have also been noted and related to both flooding and flood control structures in Brazil (Werner 1985) and North America (Gleser *et al.* 1981).

Many authors (Goddard 1973; Burton 1970; Burton and Kates 1965; among others) have pointed out that flood damage is increasing despite a massive and continuing investment in protection. Goddard (1973) suggested that annual global flood losses might be in the region of $1.75 billion. Smith and Tobin (1978) state that the flooding associated with tropical storm Agnes in 1972 might well be the most expensive flood event in history (US losses alone were estimated at $4.3 billion).

The causes of this increased damage are doubtless complex, but several can be suggested. Improved accuracy and coverage of reporting might explain 10 to 15 per cent of the increased costs (Hanke 1972). Further explanation derives from changes in the catchment hydrological response caused by expanded urban areas and modifications to the channel due to civil engineering works which for the Mississippi might have reduced capacity by 30 per cent. Possibly the most important factor is human encroachment onto the floodplain, and some 2,000 US communities are located on such sites. In 1973, Goddard claimed that 16 per cent of the entire US urban area was within the natural 100-year floodplain. White and Haas (1975) suggest that encroachment continues at 1.5 to 2.5 per cent a year, negating the nation's $9 billion expenditure on protection (Muckleston 1976). We focus on the encroachment problem in more detail below.

In this chapter we examine the scale of the probem, issues of selective location, and the types of, and responses to, flooding. Initially, however, we examine some questions of definition. There are two distinct sets of information on which adjustments to the flood hazard are based. The public has a perception based upon its subjective memory of past events. Individuals take flood-proofing measures in response to this knowledge base. The agency manager acts on more objective, but still imperfect, knowledge derived from past flow records and hydrological data. It is the difference between these two sets of information which produces the apparently irrational human responses to the flood hazard noted above. Figure 5.1 outlines these distinct areas of knowledge.

In the floodplain, the 'normal' flow occupies a channel with obvious banks. The entire floodplain is a part of the hydraulic system by which infrequent high flows are passed down the valley. Thus, while a flood that exceeds the channel may be an extreme event, it is not an extraordinary event. Definitions of a flood frequently imply that the floodplain is not a part of the hydraulic system:

a flood is a relatively high flow which *overtaxes the natural channel provided for the runoff.* (Chow 1956:134 authors' italics)

A flood is any high streamflow *which overtops the natural or artificial banks of a stream.* (Rostvedt *et al.* 1968:1 authors' italics)

We would suggest the modification of the definition given in Ward (1978) outlined below:

112

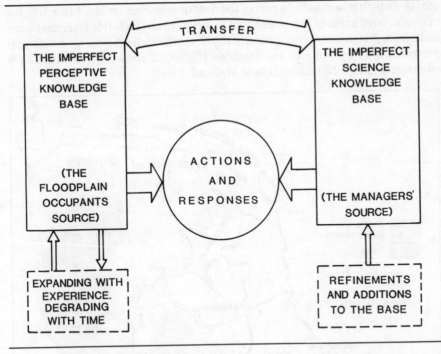

*Fig. 5.1*  Information sets and human responses of the public and the resource manager

*A flood is a body of water that inundates land that is infrequently submerged and in so doing causes or threatens to cause damage.*

## 5.2  Selective location

Many of the sites subject to flooding – coasts, estuaries, lakes and rivers – are also subject to preferential location by industry, commerce and private housing. In upland areas, river valleys are frequently a natural routeway for road and railway traffic and for the developments associated with such routeways. The floodplains provide flat building land protected by the valley sides. In larger catchments, lake and river edge sites are often selected for amenity reasons as much as for accessibility, communications and cheapness. Thus the physical, aesthetic and economic characteristics of the floodplain and other water edge land encourage the encroachment onto high flood-risk areas. Rivers attract development for reasons such as those outlined above, but many sites of development also stem from their historical importance as bridging points and watering sites.

In a number of places, developments have taken place which have released for

113

use land which is 'normally' a part of the river or estuarine system. In the UK, for example, large areas of salt marsh that lie below mean high-tide level have been reclaimed. A significant proportion of the Netherlands lies below sea level and is protected only by complex sea defences. Figure 5.2 shows the extent of such estuarine and marine reclamation in Holland.

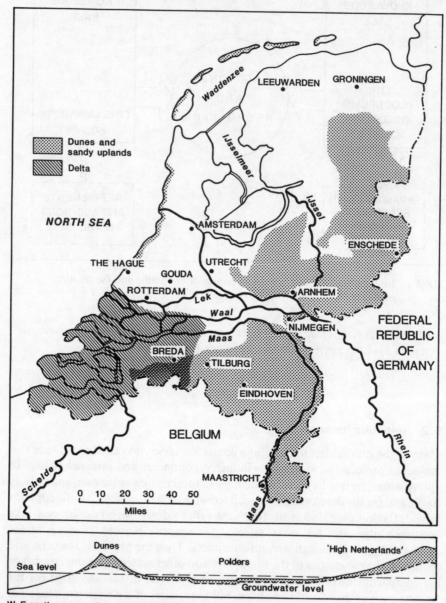

*Fig. 5.2*   The extent of estuarine and marine reclamation in Holland

114

## 5.3 Physical appraisal of flooding

A great deal is known about the physical effects and reasons for flooding. Much less is known about the socio-economic effects and responses to flooding. This section addresses the physical factors and covers the nature and processes of flood events. Flooding can be considered as being one of two types:

1. Sea floods;
2. River floods.

### 5.3.1 Sea floods

Sea floods include (i) direct coastal inundation by the sea; (ii) estuarine floods, where there is a possible interaction with high outflows from a river, and (iii) flooding along the margins of lakes which are sufficiently large to permit processes of a marine nature to operate. Sea floods involve the combination of five factors:

1. Wind direction and strength;
2. Intensity of low-pressure systems;
3. Tidal state;
4. The geometry of the sea basin;
5. The nature of the coastline.

These factors produce an actual sea level greater than expected from normal sea-level variations and in extreme circumstances the sea level overtops coastal defences and inundates adjacent land.

Sea floods are generally large-scale events. The most recent in Europe occurred on 1 February 1953 and affected the east of England and the coast of Northern Europe. Two thousand lives and 40,000 homes were lost. These losses were small in comparison to the effects of the coastal storm surges that affected Bangladesh in November 1970 killing some 225,000 people (Frank and Husain 1971).

### 5.3.1.1 Prediction and forecasting

Despite the chance combination of influences that produce sea floods, the events are predictable. As early as 1939, Wemelsfelder demonstrated the statistical nature of sea-height return intervals. Figure 5.3 shows the relationship between return interval and sea height.

Both sea height and flood damage potential information is required when designing flood-protection structures. However, for the day-to-day operation of non-static protection works, such as the Thames Barrage and the non-structural alternatives such as evacuation (section 5.4.3.2), there is a need for accurate short-term forecasting of flood events.

For the 1953 North Sea floods, Ward (1978:47) has gathered data from several sources to illustrate the chain of events leading to the flood. Since the basin shape

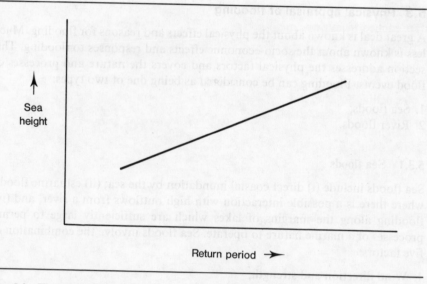

*Fig. 5.3* The relationship between return interval and sea height

and the coastlines are static, and the normal tidal range is entirely predictable, the remaining variables – the coincidental extreme meteorological events – are fundamental to overall forecasting. The last 30 years have seen great advances in remote data telemetry from radar, satellites and surface stations. Thus, forecasting of sea floods is now technically possible given early data on (i) wind direction and strength and (ii) the severity of advancing depressions. This is not a trivial task since many of the variables interact. For example, the storm surge itself modifies the timing and the size of the 'entirely predictable' normal tide.

The implementation of adequate flood forecasting for many of the world's coastlines will be a major issue for water managers in the future. Forecasting without the technical and financial resources to build structural protection systems, or without the human and financial organisation to implement non-structural plans, is currently close to a pointless exercise. However, it could be argued that forecasting itself generates political pressure for resource allocation.

### 5.3.2 River floods

Rivers flood due to the inability of the 'normal' channel to hold the discharge of water passing down the river system. Such discharges may be generated by high-intensity or long-duration rainfalls, by snowmelt or by failure of either natural or artificial stores of water, for example dam failure or the sudden release of glacial pondings. The return interval of floods can be calculated, but many drainage basins have little or no gauge data. In a major study, the Institute of Hydrology in the UK sought to provide a means of calculating the flood characteristics of ungauged catchments (NERC 1975). The problem was approached from three main perspectives:

1. Statistical, in which the statistical distribution of extreme events is examined for an areal spread of observation points;
2. Unit hydrograph, a well-established, black-box approach to hydrological modelling in which the response of a river to a unit of storm rainfall over a given time period is calculated;
3. Catchment morphometry, which combines data on catchment characteristics as a multiple regression equation to predict flood levels.

Of these approaches, the third has perhaps the greatest management potential and is outlined below.

From an examination of a large number of catchment characteristics, six were identified as the main predictors of the value of the mean annual flood. These six catchment characteristics are given in Table 5.2 and are combined as follows to determine the mean annual flood:

$$Q=R(\text{area})^{0.94}(\text{stmfrq})^{0.27}(\text{s}1085)^{0.16}(\text{soil})^{1.23}(\text{rsmd})^{1.03}(1+\text{lake})^{-0.85}$$

where $R$ is the regional multiplier, the value of which can be derived from the map given in Fig. 5.4. The flood frequency curve for a particular site can then be determined from Table 5.3 which shows the ratio of the mean annual flood to the flood expected to occur at the given flood return interval.

*Table 5.2*  Catchment characteristics identified as significant in the Flood Studies Report

| | |
|---|---|
| area | Catchment area in km² |
| stmfrq | The number of stream junctions as shown on the 1:25,000 map, divided by the catchment area |
| s1085 | The stream channel slope measured between two points 10 and 85 per cent of the stream length from gauge expressed in m/km |
| rsmd | A net 1-day rainfall of 5-year return period. The rainfall is net in the sense that a weighted mean soil moisture deficit is subtracted from it |
| lake | The fraction of the catchment draining through a lake or reservoir |
| soil | A soil index with values in the range 0.15–0.50. Soils were classified into five classes. If $S_1$ is the fraction covered by soil class i, the index is given by $(0.15\,S_1 + 0.30\,S_2 + 0.40\,S_3 + 0.45\,S_4 + 0.50\,S_5)/(S_1 + S_2 + S_3 + S_4 + S_5)$ |

Definitions of catchment characteristics selected in the final sex-variable equation.
Adapted from the Flood Studies Report (1975).
*Source*: NERC (1975)

Northern
Scotland
0.0186

Central
0.0213

Ireland
0.0172

East Anglia
0.0153

Essex, Lee
and Thames *

South Coast 0.0234

South West
0.0315

* Highly urbanised catchment has a unique equation of
the form : $Q = 0.302 \ AREA^{.7} \ STMFRQ^{.52} \ (1+urban)^{2.50}$

*Fig. 5.4* Regional multipliers for flood determination in the UK

Flood-frequency relationships derived from these data are only applicable to the UK. The approach taken may be transferable provided that data can be acquired to allow recalibration for areas not having a comparable extensive data base. The Institution of Civil Engineers, in a review of the utility of the Flood

*Table 5.3* Ratio of the mean annual flood to the flood discharge expected to occur at a given flood return interval

| Return period (years) | $Q(T)/\bar{Q}$ |
|---|---|
| 2.33 | 1.0 |
| 5 | 1.22 |
| 10 | 1.43 |
| 50 | 1.94 |
| 100 | 2.19 |
| 500 | 2.80 |

Studies Report (ICE 1981), found that the work was being used for prediction and estimation of the statistical characteristics of floods but not as a tool in studies of flood-damage economics.

To calculate the financial impact of flooding requires an assessment of the costs incurred at each stage height beyond the bankfull discharge. This is to a large degree dependent upon the area that is inundated by floods of a specific stage. In calculating the area inundated by a flood, two broad approaches may be taken. The first approach assumes that the river valley is merely an extension of the channel and that water flows through the floodplain in a manner broadly similar to that of the water in the main channel. Such an approach is fraught with difficulties, relying on a uniformity of cross-section, slope and roughness which is seldom found in other than the simplest cases. The second approach assumes that the floodplain is primarily a storage area in which flows in excess of the normal channel capacity are temporarily stored. This approach is more data demanding but operates from elementary information and is applicable to a greater range of situations (McDonald and Ledger 1981). The floodplain is examined in discrete areal units and it is able to accommodate the heterogeneous nature of the floodplain topography and occupancy.

As for sea floods, the physical characteristics of the flood, in this case, frequency and area of inundation, are relatively predictable. Forecasting and the prediction of flood damage are less well developed.

## 5.4 Types of response

For the purposes of this section, responses are categorised into three broad groups:

1. Ecological;

119

2. Engineering;
3. Economic.

### 5.4.1 Ecological responses

Ecological responses are centred in the catchment. They seek to establish a land use or to support a natural plant cover that minimises the flow of water from the land phase of the hydrological cycle. Where water cannot be retained on the land, the objective is to slow and attenuate the delivery of water from the catchment. Management then seeks to maximise the interception of water and the rate of loss of water through evaporation from the interception store. This has the effect of removing some of the incoming precipitation and delaying the point at which the interception store is full and when all flow will reach the ground surface.

When water reaches the ground surface, management should seek to maximise infiltration into the soil and thus reduce the amount that contributes to relatively rapid surface flows. Within the soil, the potential moisture storage should be maximised and that potential maintained by increasing the rate of loss of water through evapotranspiration.

Crop choice can seldom be made solely on water management grounds. However, when appropriate, the use of a crop with a low stomatal resistance and a high aerodynamic resistance will increase evapotranspirational losses. Unfortunately, the loss of water from a catchment is at its most efficient at the times when there are unlikely to be flood flows. This loss of water, as identified in Chapter 4, may well have a significant cost associated with it. Furthermore, ecological responses suffer from two other major drawbacks. The first is that the physical manipulation of the catchment surface can have a detrimental influence on flood conditions. In the UK the establishment of forest on upland grassland sites has reduced the overall yield of catchments by as much as 40 per cent (see Chapter 2). However, to establish these forests in the first instance requires the creation of a dense network of drainage ditches to produce the conditions necessary for early growth. Considerable disagreement exists regarding both the direction and magnitude of the effects of pre-afforestation drainage. Conway and Miller (1960) suggested an enhanced flood response as shown in Fig. 5.5.

Conflicting evidence was presented by Burke (1963) who demonstrated a suppressed flood response in a drained catchment. In fact, the response may be strongly related to particular site characteristics such as the origin and degree of humification of the peat, as well as the altitude and the climate of the site (McDonald 1973). The second major drawback is the lack of public recognition of the potential future benefits of land-use modification and the time taken for such modifications to have an influence. Politically motivated investment in flood control usually requires a result that is definable, obvious and immediate.

### 5.4.2 Engineering responses

Engineering solutions to flood problems may centre upon the flood site or upon upstream storage. In most cases the solutions involve the increase in the capacity

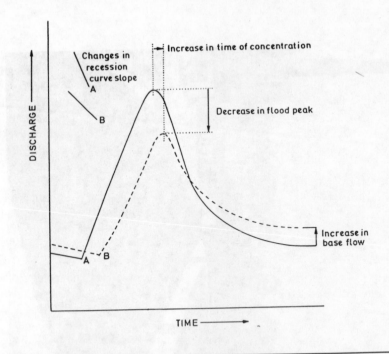

*Fig. 5.5* The characteristics of the enhanced flood hydrograph

of the channel to contain flood flows. At its simplest, this involves increasing the slope and cross-sectional area of the channel together with decreasing frictional resistance to flow. If such modification does not produce sufficient capacity, then flood walls or heightened levees of the form shown in Plate 5.1 can be built. However, this is not an option that can be exercised easily in an established urban area. The land acquisition that is involved, even in the case of a small floodbank such as that shown in Plate 5.1, could involve the loss of historic buildings which might stimulate great opposition (Bennett and Mitchell 1983; Mitchell 1981). Plate 5.2 shows the waterfront in the important historic town of York, UK. Here, buildings back directly on to the river and in some cases form part of the channel. An engineering solution of the type outlined above would clearly meet a great deal of opposition and would not be an appropriate solution to the flood problem in such a situation.

The engineering solution more applicable here would be the provision of a complete bypass channel such as has been provided for the Red River at Winnipeg, or an upstream control reservoir. The use of the reservoir option involves the problems outlined in Chapter 4.

121

*Plate 5.1*   Flood banking in Cambridge, Ontario

*Plate 5.2*  Waterfront buildings in the historic town of York, UK

### 5.4.3 Economic responses

The selection of both ecological and engineering approaches to flood control is characterised by three limitations:

1. Extensive state intervention provides capital and maintenance or planning and legislation. This is necessary because of the high costs and the need for a unified approach.
2. A significant number of the approaches are either capable of failure or are slow to take effect.
3. Engineering works reduce the flood risk and this is interpreted by the public as the removal of all risk, thus any limitation to floodplain development is removed.

Economic approaches, while not perfect, go some way to alleviate these failings and can be grouped under five headings:

1. Loss bearing and change in use;
2. Emergency evacuation, contingency planning and rescheduling;
3. Land elevation and flood proofing;
4. Insurance;
5. Floodplain zoning.

#### 5.4.3.1  Loss bearing

Loss bearing is perhaps the most widespread response to flooding. Losses can be minimised by changes in use towards that which has the lowest propensity for damage. To focus solely on the minimisation of flood damage is, however, a simplification of the necessary economic evaluation. The land use chosen should be that for which the net revenues, taking flood losses as a cost, are maximised. Figure 5.6 shows, in stylised form, the cumulative net revenues of two land uses, expressed as the difference between gross revenues and costs. It also shows the cumulative cost of flood damage for the two land uses.

If the flood costs of LU#1 were less than that of LU#2, the first land use would be the sensible option. However, if, as in Fig. 5.6, the flood costs of use LU#2 are less than that of LU#1, rational use would be determined by the relative areas A and B. Only if B>A is land use LU#2 the most economically rational option.

Such economic assessments remain, however, as simplification of reality because they ignore the many social restraints controlling land-use change. A major change in use requires a different set of skills on the part of the landowner which may not be possessed. If the skills are available, they may not be perceived as being possessed. The data on returns and on flood losses may well be seen to be of limited reliability. The markets for the alternate land-use products may be less stable. In the developed world, the perceived danger of an incorrect decision is economic failure. In the Third World, land-use decisions are often based on weaker data and are frequently on third-party advice. The perceived danger is famine rather than loss of livelihood and so land-use manipulation to limit flood

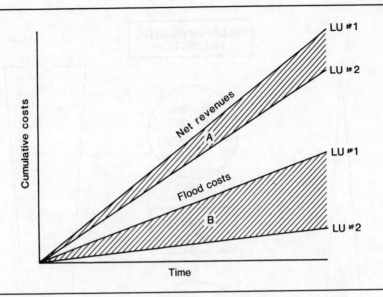

*Fig. 5.6* The cumulative net revenues of two land uses subject to flooding

damage is understandably viewed with more reserve. Individual attitudes and a collective action have been examined by Churchill and Hutchins (1984) for the Ratnapura area of Sri Lanka.

### 5.4.3.2 *Contingency planning*

Contingency planning is the rescheduling of operations to minimise stock at risk at the most flood-prone period of the year or to evacuate goods and people before the onset of flooding. The actions have to be taken in response to a situation that cannot be readily predicted and they are taken at, or shortly before, the flood event. Effective contingency planning therefore depends upon the practical implementation of the plan in the difficult circumstances prevailing during a flood. Plan implementation is dependent upon adequate warning (Smith and Handmer 1983).

In large river systems the prediction of river levels downstream from data on waters already in the upstream channel is subject to limited errors. However, in smaller river systems the prediction of flows based on gauged data upstream often allows insufficient warning time. In such cases the data which forms the basis of prediction must be taken at an earlier stage (Fig. 5.7).

The simplest improvement is to interrogate remote rain gauges. Further time may be gained by the use of predicted rainfalls from satellite or radar information. Unfortunately, the earlier warning time is gained at the expense of reliability for, as is illustrated in Fig. 5.7, with each additional set of imperfectly

125

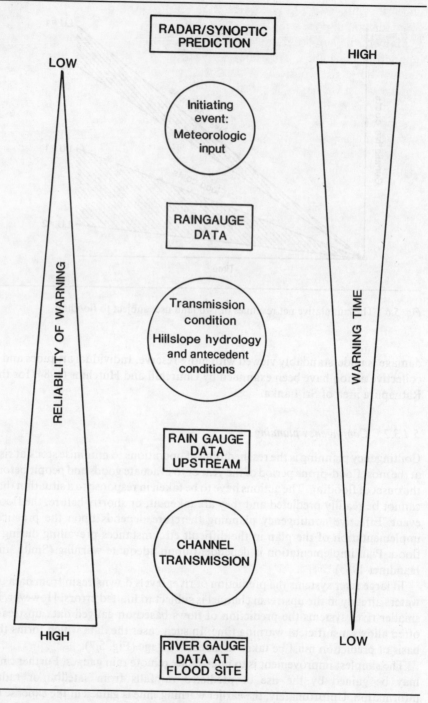

*Fig. 5.7* The reliability of warning and its relation to response time

understood processes or statistical relations, further errors are incorporated into the prediction of river levels.

Many of the non-structural alternatives discussed in this section require an input from the public. This can be beneficial as a heightened awareness of residual flood risk controls, in part, the growth of flood-damage potential. However, false warnings should be avoided where the public is involved lest they cease to respond to forms of contingency planning. A valuable future development will be to maximise not only warning times but the reliability of these warnings. Such information could be best expressed through the creation of 'stages of warning' in which the timing to the period of maximum flood danger is combined with information on the actions to be taken and the reliability of the estimate.

### 5.4.3.3 Land elevation and flood proofing

Land elevation and flood proofing does not apply to the community as a whole. In this respect it differs from both structural protection and flood warning. This is an individual or block-level response. Much of the early work in this field was carried out by Shaeffer working with Gilbert White at the University of Chicago (Shaeffer 1960). Because the beneficiaries can be charged directly, this form of protection finds favour with floodplain managers, especially at times of capital budget constraint.

Land elevation involves the raising by land fill of the ground level in individual building plots, such that the properties are raised above the expected flood level (Fig. 5.8). The fill can be extracted either external or internal to the floodplain. If the fill is external, the flood channel or the flood storage area will be reduced and this will exacerbate the flood problem in adjacent properties (Fig. 5.8(b)). Where the fill is taken internally, there should be no change in the flood level. In practice, the flood characteristics will be altered and the effects of the flood will thus differ (Fig. 5.8(c)).

Land elevation can only be implemented at the start of a building programme. It is therefore only available when the flood danger is recognised at an early planning stage. In contrast, flood proofing is available at any time in the life of a property. Thus flood proofing is potentially a tool that is available to tackle the problems of the overdeveloped floodplains that exist in many areas.

Flood proofing is the sealing of a property against flood waters. It involves the modification of entrances and windows to allow bulkheads to be fitted quickly in anticipation of a flood. Where services enter the building, waterproof grommets must be fitted and where water could flow, say in the sewage system, one-way valves must be inserted. Flood proofing depends upon an adequate flood warning in order to give time for the final sealing of the lower parts of the building. It is a technique that is only applicable to floods of limited depth and even in such cases it requires that the property is structurally capable of withstanding the lifting and displacement forces involved. As in the case of land

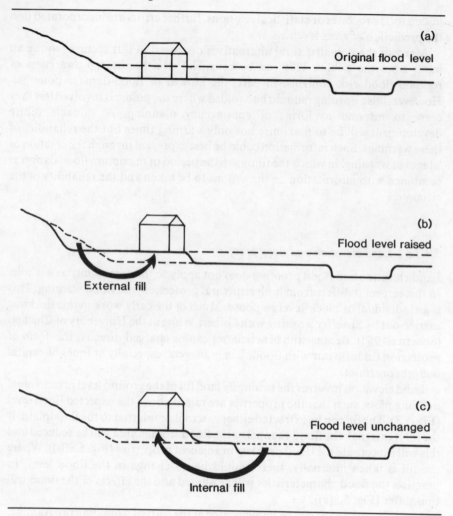

*Fig. 5.8* Land elevation and sources of land fill

elevation, a building that is flood proofed will displace water and raise the general flood level.

One form of flood proofing combines the structural modification of the property with the elevation of the sensitive, high-flood damage potential parts above the reach of the flood waters. An example of this is shown in Plate 5.3. Here the lower floor of the building is open, allowing flood waters to pass through the area. The remainder of the property is raised on stilts. There is no flood water displacement to exacerbate the problem elsewhere. The lower floor can be used to park cars which may be evacuated to higher ground at times of high flood risk.

128

*Plate 5.3*   Flood proofing on recent buildings in the flood plain of the Grand river at Cambridge, Ontario

### 5.4.3.4 Insurance

The incidence of flooding is highly localised and is extremely intermittent. Many people are at risk but the chances of being flooded in any one year are relatively small. In the event of a flood, however, the consequences to individuals and the community are severe. Such a set of circumstances is well suited to protection, or at least to financial anticipation, through insurance. Insurance involves the payment of a small premium at regular intervals to provide cover against a specified risk. To spread the risk over time and population requires that a large number of people opt for the scheme and that the scheme is large, in most cases national. Many insurance risks, for example car insurance, involve a relatively constant rate of claims and thus, although the expression of the risk may come as a shock to the individual, to the insuring organisation the constant claim flow can be anticipated and budgeted for. In flood insurance, periods can occur during which no claims arise. When a community is flooded or when there are regional floods, thousands or tens of thousands of claims have to be awarded. Because of this, the success of a flood insurance scheme relies, not only on a large spread of risk, but on extensive backing to establish a major capital fund to cover potential claims early in the project. The cost of premiums directly reflects the administrative costs of the scheme plus the real cost of claims. Premium cost can therefore be high. The rate of entrance into a scheme varies with cost in the manner shown in Fig. 5.9.

To encourage a high participation rate, which is vital to the success of the scheme, it may be necessary to introduce a subsidy. Although arguments can be introduced against the concept of subsidies, in this case they often make economic sense. In the event of a major flood, the ensuing flood relief

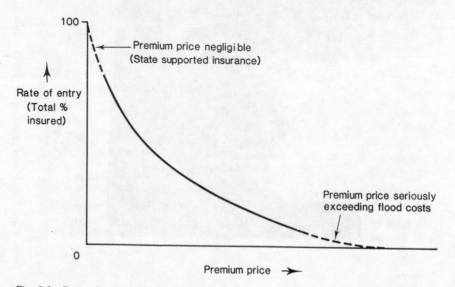

*Fig. 5.9* Rate of entry into flood insurance schemes as a function of premium price

programmes are essentially federal in character and are funded from the same public purse as insurance subsidy might draw upon. Powers and Shows (1979) state that the subsidy in the US National Flood Insurance Program amounted to two-thirds of the cost of the programme. Kunreuter (1978) argued that, in addition to the availability of real disposable income, flood insurance participation rates are influenced by age and educational attainment. In the better-educated and older sections of the community, flood insurance participation rates are higher.

Flood insurance schemes are attractive as a basis for the integrated management of the flood risk in an area. They can provide the financial basis for the integrated management of the floodplain. Premiums would be set higher in high-risk areas and lower in low-risk zones (see 5.4.3.5 below for details of flood zonation). Premiums could be reduced for the introduction of specific flood-reduction measures. This would provide an immediate and tangible return on flood-reduction expenditures by individuals and companies and at the same time it would allow the insuring agency a means of promoting other methods of flood reduction.

In the United States, a National Flood Insurance Program (NFIP) was initiated in 1968 (Arnell 1984). Walesh (1979) has given an assessment of the efficacy of the programme from the viewpoint of a floodplain management organisation, the Southeastern Wisconsin Regional Planning Commission. He identified three key beneficial features of the NFIP:

1. *Mandatory floodplain regulations.* As a part of the Program, floodplain regulations are required. This involves the identification of flood-prone areas and the creation and implementation of appropriate regulations to manage the risk.
2. *Certain flood relief.* Until the enactment of the NFIP, aid in the event of flooding depended upon federal relief. This could be provided in varying measure depending, for example, on whether the event was classed as a disaster. Such classification depends upon political circumstances, perceptions and media coverage, itself governed by the significance of the flood sites and the existence of competing news items. The NFIP gave certainty of relief.
3. *Equitable transition.* Government agencies at various levels had failed to promote a wise use of floodplains. Growth had continued and with it the increase in flood damage. Purchasers of property in floodplain areas, especially in urban environments, do not have the technical skills to recognise the dangers of flooding, far less evaluate them. Through its subsidy, the NFIP is seen as bridging the transition between government apathy and government involvement. In addition, it is a provider of information to the ill-informed floodplain resident.

Experience with the NFIP has highlighted a number of problems with the programme:

1. *Regulatory floodway.* The NFIP requires the identification of a floodway

131

through which the 100-year flood could pass with a stage increase of less than 1 ft (30 cm) beyond that which would occur if the entire natural floodplain were available with no artificial restrictions to river flow. This ensures the construction of safe structures and limits potential downstream effects. Within this corridor, Walesh (1979) identified:

(a) possible degradation of natural and cultural amenities;
(b) the promotion of extensive fringe development still on flood-risk lands or on land fills subject to erosion and undercutting; and
(c) increased downstream flood problems due to runoff from the urbanised fringe of the floodway.

2. *Administrative boundaries*. Assessments of the flood-risk information required by the NFIP were made on the basis of administrative units that seldom reflected the hydraulic or hydrologic basis of the physical system.
3. *Inflexible data base*. The programme is evaluated on the basis of current hazard and on current hydraulic characteristics. If more urbanisation takes place in either the catchment or the floodplain, the programme will become less effective. There is therefore a need for periodic updating of the data base.

Flood insurance offers an attractive means of encouraging the many components of research, evaluation, control and relief that are needed in an effective effort to control increasing flood losses. It is, however, limited in its applicability to less developed countries. The basis of the control is financial and it will function only in an economy that has a strong financial base. Even in the US, participation rates are strongly influenced by the massive subsidies.

Insurance, however, also perpetuates the damage potential by encouraging people to remain in flood-prone areas. It was for this reason that the designers of the National Flood Damage Reduction Program in Canada consciously rejected insurance as a means of damage mitigation.

### 5.4.3.5 *Floodplain zoning*

Floodplain zoning is the delineation of the floodplain into a series of areas, each experiencing a different degree of flood risk. Any flood-risk zoning system is, of course, an extreme oversimplification. The boundaries drawn will be arbitrary. For planning purposes, each zone is assumed to be homogeneous and is regulated as an entity.

For the purpose of discussion, zones of three types can be identified:

1. Exclusion zones;
2. Regulatory zones;
3. Advisory zones.

Exclusion zones are the areas in which development is considered to be against the public interest. This is the zone that must be kept clear to allow the passage of flood waters and on which any development would exacerbate the flood situation for adjacent communities. Regulatory zones are those in which development is permitted but is regulated to minimise flood problems. In the regulated zones, flood insurance, flood proofing and contingency planning may be mandatory. In the advisory zones, flood risk is lower but not negligible. Advice is provided on the degree of risk that might be anticipated and flood insurance at a lower premium would be promoted.

The NFIP, discussed in 5.4.3.4 above, incorporates a significant component of zonation. In particular, two maps are required, a Flood Hazard Boundary Map (FHBM) and a Flood Insurance Rate Map (FIRM). The FHBM provides a crude boundary of the flood-risk zone within which insurance is mandatory. These maps have been extensively challenged and Platt (1976) reports that, by 1 November 1975, 2,884 appeals had been lodged against FHBMs and, of these, 1,249 resulted in revisions. The more detailed FIRM maps correspond to the subdivision of the regulatory zones discussed above. FIRM maps, in addition to insurance subdivision, form the basis of direct planning regulation.

## 5.5 Conclusions

The loss of life due to flooding is increasing, but not in the developed world. There, increasing property losses are evident. This dichotomy of impact parallels the issues outlined in Chapter 4 concerning water supply. Energies in the developed world are devoted to minimising economic damage while developing nations struggle to prevent loss of life. Although simplistic, this division is generally true. Again the concept of appropriateness should be central to the selection of relevant management strategies. Insurance is only appropriate to a society with an advanced financial structure where the perceived danger is to property. In a less developed nation, where mortality presents the main risk, technical advice and aid in developing relevant organisational skills may offer an appropriate response to the flood hazard. Despite their many drawbacks, large flood-control structures, involving imported technology, may present the only practical solution.

In both societies, the effect of structural protection will be to engender a perception of a completely flood-free regime. This stimulates growth in flood-sensitive areas. It must be a research priority in the 1980s and 1990s to determine the nature and scale of such induced changes. The challenge will then be to integrate engineering and economic solutions in a socially acceptable framework of controls and legislation.

Although these adjustments have been discussed individually, the key to effective flood management lies in the design of a plan that combines them all to suit the particular circumstances of the community and the environment. It is not a question of choices between adjustments but rather of the selection of an appropriate group of responses.

# CHAPTER 6

# Water Quality

## 6.1 A history of changing concerns

In the United States, concern for water quality can be traced back to 1647 when the Massachusetts colony enacted legislation designed to prevent the pollution of Boston harbour. The main impetus for pollution prevention came, however, in the nineteenth century as a result of the spread of water-borne disease in the emergent conurbations of North America and Europe (Luckin 1986; Burby et al. 1983).

At a time when pathogenic micro-organisms had not been isolated and the faecal–oral route for disease transmission was not fully understood, John Snow in the UK had established the causative relationship between a polluted water supply and disease transmission (Snow 1855). He achieved this by demonstrating a higher incidence of cholera among Londoners who consumed polluted water from the Southwark and Vauxhall company. Disease rates were lower in similar social classes supplied by the Lambeth company which obtained its water from a less polluted source. Snow's study provided the essential evidence for Sedgwick (USA), Chadwick (UK) and Petinkoffer (Germany) who were campaigning for the provision of clean water supplies as a means of preventing disease epidemics (Shuval 1980).

In Britain and North America, the early supply systems were based upon a protected, or pristine, upland catchment area; a policy of 'source isolation'. This alone produced dramatic declines in disease incidence in the conurbations (Burby et al. 1983). Early treatment facilities, such as slow sand filtration, produced a further significant decline in water-borne disease. The introduction of chlorination in 1870 increased the safety of the supply and the so-called 'multiple barrier' concept of disease prevention was born. This incorporated the four lines of defence outlined in Fig. 6.1. After the Second World War, however, increased pressure from recreationists forced a relaxation of some of the more restrictive catchment-use policies (Douglas and Crabb 1972; HMSO 1948).

The new water supply systems were not without their problems. In locations

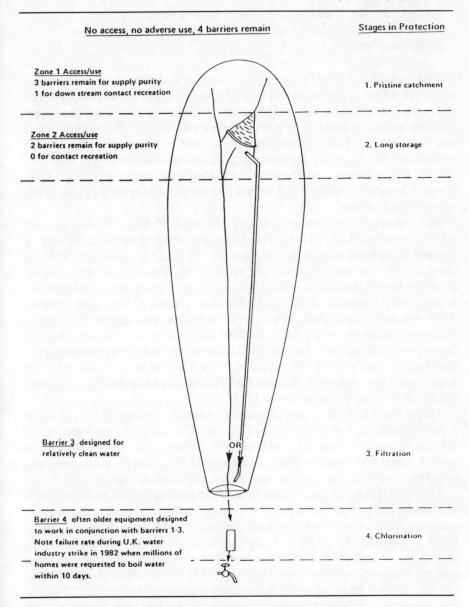

No access, no adverse use, 4 barriers remain

Stages in Protection

Zone 1 Access/use
3 barriers remain for supply purity
1 for down stream contact recreation

1. Pristine catchment

Zone 2 Access/use
2 barriers remain for supply purity
0 for contact recreation

2. Long storage

Barrier 3 designed for
relatively clean water

OR

3. Filtration

Barrier 4 often older equipment designed
to work in conjunction with barriers 1-3.
Note failure rate during U.K. water
industry strike in 1982 when millions of
homes were requested to boil water
within 10 days.

4. Chlorination

*Fig. 6.1*　The four lines of defence against pollution of a water supply.
　　　　*Source*: McDonald *et al.* (1982:65)

where the raw water supply was subject to contamination, a real danger to health
was created by the installation of the supply system itself. Berger and Divorsky
(1977:17) suggested that in the United States:

the increase of water supply systems to over 3,000 by 1900 contributed to

135

major outbreaks of disease, since such pumped supplies, when contaminated, provided a highly efficient vehicle for the delivery of pathogenic bacteria.

This problem was most frequently encountered on large lowland rivers when a municipal water supply intake was located downstream of a sewage outfall. The engineering solution to this problem was to upgrade raw water treatment facilities and, where possible, to reverse the juxtaposition of effluent outfalls and raw water intakes. Later developments in sewage treatment offered scope for improving effluent quality. By the turn of the century, the technology existed to provide a clean 'potable' water supply and to treat sewage effluents. The problem of water-borne enteric disease epidemics had therefore been solved in the newly industrialised nations.

The next set of problems came largely as a result of the growth in economic activity experienced during the twentieth century which caused a corresponding increase in effluent volume and complexity. In many instances, the effluent characteristics stressed the natural assimilative capacity of the receiving environment and the result was a disruption of aquatic ecosystems in lakes, rivers and the sea. At the turn of the twentieth century, sections of the River Thames (UK) were receiving such large quantities of effluent that the natural aquatic ecosystem had been severely degraded. This condition arose because the natural decomposition of industrial and domestic effluent had the effect of removing the dissolved oxygen from the water (Luckin 1986). This condition slowly worsened until about 1950 when some 20 km of the Thames were anaerobic during several months of the year (Gameson et al. 1972).

This overfertilization, or eutrophication, of aquatic ecosystems has presented a major problem for the developed world. The scientific examination of eutrophication first began in the mid-1920s on the Ohio river in the US (Gordon 1985; Krenkel and Novotny 1980). These studies identified the ecological basis on which predictive management models could be built (Odum 1971).

The next set of water-quality parameters to cause concern was pollutants such as lead and DDT. These are difficult to remove by common treatment processes and may accumulate in the bodies of consumers. This causes chronic effects which are difficult to relate to known periods of exposure. Often there are synergistic or antagonistic effects when water contains a mixture of these pollutants in low concentrations (Marshall 1981). For example, the presence of zinc will increase the toxicity of cadmium for crustaceans (Hutchinson 1974), and the toxic effects of dissolved aluminium for brown trout are determined by hydrogen ion concentration (O'Donnell et al. 1983). Where pollutants undergo the process of biological magnification, their presence in even non-potable water can be of great significance. Food species can be significantly affected and workers such as Airey and Jones (1982), Kudo et al. (1981) and Krenkel (1973) have reported on the human health effects of toxic chemicals in fish flesh.

The presence of organic substances (i.e. hydrocarbons or their breakdown products) is a significant cause for alarm. A link is suspected between the ingestion of traces of these compounds over protracted periods and the incidence of teratogenic and mutagenic effects in humans (Pickering 1983; Kraybill 1981; Biswas 1978; see 6.3.2 below). Similar, largely unquantified, risks are associated with the presence of natural and anthropogenic radioactive isotopes in water (Lean 1983; Miettinen 1977).

Perhaps the most insidious concern with water quality in the developed nations stems from epidemiological studies which examine 'natural' dissolved constituents of water, which would not normally be defined as pollution, with rates of disease incidence in different geographical regions. The study of Pocock *et al.* (1980) into British regional variations in cardiovascular mortality and drinking water hardness indicates that regions with the best quality 'soft' water have a significantly higher occurrence of cardiovascular mortality. While no deterministic relationship can be proven, circumstantial evidence points to a geologically determined water-quality parameter which is beyond normal treatment control. Similar epidemiological evidence linking nitrate concentrations in drinking waters with infant methaemoglobinaemia and gastric cancer has been presented by Super *et al.* (1981), Hill *et al.* (1973) and Shuval and Gruener (1972). In this case the pollution source is agricultural fertilizer. Nitrate pollution can produce adverse health effects (regional, chronic and sub-clinical) in the population of consumers. These are thought to have a major impact on the quality of life of large sections of the population (see 6.3.1).

The concern associated with nitrate pollution parallels the fears of health effects which have surrounded the deliberate addition of substances to the water supply which are designed to promote good health. The most common and controversial substance in this regard is fluoride which is added to the water supply to reduce rates of dental caries in the population. Following the addition of fluoride to the water supply of Birmingham, England, in 1964, Burk (1980) noted an apparent increase in cancer mortality. However, subsequent studies have failed to establish firm evidence for a fluoride cancer link (Kinlen and Doll 1981; Cook-Mozaffari *et al.* 1981; Cook-Mozaffari and Doll 1981; Hoover *et al.* 1976).

The most publicised water-quality issue this century has been the problem of acidic precipitation and its effects on aquatic and terrestrial ecosystems. Acid precipitation is often trans-boundary in nature and produces more concern in a recipient state than would be the case if the same ecological damage were caused by its own industries (Seip and Tollan 1985; Ellsworth 1984; Hutchinson and Havas 1980; Braekke 1976; USDA 1976). The full magnitude and continental scale of the effects of acid precipitation are only now becoming evident (UKAWRG 1986; Canadian Government 1985; Chadwick 1983; Pudlis 1983; Smith 1982).

At a more local scale, attention has returned to the concentrations of microbial pathogens in waters used for direct-contact recreation. Following the publication of the EEC (1976) and WHO (1970) standards, epidemiological investigations have been conducted to determine the potential for disease transmission via polluted bathing waters. Recreational water quality provides an excellent case study of the problems involved in water-quality data inter-pretation. There is little agreement on acceptable levels of enteric indicator bacteria in recreational waters. This is surprising since bacteria, and in particular the coliform group of organisms, comprise one of the first water-quality parameters to be used in regular water analysis (Kay and McDonald 1986a, b; Cabelli 1979; Moore 1975). This issue will be explored further in 6.2.2.

While the developed nations concern themselves with problems of water-quality aesthetics and ecological instability caused by acidic deposition, in the developing nations water-borne enteric disease is still a cause of some 10 million deaths per year and 500 million cases of illness (WHO 1986; Krenkel and Novotny 1980). The problems of gross pollution and enteric disease epidemics seen in many developing nations mirror the problems in the newly industrialised world of the nineteenth century. Feachem (1980:255) summarised the water quality experienced by many Third World consumers as follows:

> Most people in developing countries drink unchlorinated and untreated water. Where the water comes from protected groundwater or upland surface sources it may be of moderately good quality (say less than 100 faecal coliforms·100 ml$^{-1}$). In other cases the water may be highly polluted and on occasion, have an indicator bacteria concentration similar to that of weak raw sewage.

This provides an interesting comparison between the current standards for recreational water quality in the developed world and the 'moderately good' water quality for developing nations. The latter are experiencing a quality of drinking water that would not be recommended for immersion sports in North America and Europe. The application of global water-quality standards may be inappropriate at the present time.

## 6.2 Microbiological parameters

### 6.2.1 Drinking waters

The greatest danger to an individual's health from water pollution derives from enteric pathogens which are excreted in the faeces and sometimes the urine of a disease carrier. Researchers have attempted to quantify the risk of contracting disease through contact with poor-quality waters. This can be done by measuring concentrations of pathogenic organisms. However, this is a laborious and inefficient process in regular water analysis because each species of pathogen requires separate incubation and enumeration procedures. A negative result when testing for a typhoid organism does not prove that water is safe for human consumption because other pathogenic species may be present but remain undetected. A water supply may be polluted by excretal contamination but have low or zero pathogens present because there are no pathogen carriers in the faecal contributor population. A water supplier testing only for pathogens would remain unaware of the contamination and thus the 'risk' that a pathogen carrier might, at some time in the future, contribute to the pollution load. In an effort to overcome these difficulties, the water industry has adopted the use of *indicator species* of enteric bacteria. The presence of an indicator species demonstrates that contamination is taking place. The concentration of any given indicator suggests the level of risk from associated pathogens. The ideal indicator species has been defined by Mallard (1982) as follows:

1. Applicable to all types of water.
2. Present in sewage and polluted waters when pathogens are present.
3. Number is correlated with the amount of pollution.
4. Present in greater numbers than pathogens.
5. No aftergrowth in water.
6. Greater survival than pathogens.
7. Absent from unpolluted waters.
8. Easily detected by simple laboratory tests in the shortest possible time consistent with accurate results.
9. Has consistent characteristics.
10. Harmless to man and animals.

The coliform group has gained widespread acceptance among water analysts as the best measure of faecal contamination (HMSO 1969, 1983; APHA 1975). The British water industry uses a subgroup of the total coliform flora, namely *Escherichia coli*, to indicate faecal pollution. In the US, a slightly larger subgroup is defined, the 'faecal coliforms' (FC). Other indicator systems have been suggested which rely on organisms such as faecal streptococci (FS) (Geldreich and Kenner 1969), *Clostridium perfringens* (HMSO 1969) and *Pseudomonas aeruginosa* (Hoadley 1967; Sultter *et al.* 1967). All of these species indicate that pollution is taking place. They do not prove a risk from pathogens but they demonstrate the presence of future risk that a pathogen carrier might contribute to the faecal pollution. Table 6.1 shows the excretion rates and *E. coli* loadings from eight species of animal.

Standards of microbiological purity for potable waters are usually quoted as total coliform or *E. coli* concentration 100 ml$^{-1}$ of sample water. The level of risk derives from the relationship between the numbers of indicators and pathogens in a sample. The literature on indicator/pathogen relationships is sparse when compared with studies examining indicator populations alone. This has led to considerable debate over the acceptable levels of indicator bacteria for any given water resource use. Most agreement exists for drinking water. Here it is generally agreed that any *E. coli* (UK) or faecal coliforms (US) indicate a health risk which should be investigated before the supply is consumed. In most developed nations, this standard is maintained by the multiple-barrier concept outlined in Fig. 6.1. Where water-borne disease does occur in these societies it is usually traced to a small rural supply which is suffering gross pollution, often due to a broken supply line and cross-contamination with effluent (Dufour 1984; Lippy 1981).

*Table 6.1* Excretion rates of *Escherichia coli* by eight species of animal

|  | Faecal production per day (grams) | Average E. coli per gram faeces | Daily load E. coli |
|---|---|---|---|
| Man | 150.0 | $13.00 \times 10^6$ | $1.90 \times 10^9$ |
| Cow | 23,600.0 | $0.23 \times 10^6$ | $5.40 \times 10^9$ |
| Hog | 2,700.0 | $3.30 \times 10^6$ | $8.90 \times 10^9$ |
| Sheep | 1,130.0 | $16.00 \times 10^6$ | $18.10 \times 10^9$ |
| Ducks | 336.0 | $33.00 \times 10^6$ | $11.10 \times 10^9$ |
| Turkeys | 448.0 | $0.30 \times 10^6$ | $0.13 \times 10^9$ |
| Chickens | 182.0 | $1.30 \times 10^6$ | $0.24 \times 10^9$ |
| Gulls | 15.3 | $131.20 \times 10^6$ | $2.00 \times 10^9$ |

*E. coli* concentration 100 ml$^{-1}$
   Sewage          $3.4 \times 10^5 - 2.8 \times 10^7$
   Sewage effluent   $10^3 - 10_7$
*E. coli* survival times
   Freshwater      mean $T_{90}$ 62.3 hours
   Sea water       mean $T_{90}$ 2.3 hours
*Source*: White and Godfrey (1985)

Such a generally satisfactory situation is not enjoyed by the developing nations. Feachem (1980) has studied water quality in nine developing nations. Table 6.2 indicates the levels of contamination found in these countries. These data indicate the importance of the water-quality improvements which are the aim of the United Nations Water Supply and Sanitation Decade (WHO 1981; NWC 1981; Chapter 4).

### 6.2.2 Non-potable waters

Microbiological standards are defined for non-potable waters where the water is used either for recreation or as a source of shellfish. Enteric indicator standards for shellfish-growing waters are required because of the animal's ability to concentrate pathogens in its body as it filter feeds. This concentration is enhanced by the settlement of bacteria, producing high concentrations at the sediment/water interface where the animals are attached. Bacterial concentrations in shellfish of over 90 times that in the surrounding waters have been observed. In oyster flesh, Salanetz (1965) measured faecal coliform (FC) concentrations of 33 to 2,200·100 g$^{-1}$ in flesh compared to water concentrations of 1 to 29·100 ml$^{-1}$. A major US/Canadian study has suggested that shellfish-growing waters should not experience FC levels above 14·100 ml$^{-1}$ (Train 1980; Hunt and Springer 1974).

There is no internationally accepted water-quality standard for recreational waters. In part this stems from the assumptions implied in the use of any indicator of water quality to define a health risk. These assumptions include (i) uniform ingestion levels in a homogeneous population with a constant reaction to the same infective dose; (ii) identical coliform/pathogen relationships; and (iii)

*Table 6.2*  Reported concentrations of faecal bacteria in untreated domestic water
sources in developing countries

| Source | Faecal organisms (dl)* | |
| | Coliforms | Streptococci |
| --- | --- | --- |
| **Gambia:** | | |
| Open, hand-dug wells, 15–18 m deep | Up to 100,000 | NR |
| **Indonesia:** | | |
| Canals in central Jakarta | 3,100–3,100,000 | NR |
| **Kenya:** | | |
| Springs | 0 | 0 |
| Dams | 0–2 | 0–14 |
| Waterholes | 11–350 | 50–90 |
| Large rivers | 10–100,000 | 10–10,000 |
| **Lesotho:** | | |
| Unprotected springs | 900 | 1,700 |
| Waterholes | 860 | 1,610 |
| Small dams | 260 | 260 |
| Streams | 5,000 | 4,100 |
| Protected springs | 200 | 250 |
| Tap water (springs) | 9 | 29 |
| Tap water (boreholes) | 1 | 10 |
| **Nigeria:** | | |
| Ponds | 1,300–1,900 | 1,300–3,900 |
| Open hand-dug wells | 200–580 | 180–630 |
| Tap water (boreholes) | Up to 35 | Up to 6 |
| **Nigeria:** | | |
| Ponds | 4,000,000† | NR |
| Open hand-dug wells, 6–12 m deep | 50,000† | NR |
| Stored in home | 100† | NR |
| **Papua New Guinea:** | | |
| Streams | 0–10,000 | 0–4,000 |
| **Tanzania:** | | |
| Rain water | 3 | 13 |
| Waterholes | 61 | 974 |
| Ponds | 163 | 590 |
| Streams | 128 | 293 |
| Unprotected springs | 20 | 58 |
| Protected springs | 15 | 40 |
| Open wells | 343 | 1,761 |
| Protected wells | 7 | 33 |
| Boreholes | 1 | 11 |
| Treated tap water | 3 | 13 |

141

*Table 6.2* (continued)

| Source | Faecal organisms (dl)* | |
| --- | --- | --- |
| | Coliforms | Streptococci |
| Uganda: | | |
| Rivers | 500–8,000 | NR |
| Streams | 2–1,000 | NR |
| Unprotected springs | 0–2,000 | NR |
| Protected springs | 0–200 | NR |
| Hand-dug wells | 8–200 | NR |
| Boreholes | 0–60 | NR |

\*   When only a single value is given it is a geometric mean.
†   Total coliforms rather than faecal coliforms.
NR  Not recorded (or reported).

These figures are not necessarily typical of the domestic water quality in the countries concerned. They are measurements taken from selected sources during specific investigations. It is generally true, however, that people in developing countries who must use surface sources or open wells are often drinking water with >1,000 faecal coliforms/dl.

*Source*: Feachem (1980)

a uniformly bactericidal environment at all times. Only when these conditions are fulfilled is it scientifically justified to set the same water-quality level for a range of different recreational waters (ICF 1978; EEC 1976; WHO 1970). This fact has led to acrimonious dispute where recreational water-quality standards have been imposed over wide geographical areas (Kay and McDonald 1986a, b).

The definition of bacterial standards for recreational waters should be firmly based on epidemiological evidence which establishes a statistically valid relationship between the concentration of indicator bacteria and disease incidence in the recreator population. Good epidemiological studies are rare because very large sample groups are required if adequate control populations are to be established. Furthermore, it is difficult to define and detect all bathing-related disease. It is relatively simple to identify the serious or 'notifiable' (UK) diseases: however, there is a host of less serious ailments caused by sewage-polluted recreational waters, and quantification of these 'low-level' infections may be more problematical.

Opinion among many British water engineers is based upon the PHLS (1959:435) survey, the aim of which was to:

(i)   study the contamination of coastal bathing beaches by sewage,
(ii)  assess the risk to health of bathing in sewage polluted sea water,
(iii) consider the practicality of laying down bacteriological standards for bathing beaches or grading them according to the degree of pollution to which they are exposed.

During the five-year PHLS investigation, the bacteriological quality of 40 beaches was examined. The committee attempted to relate cases of poliomyelitis and enteric fever, diseases which must be notified to medical officers of health, to the known levels of sewage contamination. An examination of 150 cases of poliomyelitis failed to establish any link between the disease and recreational waters, while only four cases of enteric fever could be attributed to bathing in sewage-polluted water. From these findings, the committee concluded that:

Bathing in sewage polluted sea water carries only a negligible risk to health, even on beaches that are aesthetically very unsatisfactory ... the minimal risk attending such bathing is probably associated with chance contact with intact aggregates of faecal material that happen to have come from infected persons ... a serious risk of contracting disease through bathing in sewage polluted sea water is probably not incurred unless the water is so fouled as to be aesthetically revolting (PHLS 1959:468)

The conclusions of this study are still widely used as evidence that Britain need not implement internationally agreed standards such as the EEC Bathing Waters Directive (EEC 1976; Moore 1975, 1977). Moore (1977:270) criticised French attempts to grade their beaches, while at the same time arguing that:

At least for Britain there is no good evidence for a significant health risk from bathing in sewage contaminated sea water.

The French classification is somewhat dubious as can be seen from Table 6.3. Its nature does not excuse the dual standard adopted by Moore. He suggested that potentially expensive criteria should not be applied to his nation, while criticising the French water industry for being too lenient in its application of the same criteria. Moore's statement is still the official stance of the British government and water industry which continues to be based on the 1959 PHLS survey. This study was a *retrospective* investigation of a very narrow range of serious illnesses. A superior experimental design is a *prospective* investigation of selected groups of bathers and non-bathers. In this design, sample groups are identified at the time of bathing and the incidence of disease in both groups is then monitored for a number of days following the bathing event. In this way the total pattern of illness can be defined and incidence rates of relatively minor ailments such as gastroenteritis can be quantified.

Prospective studies of recreationist illness have been completed in the US (Dufour 1984; Cabelli *et al.* 1982), Canada (Seyfried 1980, 1984 pers. comm.) and France (Foulton *et al.* 1983). In all these studies, a significant relationship between levels of sewage contamination and recreator illness has been recognised. Figure 6.2 indicates the strength of the statistical relationship between water quality and recreator illness established by Cabelli *et al.* (1982). These data illustrate that disease transmission can occur at bacterial concentrations well below those specified in the EEC Bathing Waters Directive. Indeed,

*Table 6.3*  European bathing water-quality standards and the French 'qualitative' interpretation

| | EEC Bathing Waters Directive standards (fortnightly sampling) | | French beach classification |
|---|---|---|---|
| | Total coliform/ 100 ml | Faecal coliform/ 100 ml | |
| Guide (recommended) | 500 | 100 | Very good |
| | 80% of samples should not exceed this level | | |
| Imperative (mandatory) | 10,000 | 2,000 | Good |
| | 95% of samples should not exceed this level | | |
| | | | Average: up to 30% exceed the mandatory level |
| | | | Poor: over 33% of samples exceed mandatory level |

Increasing quality →

*Sources*: EEC (1976) and Moore (1977)

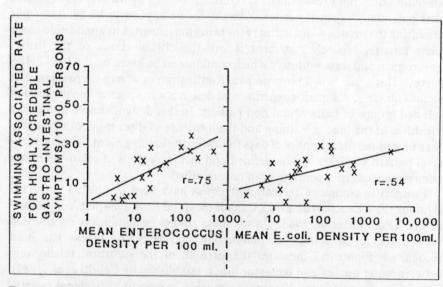

*Fig. 6.2*  The relationship between recreational water quality and disease incidence among bathers. *Source*: Cabelli *et al.* (1982)

Dufour (1984) has suggested that gastrointestinal symptoms can be detected at a mean *E. coli* level of $23 \cdot 100 \text{ ml}^{-1}$ and at a mean enterococcus level of $11 \cdot 100 \text{ ml}^{-1}$.

It is the resource manager's task to interpret these epidemiological findings and to determine the acceptable level of risk to bathers in a polluted recreational water. Strict implementation of standards based upon the results of Cabelli and Dufour's research would close many recreational beaches. This was seen in Ontario during the 1984–6 summers when recreational beaches near Toronto were closed because they exceeded a level of 100 faecal coliforms $100 \text{ ml}^{-1}$ (calculated as a ten-day running geometric mean of daily sampling at each bathing location). This caused a considerable outcry because of the loss to local businesses and communities (Baker 1985a; Hollobon 1983; Horgan 1983). The resultant political pressure has caused a re-examination of these relatively stringent standards (Baker 1985b). This pressure may result in a modification of standards to redefine the *acceptable* pollution levels. The Canadian example offers an object lesson in the interaction of scientific and political factors in environmental pollution assessment. It is clear that some modification in the acceptable level of risk to the population is likely. However, Canadian resource managers, like their American counterparts, have shown considerable courage in applying the epidemiological findings to management decisions quickly and effectively (McDonald and Kay 1984).

In Britain the response of the authorities has been very different. Initially, the Department of the Environment and the water industry showed very little willingness to implement the EEC Bathing Waters Directive (Wheeler 1986; Pearce 1982). Indeed, a government representative suggested that:

> The answer to why there was a bathing water directive was that they had not really thought it was worth arguing against. At the time major issues were being discussed in Brussels, and they had not wanted to appear too obstructive. As members of the community they had to abide by the rules, and it had seemed reasonable to accept the bathing water directive in the overall context at the time. (Barrow 1981:227, discussion)

This ambivalent attitude to the EEC Bathing Waters Directive resulted in only 27 designations of bathing waters around the coasts of the UK. Under the terms of the directive:

> 'Bathing water' means all running or still fresh waters or parts thereof and sea water, in which:
> – bathing is explicitly authorised by the competent authorities of each member state, or
> – bathing is not prohibited and is traditionally practiced by large numbers of bathers; (EEC 1976:L31/3:(Article 1))

The government interpretation of this Article was very restrictive. It required a total of 500 bathers (or, alternatively, 1,500 bathers per linear mile of beach) to be actually in the water at the time of counting. No Welsh beaches were designated and large resort beaches such as Blackpool escaped designation as bathing areas. Table 6.4 lists the numbers of designated beaches in all EEC member states in

1980 and it can be seen from these data that even landlocked Luxembourg has more designations than the UK with its extensive coastal zone.

A number of British scientists have attempted to blunt the credibility of the prospective studies by restating the results of the earlier PHLS investigation (Pike 1985:11). In fact, the two studies are not directly comparable because the PHLS investigation did not examine the same types of disease as the later American epidemiologists (Barrow 1981; Moore 1977).

There is evidence of some recent concern within the water industry and government over this issue (Evison 1985; DoE 1985a, b; Jones and White 1984; HMSO 1984; Stanfield 1982). Many British scientists have established intractable positions as a result of their irrational defence of the early British research, and the debate is likely to continue for a considerable time in the UK. Under mounting public and parliamentary pressure for action on recreational water quality, the British government has instigated a sampling programme of 330 beaches around the British coast (DoE 1985a; HMSO 1985a, b). The stated objective of this two-year study is to gather water-quality data from British beaches. This is surprising since large amounts of data already exist in water authority and Water Research Centre files (Welsh Water 1985, 1986b; Gameson *et al.* 1978). The cost of outfall improvements to clean British beaches would be at least £750 million (1986 prices) and it has been suggested that the DoE research programme is little more than a useful means of delaying the required expenditure and deflecting public pressure for water-quality improvements (Kay and McDonald 1986b).

## 6.3  Physio-chemical parameters of water quality

Many physio-chemical parameters are used to indicate the safety of a potable supply. Table 6.5 illustrates the substances which are defined by the World Health Organisation to be of management significance in a water supply. Each of these chemicals could provide the subject of a 'major issue' in its own right. However, none has received the same attention as the nitrate problem.

### 6.3.1  Nitrates

Nitrates in themselves are not poisonous but, when reduced to toxic nitrites in the stomach, two serious conditions can result. The first affects only infants because their stomach pH is particularly favourable for the microbial reduction of nitrates to nitrites. The resultant condition is known as blue baby syndrome or, more correctly, methaemoglobinaemia. This predominantly affects bottle-fed babies and Jagerstad (1977) noted some 2,000 cases reported in the literature from 1945. There is no simple dose/response relationship between nitrate levels and infant methaemoglobinaemia and, where careful epidemiological investigations have been conducted, other factors which influence infant morbidity rates have been found (Magee 1982). For example, Super *et al.* (1981) studied the incidence

*Table 6.4*  Bathing beaches and sampling locations designated under the terms of the EEC Bathing Waters Directive

| Member state[a] | No. of inland bathing waters | No. of coastal bathing waters |
|---|---|---|
| Luxembourg | 39 | 0 |
| Belgium | 41 | 15 |
| Netherlands | 323 | 60 |
| FR Germany | 85 | 9 |
| Ireland | 0 | 6 |
| Denmark | 139[b] | 1,117[b] |
| France | 1,362[b] | 1,498[b] |
| Italy | 57[b,c] | 3,308[b,d] |
| United Kingdom | 0 | 27 |

*Notes:*
[a]  Greece was not a member state when these data were collected.
[b]  Number of sampling points. Not directly comparable with other data.
[c]  Although all the major lakes in northern Italy have identified bathing waters, the number of sampling points is specified for Lake Garda only.
[d]  Excludes Sicily, for which the number of sampling points is not specified.

*Source*: Water Research Centre (1985)

*Table 6.5*  Physio-chemical parameters of potable water quality identified by the World Health Organization

| Constituent | Unit | Guideline value | Remarks |
|---|---|---|---|
| Arsenic | mg/l | 0.05 | |
| Asbestos | — | No guideline value set | |
| Barium | — | No guideline value set | |
| Beryllium | — | No guideline value set | |
| Cadmium | mg/l | 0.005 | |
| Chromium | mg/l | 0.05 | |
| Cyanide | mg/l | 0.1 | |
| Fluoride | mg/l | 1.5 | Natural or deliberately added; local or climatic conditions may necessitate adaptation |
| Hardness | — | No health-related guideline value set | |
| Lead | mg/l | 0.05 | |
| Mercury | mg/l | 0.001 | |
| Nickel | — | No guideline value set | |
| Nitrate | mg/l (N) | 10 | |
| Nitrite | — | No guideline value set | |
| Selenium | mg/l | 0.01 | |
| Silver | — | No guideline value set | |
| Sodium | — | No guideline value set | |
| Aldrin and dieldrin | $\mu$g/l | 0.03 | |
| Benzene | $\mu$g/l | 10 | |

*Table 6.5* (continued)

| Constituent | Unit | Guideline value | Remarks |
|---|---|---|---|
| Benzo[*a*]pyrene | μg/l | 0.01 | |
| Carbon tetrachloride | μg/l | 3 | Tentative guideline value |
| Chlordane | μg/l | 0.3 | |
| Chlorobenzenes | μg/l | No health-related guideline value set | Odour threshold concentration between 0.1 and 3 μg/l |
| Chloroform | μg/l | 30 | Disinfection efficiency must not be compromised when controlling chloroform content |
| Chlorophenols | μg/l | No health-related guideline value set | Odour threshold concentration 0.1 μg/l |
| 2,4-D | μg/l | 100 | |
| DDT | μg/l | 1 | |
| 1,2-dichloroethane | μg/l | 10 | |
| 1,1-dichloroethene | μg/l | 0.3 | |
| Heptachlor and heptachlor epoxide | μg/l | 0.1 | |
| Hexachlorobenzene | μg/l | 0.01 | |
| Gamma-HCH (lindane) | μg/l | 3 | |
| Methoxychlor | μg/l | 30 | |
| Pentachlorophenol | μg/l | 10 | |
| Tetrachloroethene[d] | μg/l | 10 | Tentative guideline value |
| Trichloroethene | μg/l | 30 | Tentative guideline value |
| 2,4,6-trichlorophenol | μg/l | 10 | Odour threshold concentration, 0.1 μg/l |
| Trihalomethanes | | No guideline value set | See chloroform |

*Source*: WHO (1984)

of methaemoglobinaemia in 468 children drinking well water of varying nitrate concentrations in Namibia and West Africa. While they did identify a strong positive relationship between levels of ingested nitrate and methaemoglobinaemia, they also suggested that the general health of the infant and vitamin C intake significantly affected susceptibility. Other workers have suggested that methaemoglobinaemia morbidity patterns are affected by respiratory infections, diarrhoea and diet (Shuval and Gruener 1972).

The second condition derives from the association between nitrates and nitrosamines which are carcinogenic and induce extensive malignant tumours (Jagerstad 1977). Nitrosamines are formed in the human stomach when nitrite reacts with the parent amine, producing nitrosamines; they are also taken into the body directly in foodstuffs. Hill *et al.* (1973) suggest that in 'normal' areas, where nitrate levels in potable waters are low, the nitrate in foodstuffs contributes 70–80 per cent of the weekly intake of 400–500 mg. However, in areas of high nitrate concentrations in the water supply, the total average weekly intake rises to 998 mg of which 70 per cent is water derived (Table 6.6).

Hill *et al.* (1973) investigated the relationship between high drinking water nitrate and cancer. They used data from Worksop, UK, where the drinking water nitrate concentration was about 90 mg·l⁻¹ NO₃. Morbidity patterns for Worksop were compared with eight similar towns which experienced drinking water nitrate levels of less than 10 mg·l⁻¹ during the study period. Table 6.7 illustrates the higher levels of cancer mortality in Worksop which particularly affected

*Table 6.6* Estimated weekly nitrate intake of people living in control towns with low drinking water nitrate levels and in Worksop with high drinking water nitrate levels

| Source | Weekly intake | Control towns | | Worksop | |
| --- | --- | --- | --- | --- | --- |
| | | Nitrate (ppm) | Weekly nitrate intake (mg) | Nitrate (ppm) | Weekly nitrate intake (mg) |
| Meat | 220 g | 500 | 110 | 500 | 110 |
| Vegetables (excluding potatoes) | 450 g | 500 | 225 | 500 | 225 |
| Water | 71 | 15 | 105 | 93 | 645 |
| Total | | | 440 | | 980 |

*Source*: Hill *et al.* (1973)

*Table 6.7* Stomach cancer deaths in ten towns for the years 1963–71

| Town | Males | | Females | | Total | |
| --- | --- | --- | --- | --- | --- | --- |
| | Observed | Observed Expected | Observed | Observed Expected | Observed | Observed Expected |
| Chesterfield | 99 | 0.95 | 94 | 1.32* | 193 | 1.10 |
| Doncaster | 121 | 1.00 | 78 | 0.98 | 199 | 1.00 |
| Lincoln | 96 | 0.86 | 71 | 0.88 | 167 | 0.87 |
| Mansfield | 74 | 0.95 | 53 | 1.06 | 127 | 0.99 |
| Newark | 34 | 0.94 | 29 | 1.14 | 63 | 1.03 |
| Rotherham | 120 | 1.12 | 65 | 0.88 | 185 | 1.02 |
| Scunthorpe | 65 | 0.86 | 49 | 1.03 | 114 | 0.93 |
| Sutton-in-Ashfield | 73 | 1.28* | 46 | 1.23 | 119 | 1.26* |
| Wakefield | 93 | 1.07 | 78 | 1.21 | 171 | 1.13 |
| Worksop | 50 | 1.08 | 43 | 1.60† | 93 | 1.27* |

\* $P < 0.05$.
† $P < 0.01$.
*Source*: Hill *et al.* (1973)

women (observed/expected of 1.6). These data are even more striking when the cancer incidence rates are broken down by age (Table 6.8).

Hill *et al.* (1973) explained the observed pattern by reference to the incidence of urinary infections in the defined age groups which encourage nitrosamine formation in the bladder and hence the development of gastric cancer. Subsequent workers have suggested that social differences between the study towns may account for some of the morbidity differentials observed by Hill *et al.* (1973) (Royal Society 1983). This remains an unresolved question which is central to the debate on what constitutes an acceptable concentration of nitrates in drinking water.

The epidemiological significance of drinking water nitrate concentrations was recognised in the early 1970s. During that time, trends in nitrate fertilizer applications and increases in surface and groundwater nitrate concentrations were being observed in the UK (Wilkinson and Greene 1982; Young 1981; Marsh 1980; Casey and Clarke 1979; Walling and Foster 1978; Greene 1978; Foster and Crease 1974; Tomlinson 1970), in the Netherlands (Frissel 1977), in France (Probst 1985), in Italy (Gilli *et al.* 1984) and in North America (Hill 1978; Klepper 1978; Commoner 1977; Abrams and Barr 1974; Harmeson *et al.* 1971; Kohl *et al.* 1971).

Fears were expressed by these authors of a potential 'time bomb' (Anon 1980) in the existing environmental nitrate concentrations. The reason for this view of the problem has been expressed by Foster and Crease (1974:178) who studied the East Yorkshire chalk aquifer. They stated:

the steady increase in applications of nitrogenous fertiliser since 1959 gives rise to a most pressing question. How much nitrate is contained in the groundwater of the unsaturated zone, already in transit to the water table?

In Britain this concern resulted in the formation of a Royal Society study group to review the nitrogen cycle in the UK and define the main environmental problems. The group was formed in 1979 and reported in 1983 (Royal Society 1983). That report provides an excellent compilation of ecological research on nitrogen cycling. The study group also noted the rapid rise in UK nitrate usage in the period from 1943 to 1981 (see Fig. 6.3). This increase was mirrored by a rise in river nitrate levels over the same period, with peak levels in the Midlands and the south-east of England. Figure 6.4 illustrates this regional pattern for surface waters.

The Royal Society also presented data on groundwater nitrate concentrations projected into the next century (Fig 6.5). These projections reinforced the earlier fears expressed by Hill *et al.* (1973). The Royal Society (1983:165) stated:

The model predictions are relatively insensitive to future trends in land use and fertilizer application rates because of the long transit times through the unsaturated zone.

There is little sign of a decrease in nitrate applications, and Hood (1982) has suggested that ceilings in biological productivity are unlikely to produce a brake

*Table 6.8* Deaths from cancer of the stomach, and all neoplasms other than gastric cancer in Worksop 1963–71

| Age group | Males | | | Females | | | Total | | |
|---|---|---|---|---|---|---|---|---|---|
| | Observed | Expected | Observed/Expected | Observed | Expected | Observed/Expected | Observed | Expected | Observed/Expected |
| *Stomach cancer* | | | | | | | | | |
| Less than 55 | 4 | 5.00 | 0.70 | 5 | 2.59 | 1.93 | 9 | 8.29 | 1.09 |
| 55–64 | 12 | 14.00 | 0.81 | 5 | 5.40 | 0.93 | 17 | 20.25 | 0.84 |
| 65–74 | 15 | 16.34 | 0.92 | 13 | 8.57 | 1.52 | 28 | 24.91 | 1.12 |
| Over 75 | 19 | 9.29 | 2.05 | 20 | 10.25 | 1.95 | 39 | 19.54 | 2.00 |
| Total | 50 | 46.19 | 1.08 | 43 | 26.81 | 1.60 | 93 | 73.00 | 1.27 |
| *All cancers other than stomach* | | | | | | | | | |
| Less than 55 | 44 | 53.33 | 0.83 | 64 | 58.23 | 1.10 | 108 | 111.56 | 0.97 |
| 55–64 | 75 | 106.02 | 0.71 | 41 | 63.02 | 0.65 | 116 | 169.04 | 0.69 |
| 65–74 | 87 | 109.43 | 0.80 | 47 | 62.97 | 0.75 | 134 | 172.40 | 0.78 |
| Over 75 | 61 | 58.90 | 1.04 | 49 | 53.64 | 0.91 | 110 | 112.54 | 0.98 |
| Total | 267 | 327.68 | 0.81 | 201 | 237.86 | 0.85 | 468 | 565.54 | 0.83 |

*Source:* Hill et al. (1973)

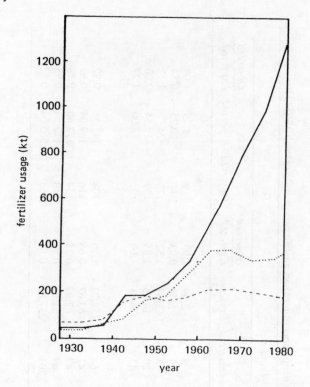

*Fig. 6.3* The trends in annual fertilizer usage in the UK in the period 1928–80.
*Source*: The Royal Society (1983)

on nitrate use in the near future. Political and economic forces are required to halt the alarming trends identified in UK nitrate pollution.

Long-term trends in nitrate concentrations offer the most cause for potential concern. However, short-term cycles, with return periods of less than one year, cause significant operational management problems. Short-term changes in stream nitrate concentration are determined by discharge levels. Where the input is largely derived from agriculture, the concentrations increase with increasing flow. Where the dominant nitrate source is sewage effluents, a dilution effect occurs under high flows. The seasonal patterns also demonstrate regional variations which are determined by land use and catchment hydrology. The greatest annual variation is found in the rivers in the south-east of England which exhibit a marked winter peak in nitrate concentrations as the autumn rains mobilise fertilizer from the arable lands (see Fig. 6.6 (iii) and (iv)). In the higher rainfall of north-west England, a reverse pattern is seen: nitrate concentrations in the River Mersey at Flixton exhibit a later summer peak (Fig. 6.6) caused by the higher summer rainfall.

The magnitude and duration of peak nitrate loads in rivers is a matter of

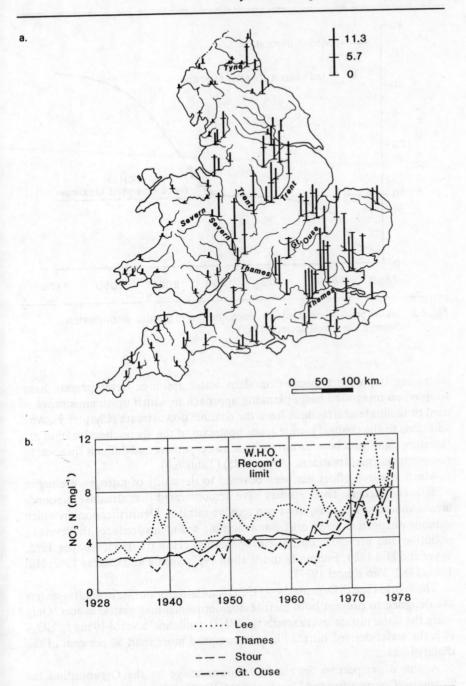

*Fig. 6.4* Nitrate concentrations in British rivers: (a) areal distribution; and
(b) long-term trends. *Source*: The Royal Society (1983)

153

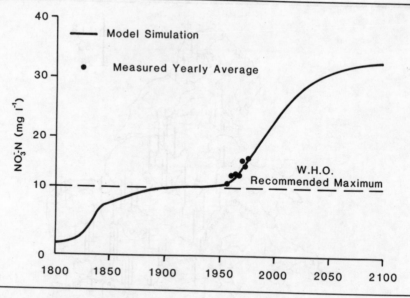

*Fig. 6.5*  Model predictions of nitrate concentrations in potable groundwaters.
*Source*: The Royal Society (1983)

increasing importance because modern water resource developments have adopted an integrated basin-planning approach in which upstream storage is used to facilitate abstractions from the channel downstream (Chapter 9). Any additions to the channel nitrate loads upstream of the abstraction location are therefore significant because nitrate is such an expensive and difficult chemical to remove by normal treatment (Anon 1985) (Table 6.9).

Much research effort has been devoted to the study of nitrogen cycling in aquatic ecosystems. These studies have demonstrated that streams, impoundments, inland seas and aquifers can remove nitrates. Denitrification, in which gaseous nitrogen is given off from anaerobic sediments, reduces the levels of pollution and prevents cultural eutrophication (Howard 1985; Ronner 1985; Wyer and Hill 1984; Edmunds and Walton 1982; Swank and Caskey 1982; Hill 1981, 1982; Van Kessel 1977).

The World Health Organization (1984) standards for nitrate in potable waters are designed to prevent both methaemoglobinaemia and gastric cancer. Only when the water nitrate level exceeds the WHO 'guideline' level of 10 mg·l$^{-1}$ NO$_3$–N is the water-derived nitrate likely to comprise more than 50 per cent of the dietary intake.

A global perspective on nitrate fertilizer usage by the Organization for Economic Cooperation and Development (OECD) (1986) indicates that upward trends are likely to continue in both the developed and developing worlds. Perhaps the most significant trend identified is the consumption of nitrate

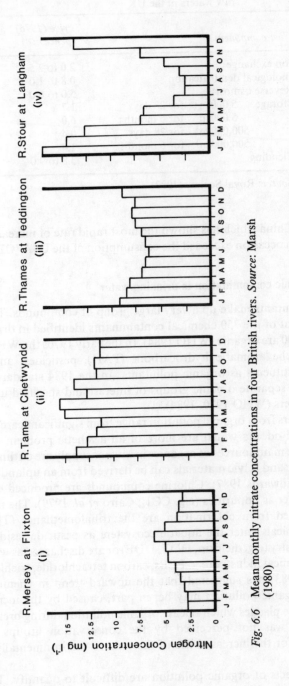

Fig. 6.6  Mean monthly nitrate concentrations in four British rivers. Source: Marsh (1980)

*Table 6.9*  Water-treatment costs of removing nitrate from
raw waters in the UK

| Cost component | | Price (1976) (pence m$^{-3}$) |
|---|---|---|
| Ion exchange | | 2.0 to 2.5 |
| Biological denitrification | | 0.8 to 1.0 |
| Reverse osmosis | | 5.0 to 6.0 |
| Storage: 5,000 m$^3$ | for 28 days | 1.7 |
| 5,000 m$^3$ | for 6 months | 6.0 |
| 500,000 m$^3$ | for 28 days | 0.4 |
| 500,000 m$^3$ | for 6 months | 1.4 |
| Blending | | 3.8 to 9.0 |

*Source*: Royal Society (1983)

fertilizer in China which has shown the most rapid rate of increase to 1985 and which has on occasion exceeded the consumption of the USA (OECD 1986:33).

### 6.3.2  Organic contamination in drinking water

Organic pollutants make up a very large group of compounds. The WHO has estimated that of the 750 chemical contaminants identified in drinking waters, more than 600 are organic (WHO 1984). In the early 1970s the WHO recognised only polycyclic aromatic hydrocarbons (PAH), pesticides, and extractable organic constituents as organic pollutants. In the 1984 standards, the WHO identified 21 separate organic groups of interest and specified upper limits in drinking waters (WHO 1970, 1984).

The dangers from organic pollution range from significant carcinogenic risks to tastes and odours which are more of an aesthetic problem for the water industry. The main sources of organics in a water supply are outlined in Fig. 6.7.

The humic and fulvic materials can be derived from an upland peat-covered catchment (Edwards 1987). Chlorine compounds are produced during chlorination or enter as impurities (e.g. $CCl_4$; Cairo *et al.* 1979). The main problem species derived from chlorination are the trihalomethanes (THMs). Other organic chemicals enter the aquatic ecosystem as pesticide residues from the farming industry (e.g. dieldrin, DDT, DDE) or are discharged as waste products from the chemical industry (e.g. PCBs, carbon tetrachloride, trichloroethylene). Pickering (1983) has suggested that the upward trend in chemical industry-generated organic pollution may be, in part, caused by the increased use of biodegradable plastics which release organic pollution during breakdown. This consequence was not perceived by the conservation groups which have campaigned for the increased use of these more 'environmentally acceptable' plastics.

Health effects of organic pollution are difficult to quantify. The available epidemiological evidence is not conclusive because prospective human studies

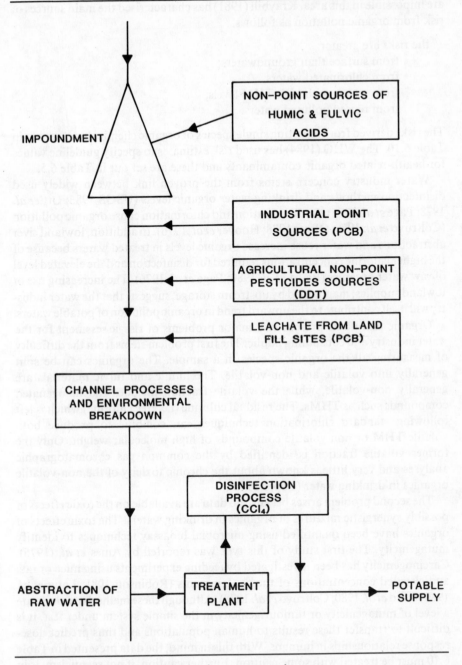

NON-POINT SOURCES OF
HUMIC & FULVIC
ACIDS

IMPOUNDMENT

INDUSTRIAL POINT
SOURCES (PCB)

AGRICULTURAL NON-POINT
PESTICIDES SOURCES
(DDT)

LEACHATE FROM LAND
FILL SITES (PCB)

CHANNEL PROCESSES
AND ENVIRONMENTAL
BREAKDOWN

DISINFECTION
PROCESS
(CCl₄)

ABSTRACTION OF
RAW WATER

TREATMENT
PLANT

POTABLE
SUPPLY

*Fig. 6.7* Sources of organic pollution in a water supply system

are impossible in this area. Kraybill (1981) has characterised the main sources of risk from organic pollution as follows:

the risks are greater:
from surface than groundwaters;
from chlorinated waters;
from waters with high THM levels;
from reused polluted waters.

The risks derived from ingesting single species of organic chemicals are set out in Table 6.10. The WHO (1984) has used risk estimates to specify guideline values for health-related organic contaminants and these are set out in Table 6.5.

Water industry concern stems from the proven link between widely used disinfection methods and drinking water organic levels (USGS 1983; Ott *et al.* 1978; Page *et al.* 1976). Both ozonation and chlorination cause organic pollution (Coltruvo *et al.* 1978; Oliver 1978; Hoover *et al.* 1976). In addition, lowland river abstractions and water reuse increase organic levels in treated waters because of the higher chlorine concentrations required for disinfection and the elevated level of raw water organics (Baird *et al.* 1980; Page *et al.* 1976). The increasing use of lowland supplies, maintained by upstream storage, suggests that the water industry will itself contribute to the upward trend in organic pollution of potable waters.

Organic pollutants present two major problems of risk assessment for the water industry and consuming public. The first problem stems from the difficulty of measuring all the organic species in a sample. The organics can be split generally into volatile and non-volatile. The humic and fulvic materials are generally non-volatile, while the volatile fraction includes the halogenated compounds such as THMs. The residual chlorine (i.e. free chlorine) which is left following standard chlorination techniques can combine to produce both volatile THM or non-volatile compounds of high molecular weight. Only the former volatile fraction is identified by the common gas chromatographic analyses and very little is known about the chronic toxicity of the non-volatile organics in drinking water (Loper 1980).

The second problem arises because no data are available on the toxic effects of possibly synergistic mixtures of organics in drinking waters. The toxic effects of organics have been quantified using microbial bioassay techniques to identify mutagenicity. The first study of this type was reported by Ames *et al.* (1975). Carcinogenicity has been investigated by feeding experiments using mice or rats and elevated concentrations of the contaminants (Robinson 1981; Lang *et al.* 1980; Baird *et al.* 1980; Coltruvo *et al.* 1978). Although these methods can indicate a level of mutagenicity or tumourigenicity in the simple system under test, it is difficult to transfer these results to human populations and thus predict dose-response relationships in humans. With this in mind, the data presented in Table 6.10 must be treated with some caution. Further caution, if not scepticism, is in order when one also considers that these data are presented for individual organic species. Rarely would an organism be presented with a single pollutant in the environment (Kraybill 1981).

*Table 6.10* Known or suspected organic carcinogens found in drinking waters with the associated level of risk

| Compound | Highest observed concentrations in finished water (µg/l) | Upper 95% confidence estimate of lifetime cancer risk per µg/l $\times$ $10^{-7}$ |
|---|---|---|
| Vinyl chloride | 10 | 4.7 |
| Dieldrin | 8 | 2,600 |
| Kepone | ND | 440 |
| Heptachlor | D | 420 |
| Chlordane | 0.1 | 180 |
| DDT | D | 120 |
| Lindane ($\zeta$-BHC) | 0.01 | 93 |
| $\beta$-BHC | D | 42 |
| PCB (Aroclor 1260) | 3 | 31 |
| Ethylenethiourea | ND | 22 |
| Chloroform | 366 | 17 |
| $\alpha$-BHC | D | 15 |
| $\rho$-Chloronitrobenzene | ND | 1.4 |
| Carbon tetrachloride | 5 | 1.1 |
| Trichloroethylene | 0.5 | 1.1 |
| Bis-(2-chloroethyl)ether | 0.42 | 12 |
| Acrylonitrile[a] | — | 13 |
| 1,2 Dichloroethane[a] | 8 | 7 |
| Ethylenedibromide[a] | — | 91 |
| Tetrachloroethylene[a] | 5 | 1.4 |
| Hexachlorobenzene[a] | 0.006 | 290 |
| Benzene | 10 | ID |
| Benzo[$\alpha$]pyrene | D | ID |
| Diphenylhydrazine | 1 | ID |
| Aldrin | D | ID |
| Endrin | 0.08 | ID |
| Heptachlor epoxide | D | ID |

*Source*: Loper (1980)

### 6.3.3 Acidic precipitation

Acidic precipitation is derived from vehicular and industrial emissions containing the oxides of nitrogen and sulphur ($NO_2$ and $SO_2$). It is a relatively recent problem which has caused significant environmental concern in North America and Europe. Acid input to a river basin is a water resource management problem because it produces aquatic ecosystem damage as well as reducing the

159

quality of potable waters (McDonald 1985). The form of this input can be either 'wet' or 'dry': wet deposition occurs as rainfall and mists while dry deposition takes the form of particulate material. Adjacent to emission sources, the dry form of input dominates; but at distance, the balance changes in favour of wet deposition (Seip and Tollan 1985). It is the ability of this pollution to travel great distances across international boundaries that has generated such political controversy between the producers and recipients of 'acid rain'.

The presence of 'acid rain' in Europe was first identified in Manchester (UK) by Robert Angus Smith in 1872. This nineteenth-century phenomenon was very localised, but the increasing use of fossil fuels in Europe since 1950 has resulted in a vast increase in absolute pollution levels (Fig. 6.8). The contemporary use of higher power plant smoke stacks has increased the distances travelled by acidic precipitation.

The impact of this pollution can be identified in:

1. Increased corrosion of man-made structures (Kucera 1976);
2. Apparent forest damage (Binns and Redfern 1983); and
3. Major changes in aquatic ecosystems (Drablos and Tollan 1980)

These effects stem from the increased hydrogen ion concentrations (i.e. acidity) caused by acidic deposition. The *natural* acidity of rainfall, caused by dissolved $CO_2$, is between 5.5 and 5.6. In Canada, rainfall pH has been measured at 2.9 in the La Cloche Mountains (Beamish 1976) and in Scotland (UK) rainfall with a pH of 2.4 was recorded on 10 April 1974. Tollan (1981) suggested that large areas of North America and Scandinavia experience average rainfall pH levels below

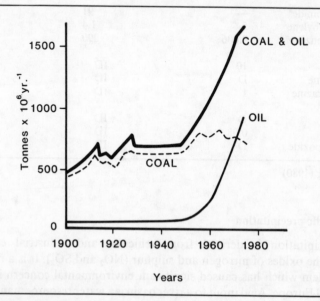

*Fig. 6.8* The usage rate of fossil fuels in Europe. *Source*: Drablos and Tollan (1980)

4.3. The recent nature of this change in precipitation chemistry is evident from Greenland ice cores (Busenberg and Langway 1979) and diatoms preserved within lake sediment profiles (Jones *et al.* 1986; Batterbee *et al.* 1985).

Although rainfall acidity is a significant problem, the major determinant of aquatic ecological damage is not precipitation acidity but rather the ability of the catchment area to buffer or neutralise the weak acidic input. Catchments with a good supply of basic cations from rock weathering will experience little damage to aquatic ecosystems from acidic precipitation. It is the areas of hard, base poor, rocks with thin soils and high rainfall totals that are most susceptible to acidification of surface waters. Approaches to the definition of acidic susceptibility have centred on soils and geology (McFee 1983). When acidic precipitation falls on such *susceptible* areas, $SO^{2-}$ becomes the 'driving' anion which is balanced by $H^+$ and $Al^{3+}$ cations from the soils producing acidic waters rich in dissolved aluminium. (For a fuller explanation of catchment ionic balance concepts, see Rosenqvist (1981).) The combined effects of low pH ($<5.5$) and high $Al^{3+}$ concentrations ($>0.2$ mg·l$^{-1}$) produce conditions toxic to salmonid species which experience gill irritation and difficulty in regulating blood salt concentrations. These effects are more marked when the waters have very low dissolved $Ca^{2+}$ concentrations of $<2$ mg·l$^{-1}$ (O'Donnell *et al.* 1983).

Canada has claimed significant environmental damage to salmonid species in Nova Scotia and Ontario. This was identified by Beamish and Harvey (1972) who observed the effects of recent acidification on fisheries in Lumsden Lake in the La Cloche Mountains in the late 1960s. This area is some 65 km to the south-west of the world's largest emitter of sulphur dioxide, the International Nickel Company (INCO) plant at Sudbury, Ontario. The lakes are within a wilderness area, the Killarney Provincial Park, and the geology of the area comprises quartzite ridges, a hard rock of low base status. The pH of Lumsden Lake had fallen from 6.8 in 1961 to 4.4 in 1971, which represented a hundred-fold increase in acidity, causing severe fisheries decline. Similar acidification was noted in many other lakes in the wilderness area to the north of Georgian Bay. Analysis of wind tracks suggested that significant amounts of the 2.6 million metric tonnes of $SO_2$ released into the atmosphere (1969) from nickel smelters at Sudbury could be reaching the area of lake acidification. This realisation of rapid environmental deterioration resulted in agreements to reduce $SO_2$ levels in Eastern Canada (Environment Canada 1984a, b).

Canadian attention turned to its southern neighbour, the USA, which was producing vast amounts of $SO_2$ from the burning of sulphur-rich Appalachian coal for power generation. This was causing ecological damage within the USA in the Adirondak Mountains of New York State. Here, 180 resort-area lakes are now devoid of fish life due to acid precipitation damage (Canadian Government 1985). Canadian concern centred on the degree to which US pollution was blown into Canada, adding to the existing levels from Sudbury smelters and Ontario hydro-power plants (Environment Canada 1984a). Initially, this concern was expressed by vociferous environmental groups rather than at an 'official' level. It has been suggested that, at first, the Canadian federal and provincial

161

administrations did not wish to press the case for controls within the USA because this could lead to embarrassing questions about emissions policy within Canada and in particular the lack of effective measures to reduce pollution from the Sudbury nickel smelters and Ontario hydro-power plant at Atikokan. It was not until the late 1970s that this environmental pressure was translated into Canadian government action which eventually resulted in pressure to limit industrial acidic emissions on both sides of the border.

The Canadian government is at the forefront of those pollution-recipient nations calling for international agreement on abatement targets. This stance stems partly from the scale of potential damage within Canada. In 1984, Environment Canada (1984a) estimated that 48,468 lakes in Ontario were susceptible to acidification (see Fig. 6.9) and 30 per cent of Nova Scotian salmon fisheries have disappeared or are declining. Potential reductions in forest productivity in Eastern and Atlantic Canada were estimated at 8–11 per cent given no additional pollution control and 0–2 per cent given effective control measures (Canadian Forestry Service 1985). In addition, 50 per cent of Ontario and 87 per cent of Quebec soils have been classed as susceptible to acidification. The economic impacts of this ecological problem have been estimated at (i) 9,000 jobs and $8 million Cdn at risk in the Ontario fishing industry; (ii) 600 (from a total 1,600) fishing camps and lodges in Ontario could be lost by the year 2000; and (iii) potential crop losses are estimated at $3 billion Cdn from Ontario and Quebec (Canadian Government 1985; Environment Canada 1984a).

Having identified the problem, sections of the Canadian polity have been swift to suggest control strategies designed to limit $SO_2$ deposition in vulnerable areas to $20 \text{ kg·ha}^{-1} \cdot \text{yr}^{-1}$. Of particular importance has been the work of the Federal House of Commons Sub-Committee on Acid Rain. This body was formed on 18 July 1980 and its first report, entitled *Still Waters*, was issued in October 1981. Very little action resulted and the committee was reformed on 9 March 1983, publishing a second report entitled *Lost Time* in 1985. This committee continues to hold hearings and publish its findings (Canadian Government 1986). In their 1985 report, this group of parliamentarians stated that:

> The sub committee emphatically rejects the proposition that more research is necessary before control programmes can be adopted. With more than 3,000 studies published on this subject we maintain that an adequate data base for positive action already exists.
>
> ... our Federal Government, with the support of provincial administrations has for some years been attempting to reach an agreement with the United States Government on acid rain control. The failure of this initiative due largely to the Reagan administration has been a bitter subject for all Canadians.
>
> ... For those Canadians, including members of this sub committee who have travelled to the United States to argue for more stringent controls on American polluters, Canadian government inaction and/or obstinacy with respect to domestic controls have been, quite frankly, an embarrassment.
> (Canadian Government 1985:7)

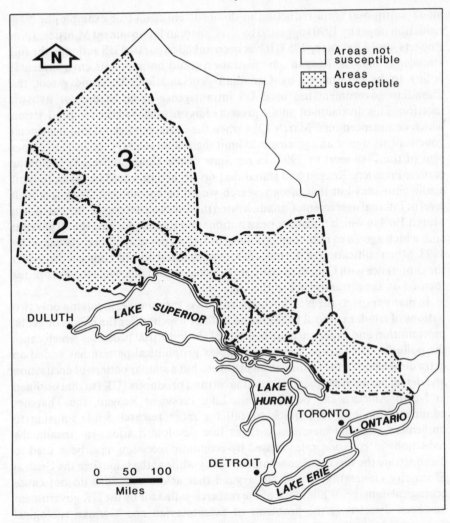

*Fig. 6.9* Ontario lakes susceptible to acidification. *Source*: Ontario Ministry of Environment (1980)

This quotation summarises much of the debate on acidic precipitation in Canada. Although many have identified the problem, specific action has been slow. Often much energy has been devoted to the search for a bilateral agreement with the USA on emission controls. However, this has led to relatively worthless documents such as the 1980 Memorandum of Intent in which both governments stated their intention to enforce current air-quality control standards and to work towards bilateral agreement.

Too often the Canadian position has been weakened by the lack of firm action to limit domestic pollution (Canadian Government 1985). Where Canada has made a proposal for a reduction in domestic emission (for example the 50% reduction target by 1990 suggested by the Canadian Environment Minister, John Roberts, on 15 February 1983) it has been linked to parallel US action in the full knowledge that the Reagan administration could not allow its environmental policy to be determined by Canadian proclamation. To some extent the Canadian government has used US intransigence as an excuse for its own inaction. This diversion of public pressure has only delayed the required action which commenced on 6 March 1984 when the Canadian federal and provincial governments signed an agreement to limit their domestic $SO_2$ emission to 50 per cent of the 1980 level by 1994. In his State of the Union address two months earlier, President Reagan had stated that no US action would be taken to limit acidic emissions but that more research would be encouraged. With this high level of internal agreement, Canada hosted the Ottawa conference on acid rain in March 1984 in which nine European nations and Canada formed the 30 per cent club which agreed to reduce emissions of $SO_2$ to 30 per cent of their 1980 level by 1993. Much vilification of the main $SO_2$ exporters outside the club was evident at the conference with Canadian criticism directed at the USA while the Europeans focused on the intransigence of the UK.

In many respects the North American case is very simple, involving only two nations of similar cultural background both of which suffer the effects of acidic precipitation and experience the benefits of the industrial processes which cause the pollution. In Europe the more complex geopolitical pattern has added an extra dimension to the acidification problem, but a similar pattern of accusation and denial between recipients (Scandinavia) and producers (UK) to that outlined in North America can be identified. Like President Reagan, the Thatcher administration has been quick to call for more research while refusing to implement remedial measures such as flue desulphurisation. In Britain, the reductions in emission rates caused by economic recession have been used to demonstrate the *success* of government policy while at the same time the Central Electricity Generating Board has argued that acidic emissions do not cause ecological damage. While some of the research called for by the UK government has been directed at the problems of Scandinavian and German ecological damage, it is increasingly evident that significant ecological damage has taken place in Scotland, Cumbria and Wales.

Concern over the declines in salmonid numbers in Scotland led to a major study which defined fisheries districts with serious problems of salmonid decline. Figure 6.11 was produced by the United Kingdom Acid Waters Review Group and shows the main acid-susceptible areas in the UK. This map was based on the solid and surficial geological deposits of the UK. Figure 6.12 shows the extent of recent salmon-catch declines in Scottish fishery districts.

Gee and Stoner (1985) used three water-quality parameters to quantify the degree of environmental toxicity of upland Welsh streams to brown trout and salmon in terms of the $LT_{50}$ (time taken to kill 50% of a test population) which can be predicted from the concentrations of hydrogen ions, aluminium and calcium as shown below:

*Fig. 6.10* A graphical comment on the US attitude to emission control measures.
*Source*: *Environment Canada* (22 March 1984)

Trout: $R^2 = 0.964$, $Df = 5$
Mortality $(1/LT_{50}) = 0.051 + 0.0058(H) + 0.0019(Al) - 0.00045(Ca)$

Salmon: $R^2 = 0.521$, $Df = 5$
Mortality $(1/LT_{50}) = 0.032 + 0.0099(Al)$

where (H), (Al) and (Ca) represent the 50th percentile concentrations of hydrogen, aluminium and calcium in equiv. $l^{-1}$.

The prevalence of toxic conditions is highly episodic. Toxic episodes are associated with snowmelt events when accumulated dry and wet deposition can enter a watercourse, often without passing through the soil system which may be frozen and hence incapable of producing any buffering reaction on the acid input. Significant fish kills have been reported due to snowmelt events in Norwegian rivers by Henriksen *et al.* (1984) and highly toxic conditions have been observed following snowmelt in British catchment streams. Figure 6.13 shows the pH and $Al^{3+}$ concentrations in a small afforested catchment stream in West Wales during a snowmelt event following a two-month period of light snow accumulation.

Although snowmelt produces the most dramatic changes in stream water chemistry, autumn and winter rainfalls will produce similar patterns of depressed

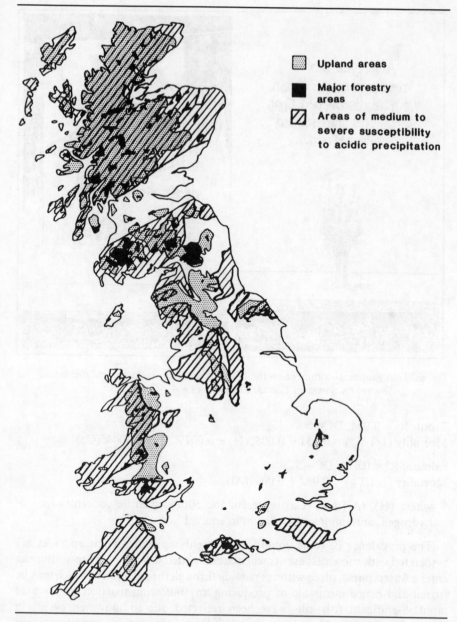

*Fig. 6.11* Regions of acid susceptibility in the UK. *Source*: UKAWRG (1986)

pH and elevated Al$^{3+}$ in acid-susceptible areas. Fish kills can follow from such events as documented by Robinson (1984) in the Cumbrian rivers Duddon and Esk. In Britain, the removal of the agricultural lime subsidy in 1976 and the consequent decline in lime application rates to upland catchments has been

166

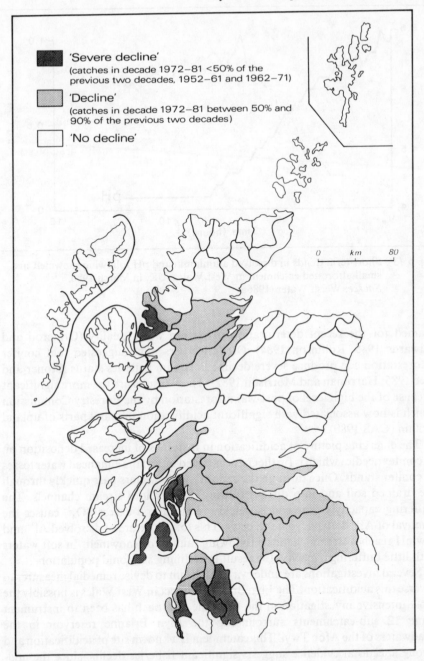

'Severe decline'
(catches in decade 1972–81 <50% of the
previous two decades, 1952–61 and 1962–71)

'Decline'
(catches in decade 1972–81 between 50% and
90% of the previous two decades)

'No decline'

0    km    80

*Fig. 6.12*  Trends in salmon catch by all methods (rod and line, net and cable and
            fixed engine) and all ages (i.e. grilse and salmon combined) over the period
            1952–81 for the 54 districts on the Scottish mainland. *Source*: UKAWRG
            (1986)

167

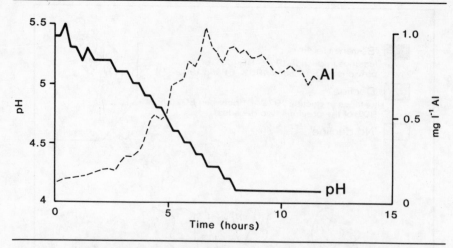

*Fig. 6.13* Short-term trends in dissolved aluminium and pH following snowmelt in a small afforested catchment in West Wales, UK, in March 1986.
*Source*: Welsh Water (1986a)

blamed for the recent deterioration of stream water quality (Ormerod and Edwards 1985; Robinson 1984). Other workers have suggested that conifer afforestation can produce severe decline in stream fisheries status (Stoner and Gee 1985; Harriman and Morrison 1982). These results are the more significant because of the high level of post-war afforestation by the Forestry Commission which is now associated with significant acidification in many parts of upland Britain (CAS 1980).

The emerging picture of acidification in Britain is of increased deposition on to conifer needles which is further concentrated due to the enhanced water losses of conifer stands. Once through the canopy, acidic waters pass quickly through the drained soil and into ditches flowing directly into stream channels. The buffering capacity of the soil is quickly reduced and excess $SO_4^{2-}$ causes the removal of $Al^{3+}$ derived from soil clays. This toxic mixture of dissolved $Al^{3+}$ and low pH reaches stream channels following rainfall or snowmelt. In soft waters with little buffering capacity, the result is declining salmonid populations.

Several investigations are underway which aim to devise remedial measures to reverse this acidification. The Llyn Brianne project in West Wales is possibly the most intensive investigation in the UK. The approach has been to instrument some 12 sub-catchments surrounding the Llyn Brianne reservoir in the headwaters of the Afon Twyi. This catchment is a known site of acidification and strong anecdotal evidence suggests significant fisheries decline since the mid-1970s. The research design involved a comparative study of afforested and grassland catchments for a one-year calibration period followed by a series of catchment modifications in the summer of 1986. The individual catchments and the modifications are shown in Fig. 6.14. The objective is to design practical

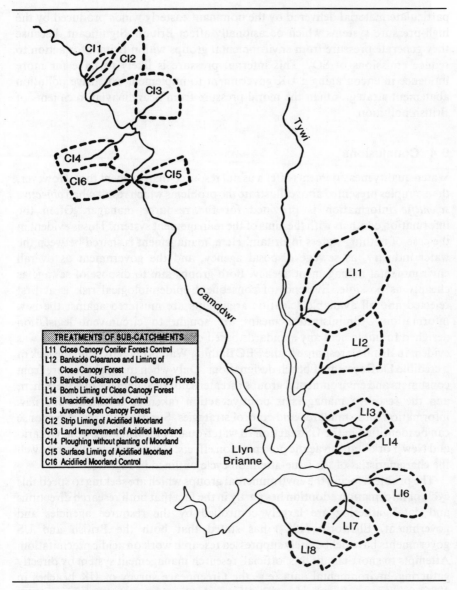

*Fig 6.14* Sub-catchments and land treatments underway as part of the Llyn Brianne study in West Wales, UK. *Source*: Welsh Water (1986a)

management strategies which could be implemented over wide areas of upland Britain to reverse acidification effects.

The results of ecological studies in western and northern Britain are surprising and significant. Surprising, because they indicate that areas upwind of the major pollution sources are under threat of acidification which may derive from

169

rticulate material delivered by the dominant easterly winds produced by the gh-pressure systems which occasionally affect Britain. Significant, because they generate pressure from environmental groups within Britain for action to reduce emissions of $SO_2$. This internal pressure is likely to have far more influence in encouraging a UK government to implement expensive pollution abatement strategies than the moral pressure from Scandinavian recipients of British pollution.

## 6.4 Conclusions

Water-quality measurements offer a useful resource-management tool. However, the examples presented above illustrate the problems which result when *objective scientific* information is provided for the resource manager. Often the information conflicts with the aims of the management system. This is evident in the case of bathing waters in Britain. Here, management is shared between the water industry, as sewage disposal agency, and the government as overall environmental management agency. Both groups aim to dispose of sewage as cheaply as possible. Evidence of consequent epidemiological risk is at first rejected and all available scientific arguments are mustered against the new information. Administrative means are sought to circumvent legislation designed to implement any standards based on the new information. This was evident in Britain's response to the EEC Bathing Waters Directive and the lack of a credible DoE system of beach designations. Only when internal pressure from consumers and environmental groups threatens political damage to government and the resource managers is positive action taken to assimilate the new information into standards and control strategies. Similar patterns of response can be identified in the US reaction to water-quality information from Ontario and New York State on acidic precipitation effects. Both examples illustrate well the characteristics of the issue-attention cycle outlined in Fig. 1.1.

The problem facing the environmental groups which are seeking to speed this cycle of information adoption lies partly in the fact that both research directions and data gathering are largely controlled by the resource agencies and government. Ellsworth (1984) has stated that both the British and US governments have deliberately suppressed research work on acidic precipitation. Attempts to short-circuit this 'official' research management system by directly gathering environmental data (e.g. the Greenpeace survey of UK beaches in 1986) are open to charges of unscientific method and low volumes of data. Such groups might do well to utilise properly the available data before producing additional information of low quality. Notwithstanding the problems, the importance of environmental pressure groups, within a plural democratic society, in promoting improvements in water quality is evident (Lowe 1975a, b, 1977). The plural democratic model of society does not apply to many Third World nations, where the order of magnitide of the problem is so much greater (see 6.2.1 and Table 6.2), or in socialist societies where environmental quality improvement has not, to date, been a high priority (Sandbach 1980).

# CHAPTER 7

# Water as a power resource

## 7.1 Introduction

The use of energy derived from falling water is one of the earliest examples of human endeavour to harness natural power. Traces of such use exist from pre-classical Rome where the power from the horizontally shafted wheel was used for cereal grinding (Forbes, 1956). The mechanical use of hydro-power dominated well into the early industrial revolution. The development of the smaller towns of the Yorkshire and Lancashire Pennine valleys, the cradle of this revolution, was based upon abundant water power, and today the majority of the impoundments found in the area are, in fact, the storage ponds for the mills of that era. Direct mechanical power has now given way to hydro-electric power. Although the potential of hydro-power as a source of electricity is limited, it will be an important source of future power because: (i) it is the only renewable source that uses commercially proven technology at a significant scale; and (ii) it has the capacity to store energy through pump storage and can, therefore, use the residual power from thermal stations or, in the future, from alternative renewable sources.

Hydro-power is, like the wind, an indirect form of solar energy. It is the solar input that powers the hydrological cycle, lifting water to higher levels where the energy it possesses is released during flow to the sea and can be 'captured' in a usable form. It is the potential of this cycle and the consequences of its development on the social and natural environment, rather than the technology of hydro-power, that is the focus of this chapter. However, before proceeding it would be appropriate, in view of the developing interest in tidal power, to comment on this parallel but essentially different form of hydro-power.

## 7.2 Tidal power

Water held above some base elevation contains gravitational potential energy which is released as it falls to a lower elevation. The amount of energy is a function of the head of water and the mass of that water. In tidal power, the gravitational effects from sun–moon interactions move very large bodies of water. Despite the relatively low head of water involved, the massive volumes make power generation feasible, given a suitable topography. The potential of tidal power is immense. Because the sites are lowland and relatively accessible, it is likely that capital costs per unit of generation would be no higher than that expected of a river power plant. Indeed, Hafele (1981) suggests that the costs could be much lower (Table 7.1).

Table 7.1  Comparative capital costs of alternative power sources

| Power source | Plant capacity | Investment costs | Technical status |
|---|---|---|---|
| Hydro-electricity: | | | |
| High head | 250 MW | 800 | Mature and |
| Low head | 250 MW | 1,400 | deployed |
| Tidal power | 1.6 GW | 400 | Proven technology, limited application |
| Wind: | | | Development studies and projects, |
| Small scale | 6 kW | 1,600 | some commercial |
| Large scale | 3 MW | 450 | experience |
| Direct solar | 100 MW | 3,000 | Prototypes |

For similar bodies of water, the tidal range determines the hydro-power potential. Consequently, the large tidal oscillation of the Bay of Fundy in Canada, with an extreme range of 15 m, has attracted the attention of power interests. A pilot plant on the Annapolis river (Fig. 7.1) has been constructed by the governments of Canada and Nova Scotia at a cost of $57 million with an expected initial annual output of 50 GW·hrs. If the pilot scheme reaches its potential, a subsequent implementation of the full scheme, using an 8 km dam with as many as 100 turbines, will produce a much larger power output, approaching the tidal power potential of the Annapolis river, estimated by MacMullan et al. (1983) as 6,710 GW·hrs yr$^{-1}$.

Global tidal power potential has been estimated by various authors. MacMullan et al. (1983), for example, quotes 62,125 MW. These figures are as much a reflection of the state of current studies as they are of the true potential of sites as yet unevaluated and, thus, these estimates are of limited value at the present time.

## 7.3  The status of hydro-power

In the United States, a world leader in energy consumption, the place of hydro-electric power in overall electrical production has fallen steadily over the last 50

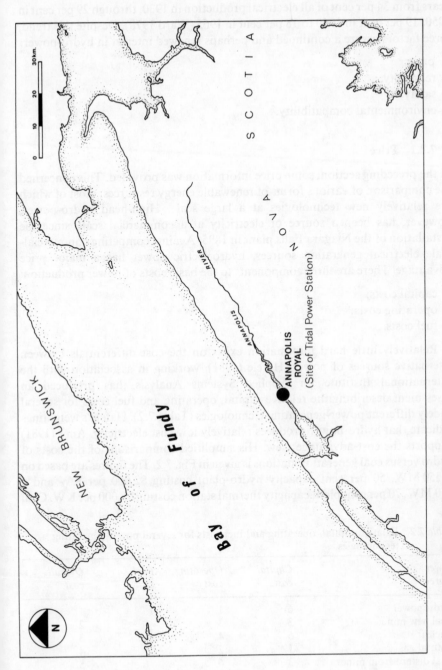

*Fig. 7.1* Tidal power in the Bay of Fundy

years from 34 per cent of all electrical production in 1930, through 29 per cent in 1950, 19 per cent in 1960 to 18 per cent in 1965 (Ward 1978). Despite this trend, three factors assure a continued and perhaps renewed interest in hydro-power:

1. price;
2. reliability;
3. safety;
4. environmental compatibility.

### 7.3.1 Price

In the preceding section, some price information was provided. This concerned the comparison of various forms of renewable energy resources, most of which are relatively new technologies at a large scale. High-head hydro-power, however, has been a source of electricity at a commercial scale since the installation of the Niagara Falls plant in 1895. Against competing commercial-scale electrical generation sources, hydroelectric power has a major price advantage. There are three components to the basic costs of power production:

1. capital costs;
2. operating costs;
3. fuel costs.

Relatively little hard information exists on the cost differentials between alternative sources of power. Hafele (1981), working in association with the International Institute for Applied Systems Analysis, has produced an assessment describing the relative capital, operating and fuel costs for several widely different power-generating technologies (Table 7.2). Hafele's weightings indicate that hydro-power produces relatively low-cost electricity. Auer (1981) supports the cost-advantage view. His simplified comparisons of the costs of hydro versus coal generation stations is given in Fig. 7.2. The figures are based on a 350 MW, 50 per cent capacity hydro-plant costing $2,000 per KW and a 250 MW, 70 per cent plant capacity thermal station costing $1,000 per KW. Coal

*Table 7.2*  Relative capital, operating and fuel costs for several power-generating technologies

| Power source | Capital costs | Operating cost | Fuel cost | Overall cost |
|---|---|---|---|---|
| Hydropower | 6 | 1 | 1 | 1 |
| Coal new mine | 3 | 3 | | 2 |
| Nuclear | 5 | 4 | $\frac{2}{3}$ | 3 |
| Natural gas | 1 | 2 | | 4 |
| Coal distant from mine | 3 | 6 | | 5 |
| Wind | 6 | 1 | 1 | 6 |
| Oil | 2 | 2 | | 7 |
| Direct solar | 7 | 1 | 1 | 7 |

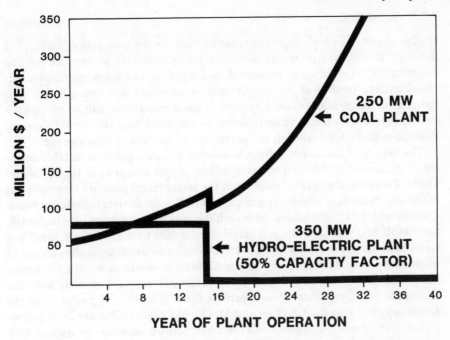

*Fig. 7.2* Cost comparisons between hydro-power and thermal generation stations

price is assumed to escalate by 8 per cent per year and has an initial price of $50 per tonne. Finance is at 8 per cent over 15 years. Hydro-power is initially more expensive, but costs equate in the seventh year and thereafter thermal power is much more costly. Actual cost comparisons (Table 7.3) for the regional performance of several generating station types for the financial year 1983–4 support both the subjective cost advantage assertions.

The demand for electricity is variable but can be viewed as base load and peak load in much the same way as a simplified river record. Thermal stations are best suited to base-load provision since they take a considerable lead time to produce electricity. Hydroelectric power is, however, much more responsive and can satisfy peak demands as well as base load. Electricity at peak times commands a price premium. Hence, hydro-power, already a low-cost provider of electricity, is given a further cost advantage.

*Table 7.3* Actual cost comparisons for the generating performance of several station types, pence per unit

|  | 'All-in costs' | Total works costs |
|---|---|---|
| Coal/oil/gas | 2.99 | 2.442 |
| Nuclear | 1.90 | 1.184 |
| Hydroelectric | 0.68 | 0.558 |

### 7.3.2 Reliability

Hydro-power has a high degree of reliability both in the provision of fuel and in the capability of the equipment. Since fuel for hydroelectricity does not have to be extracted, transported or processed, fuel supply is, to a great extent, assured. However, the quality of the supply may be modified, for example, by high sediment concentrations caused by natural phenomena or human activity on the catchments. This could have detrimental effects which may be especially crucial in small-scale systems without the protection of barriers or long storage.

The supply of fuel is not subject to market vagaries, political instabilities or the formation of cartels that so disrupted oil supply and price in the 1970s and 1980s. There are always exceptions and the larger transboundary rivers are not entirely without 'fuel' reliability questions. The Columbia river is shared between Canada and the United States. Although the bulk of the catchment is in the US, the runoff and the head drop is largely controlled by Canada and there is a significant history of threat, both overt and by 'rumour', that, in the absence of satisfactory boundary agreements, the Canadians would divert the Columbia (Swainson 1979) into the Frazer river (unlikely) or the Kootenay into the Columbia at Canal Flats, thus depriving the US utilities of power from the Kootenay loop into the US (Kay and McDonald 1982a) (Chapter 2). If hydro-power developments and potentials can cause conflict between two nations with a long history of good relations and which have broadly similar political and economic processes and aspirations, then the reliability of fuel supplies over less stable international boundaries must remain a question in the mind of water planners.

The equipment used in the generation of hydroelectric power has evolved in detail, grown greatly in size, and is often now installed in multiple units. The fundamental technology, however, remains little changed over this century and there is an established body of experience from which to maintain the reliability of the system.

### 7.3.3 Safety

Safety is a question of great public concern at the present time. The power industry, probably due to its increasing development of the nuclear technologies, is one that has been particularly subject to these concerns. There are two, often quite separate, threads to the question. The first is the public perception of the safety of different technologies and the second is the real risks associated with these technologies.

Thomas et al. (1980) examined the attitudes of two Austrian sample groups towards five different sources of energy. The groups were 'supporters' and 'antagonists' of nuclear power. In both these groups the support for hydro-power exceeded that given to any other source (Table 7.4).

Mean values hide a considerable amount of information, and Hafele (1981) in a similar questionnaire-based survey explored the distribution of attitudes

*Table 7.4* The public support for hydroelectric power sources

|  | Hydro-power | Nuclear | Solar | Thermal |
|---|---|---|---|---|
| Nuclear supporters | 12.3 | 10.2 | 12.2 | 9.0 |
| Nuclear rejectors | 11.2 | −10.1 | 11.1 | 4.7 |
| Total | 11.75 | 0.05 | 11.65 | 6.9 |

towards various energy sources. Figure 7.3 demonstrates the extreme support for the technologies perceived as clean and pollution free, the lower support for the thermal technologies and the extreme variation in the support for the nuclear option.

The real risks of hydroelectric power generation appear to be low. Hydro-power is seldom considered worthy of comparative risk assessment with alternative sources. Table 7.5, derived from a lecture on risk given by Lord Rothschild (1979), shows the wide variation in risk which can be calculated for a variety of power sources. The risks associated with hydro and natural gas generation of electricity are similar. Certainly there are few fuel risks or waste risks associated with hydro-power. The risk associated with turbine production and operation will be no different from, say, thermal electricity production. There will, however, be risk associated with the construction of the massive civil

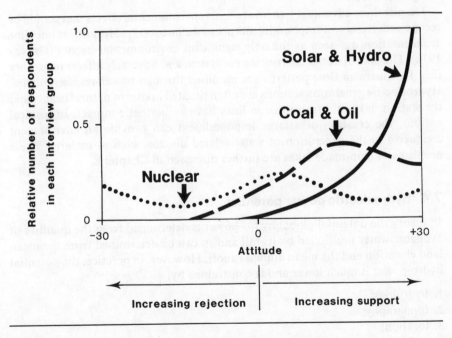

*Fig. 7.3* Public perceptions of the safety of various energy sources

177

engineering works commonly associated with hydroelectric facilities and with the possibility of future dam failure.

| Table 7.5 | The risks of various power sources |
|---|---|

| Energy source | Number of deaths |
|---|---|
| Coal | 50–1,600 |
| Oil | 20–1,400 |
| Wind | 230–700 |
| Solar | 80–100 |
| Uranium | 2–5–15 |
| Natural gas | 1–4 |

### 7.3.4 Environmental compatibility

After the early construction phase, hydroelectric power has a high degree of environmental compatibility. It is generated on-site and thus has no input requirements that demand transportation. In this respect it differs from the fossil thermal technologies through the absence of coal and oil trains. In addition, there are no waste flows and so problems such as acid precipitation and nuclear waste disposal are avoided. The creation of a large impoundment also has a flood mitigation effect.

Despite these advantages, there are some environmental effects that should be recognised. Reservoir impoundments act as sediment traps. Indeed, at one time sedimentation was seen as the only significant environmental impact (Garvey 1972). The lake disrupts the riverine ecosystem and adversely affects migratory fish. Downstream flow patterns are modified through power-release policies. Hydroelectric generation stations are often situated in sites of natural beauty and the station, lake and transmission lines have an aesthetic impact. In tropical nations, the creation of a large impoundment can provide an environment conducive to the generation of water-related diseases such as malaria. These problems of man-made lakes are further discussed in Chapter 8.

## 7.4 Hydroelectric power potential

In theory the potential global hydro-power is determined from the quantity of available water multiplied by its fall and so can be determined from the mean land elevation and the mean annual runoff. However, in practice, the potential hydro-power is much lower and is constrained by:

1. hydrology;
2. topography;
3. location;
4. technology.

178

### 7.4.1  Hydrology

The flow of water in any river is not constant: it varies with short-term and seasonal fluctuations in precipitation, temperature and vegetation cover. The mean flow of the river can often be a misleading guide to potential power production. The $G_{av}$, the power production attainable under average flow conditions, is often substantially more than could be achieved from flows which occur 95 per cent of the time, i.e. the $G_{95}$. As the proportion of the flow that arises from seasonal flooding or snowmelt increases, $G_{av}$ and $G_{95}$ diverge. To attain the full potential in a river of variable regime, more storage needs to be provided. In complex river systems, where storage exists for a mix of power, supply, flood control and irrigation interests, downstream flows will be modified by the storage and release policies of the various users and power production will not be optimised.

### 7.4.2  Topography

Power can be generated by modest flows of water falling over large distances or large volumes of water falling over modest distances. The former dominate in the upstream areas. Downstream, run of the river stations predominate: these use minimal storage and small head fall. The balance between the long profile and the flow at each point determines the potential power of each reach of the river. The need for storage controls the number of sites at which power can be generated. Both the natural reduction in flow variability from source to mouth and the increase in man-made regulations controls the type of system that is installed in each part of the long profile of the river. High-storage, high-head stations dominate in the upper reaches, lower storage systems dominate in the middle reaches and run of the river systems in the lower reaches. A lack of suitable storage sites in the upper reaches will limit the potential production in the lower river (section 4.2.2.2). Topographically limited power production can be observed in the Amazon which has a lower power potential than the Congo despite a flow several times larger. See, for example, the data for Zaire and Brazil listed in Table 7.8.

### 7.4.3  Location

The spatial distribution of hydroelectric power resources and population differ. Population tends to be concentrated in lowland areas while the power potential, defined by the possession of high precipitation and elevation, is often associated with uplands. As distances between power sources and centres of utilisation increase, so the technical and economic feasibility of transmission decrease. Thus, for example, in relation to the Seven Mile Project on the Pend Oreille river in British Columbia, Seattle City Light estimated that wheeling (or transmission) costs will make up 29 per cent of the annual costs of the project. Table 7.6 shows the projected costs of the scheme. It may be argued that in the developed world, geography is the most serious limitation on hydro-power development.

179

Table 7.6    Projected costs of the Seven Mile
Project on the Pend Oreille river

| Cost component | Cost ($) |
|---|---|
| Annual capital payment | 2,511,000 |
| Operation and management | 826,000 |
| Wheeling costs | 1,380,000 |
| Total | 4,717,000 |

### 7.4.4 Technology

Until very recently, technology has limited hydroelectric power generation to high-head sets and to large-volume, run of the river stations with a minimum head of approximately 7 m. Advances in technology and economics have permitted an expansion in small stations, sometimes known as micro-hydro stations, and in low-head stations. Keevin (1982) stated that the minimum head required to generate power at new low-head hydroelectric stations on the Mississippi can be only 5.2 m. Kiely (1981), listing the range of generator sets developed by the People's Republic of China, gives a head range starting as low as 2.0 m for the smallest, 18–125 kW installations (Plate 7.1). Technology has, to a limited extent, counteracted the effects of topography and location by expanding the number of possible sites.

The small-scale technology has been most widely applied in China. Growth in small-scale hydro-plants began in the late 1950s but did not expand rapidly until the 1970s. Figure 7.4 from Xiaozhang et al. (1982) shows the growth in installation of small hydro-plants in China and the initial effect of this on the average capacity of each station. The definition of small hydro-power is a unit capacity below 6 MW and total plant capacity of 12 MW. However, the bulk of the stations are much smaller than this limit with over 98 per cent having units rated at less than 0.5 MW. Table 7.7 shows the distribution of these very low-capacity Chinese stations in 1981.

### 7.4.5 Global estimates

All estimates of world potential hydro-power incorporate some assessment, usually unquantified, of the proportion of the potential that can be realised given advances in demand and technology. The estimates have been provided in a variety of units, but here are expressed in exajoules (EJ, $10^{18}$ joules: for example, 1 EJ would power a 1 kW domestic heater for 3 million years) for comparability. Estimates of ultimate potential range from 25–50 EJ, but the most specified estimates lie in the range 28–36 EJ.

The distribution of hydroelectric resources is not equitable: about 50 per cent of world resources are held by six nations. However, the particular ranking of these nations depends upon whether the $G_{av}$ or $G_{95}$ is used as the basis of the

*Plate 7.1* A small head hydro-power plant in the Peoples Republic of China (photographed by Prof. Bruce Mitchell)

181

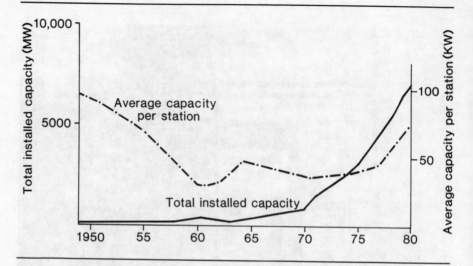

*Fig. 7.4* Growth in the installation of small hydro-power plants in China (per cent)

*Table 7.7* Distribution of very low-capacity hydroelectric stations in China

| | Number of stations | Installed capacity (MW) | Proportion of total capacity (%) |
|---|---|---|---|
| Stations with units < 500 kW | 84,175 | 4,447 | 59 |
| Stations with units > 500 kW | 1,235 | 3,126 | 41 |
| Total | 85,300 | 7,573 | 100 |

ranking (Table 7.8). For example, Zaire ranked as fourth, with 6.7 per cent of world resources, on a $G_{av}$ basis, but is placed first, with almost 14 per cent of world resources, when ranked on a $G_{95}$ basis. In all cases, the $G_{95}$ as a basis for the measure of hydroelectric potential produces a lower estimate than $G_{av}$.

The difference in the two measures is least marked in the steady regimes of areas without significant seasonality. In Table 7.8, only Zaire and Brazil improve in rank between $G_{av}$ and $G_{95}$ while the USA, USSR and China decline. The change in ranking is due to the variable nature of the flow in these countries, caused largely by extreme winter low-flow conditions and marked seasonal rainfall.

## 7.5 Hydroelectric resources and development

For most developed countries the share of the global hydroelectric resource is small and has already been significantly developed. Furthermore, hydro-

*Table 7.8*  National hydroelectric rankings on the basis of $G_{av}$ and $G_{95}$

| | $G_{av}$ | | | $G_{95}$ | | |
|---|---|---|---|---|---|---|
| | Capacity (EJ) | Rank | Global capacity (%) | Capacity (EJ) | Rank | Global capacity (%) |
| China | 4.75 | 1 | 13.5 | 1.73 | 2 | 10.84 |
| USSR | 3.94 | 2 | 11.1 | 0.44 | 3 | 9.02 |
| USA | 2.52 | 3 | 7.2 | 0.78 | 6 | 4.89 |
| Zaire | 2.38 | 4 | 6.7 | 2.23 | 1 | 13.97 |
| Canada | 1.93 | 5 | 5.5 | 0.87 | 5 | 5.45 |
| Brazil | 1.87 | 6 | 5.3 | 1.37 | 4 | 8.58 |
| World | 35.3 | | 100 | 15.96 | | 100 |

electricity typically plays a relatively small part in the overall energy budget of such developed countries. In the EEC, for example, hydroelectricity, concentrated largely in France and Italy, provides only about 3 per cent of the overall energy budget (Evans 1978). In a review of future energy sources, Sellars and Newsum (1980:228) typify the Western view of hydro-power potential, dismissing it in a few lines:

> ... sites for such plants are restricted. Schemes have been successfully implemented in Scotland and in Scandinavia, and run in connection with a water supply scheme, are locally acceptable and economically useful.

This blinkered appraisal suggests a European distribution that is more limited than is the case, and a viability dependent upon multiple use with a water supply.

The potential value of hydro-power for the less developed countries has been voiced by Goldemberg and reported by Daglish (1979:209):

> Self sufficiency in energy supplies could be achieved in a few large LDCs using indigenous supplies such as coal in India, hydro-power in Brazil ... as a group non OPEC LDCs were self sufficient in all primary energy sources with the exception of oil and regional cooperation ... could lead them to energy independence in most areas. This was particularly true in the case of hydroelectricity whose role had been grossly under-estimated not only in most countries but in most regions.

Sabato and Ramesh (1979:209) suggest that hydro-power, in common with other renewable energy sources, is more appropriate to LDCs because it can:

> be decentralised and made compatible with the local ecological and socio-economic milieu.

Some contrasting arguments were set out in 4.2.2 above. The detailed distribution of the hydroelectric potential among the DCs and LDCs is partly a matter of definition. The DCs have about 35 per cent of global hydroelectric potential and the LDCs 65 per cent (Table 7.9). These percentages do not alter

*Table 7.9* Hydroelectric potential of developed and less developed countries

| | $G_{av}$ | | $G_{95}$ | |
|---|---|---|---|---|
| | *EJ* | *% world* | *EJ* | *% world* |
| Developed nations | 12.42 | 35 | 5.29 | 33 |
| Developing nations | 22.87 | 65 | 10.68 | 67 |
| World | 35.29 | 100 | 16.97 | 100 |

*Source*: Ion (1980) quoting from World Energy Conference figures (1974)

significantly between the $G_{av}$ and the $G_{95}$ basis of measurement. Despite the promising power potential, there are a significant number of problems facing LDCs in the development of that power. These may be grouped into three headings:

1. financing;
2. appropriateness;
3. environment.

### 7.5.1 Financing

Although in the long term the cost advantages of water power may be clear, the initial capital costs of large hydroelectric projects are often beyond the financial capability of the countries concerned. The result is that finance is sought from abroad and is provided, not in recognition of the needs of the country or, indeed, of the inherent financial attractiveness of the project, but rather as a means of promoting the political standing of the donor nations. The resulting debt burden can distort the internal economic structure of the recipient nation (Chapter 4).

Some examples exist of the promotion of a hydroelectric project to provide power for a neighbouring country. South Africa uses the power that is generated by the Cabora Bassa project on the Zambeze river in Mozambique (Boulton 1986) (Fig. 7.5). This appears to be a successful arrangement to both sides despite the potential for disharmony between two countries with significantly different political systems. Kiely (1981) urged the development of these bilateral agreements between Third World countries in which power-rich but generally mountainous, thinly populated and industrially weak nations sell power to neighbouring states. Nepal, for example, is seen as capable of providing power for the adjacent areas on the Indian subcontinent.

### 7.5.2 Appropriateness

Concern for what is appropriate to a Third World country has grown over the last decade since the publication of Schumacher's *Small is beautiful* (1973) and the growing impact of the appropriate and intermediate technology groups (Table 4.3). The scale of many of the water resource developments in Asia, Africa

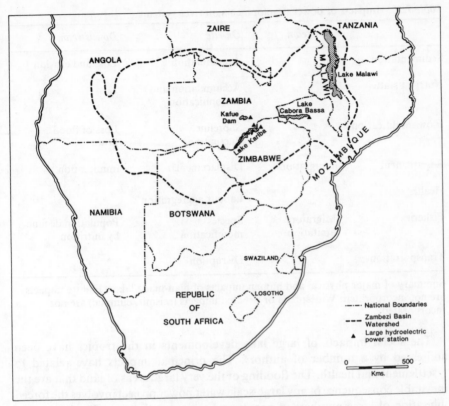

*Fig. 7.5* The Cabora Bassa project on the Zambeze river

and South America has not been such that the projects fitted into the social, environmental or economic life of the country. Hart (1977) has argued that in the case of the Volta river project the development has been a disaster from almost every viewpoint (section 8.3).

### 7.5.3 Environment

In addition to significant economic impacts, there are important social and physical environmental consequences (Goldsmith and Hildyard 1984). Table 7.10 provides a summary of these problems. The division into upstream, on-site and downstream impacts is arbitrary but serves to indicate the spatial extent of the problems encountered. The exact balance of these effects is site specific.

In one of the largest proposed hydro-power projects in China – the Three Gorges Project on the Yantze river (La Bounty 1982) – the problems of sedimentation are so severe as to bring the whole viability of the development into question (Gu 1986, pers. comm.). In the Nile, the denial of sediment to the delta regions has caused fisheries decline and marine incursion to agricultural land (El-Hinnawi 1980).

185

Table 7.10  Impacts of power developments on river systems

|  | Upstream | On-site | Downstream |
|---|---|---|---|
| Sedimentation |  | Accumulation | Loss and erosion |
| Nutrient status |  | Accumulation and entrophication | Loss |
| Flow modification |  | Shoreline fluctuation | Loss of flood flows |
| Resettlement | Immigration | Displacement | Immigration |
| Health |  | Labour aggregration |  |
| Fisheries | Migratory limitation | Species modification | Population decline by nutrition |
| Transportation |  | Disruption |  |

Summary of major physical and human impacts of man-made lakes. Failure impacts are not incorporated. Widespread or debated impacts (seismic/climatic) are not incorporated.

The social impacts of large lake developments in the tropics have been addressed by a number of authors. The principal impacts have related to resettlement and health. The flooding of the very large areas of land that are the inevitable consequence of any large-scale water power project involves the forced migration of large numbers of people and their resettlement often in areas of alien cultures where their intrusion into established patterns of land tenure is resented. Table 7.11 shows that in many cases the numbers of people involved in the resettlement are so large as to make a successful outcome unlikely without a carefully planned and well-supported pre-development operation. This is, however, seldom the case as the project itself rather than the people involved is usually the most pressing objective. If benefits accrue to the nation it is often not to the regions or social groups involved in the resettlement (Chapter 8).

The impact on health from man-made lakes is well established. The change from a riverine to a lacustrine environment and the associated modifications to the patterns of human use encourage the spread and redistribution of disease. Previous projects have been criticised because they were planned for a single power-generation purpose. The negative aspects have seldom been formally costed and integrated into the project assessment. In the future, planners should aim to maximise the net social benefits to all recipient groups. This can only result from an integrated approach to the management of river basins. This issue is addressed further in Chapter 8.

### 7.5.3.1  The Gordon–Franklin river system

The proposed development of the hydroelectric resources of the Gordon–

186

*Table 7.11*  Numbers of people involved in resettlement
following hydroelectric projects

| | Number of evacuees | |
| Project | Households | People (est.)[a] |
| --- | --- | --- |
| Yanhee (Bhumipon) | 4,035 | 24,210 |
| Nam Pong (Ubonrat) | 5,012 | 30,072 |
| Lam Pao | 5,459 | 32,754 |
| Lam Takong | 444 | 2,664 |
| Kiew Lom | 496 | 2,976 |
| Lam Nam Oon | 1,639 | 9,834 |
| Lam Dom Noi | 1,317 | 7,902 |
| Nan (Sirikhit) | 2,797 | 16,782 |
| Huai Luang | 612 | 3,672 |
| Krasiaw | 313 | 1,878 |
| Kwae Yai (Chao Nen) | 1,200 | 7,200 |
| Total | 23,324 | 139,944 |

[a]Numbers of people are estimated on the assumption
that households consist of a mean of six people.
*Source*: Lightfoot (1981)

Franklin river system in Australia during the 1980s generated one of the most
controversial environmental issues in the southern hemisphere perhaps in all
time (Editorial Comment, *Environmental Conservation* 1986, **10**, 197). High
rainfall totals and a topography suited to impoundments have encouraged the
development of hydroelectric power in Tasmania. Pigram (1986) noted that 98
per cent of Tasmania's electrical energy has been generated by hydroelectric
schemes. This accounts for over half the hydroelectricity produced in Australia.

The upper reaches of the Gordon–Franklin system are already controlled by
large storage reservoirs. The debate concerned the development of the water
resources of the lower river (Fig. 7.6). These developments would have the
impacts outlined in Table 7.12. The most significant potential impact related to
the effects of the impoundment on south-west Tasmania as a wilderness area.
This impact would arise through direct inundation and by the establishment of
new routes for access. This improved access would increase human contact and
thus increase the incidence of both fire and the erosion of the deep fibrous peats
which are vital to slope stability. In addition to human encroachment, the access
would encourage invasion and competition from introduced plants, feral
animals and parasitic organisms. The impacts on the existing 'island bio-
geographic' community could be very damaging (Miles 1981).

The inundation would also reduce the capacity of the river system for white-
water rafting and canoeing (Dragun 1983), and important archaeological sites

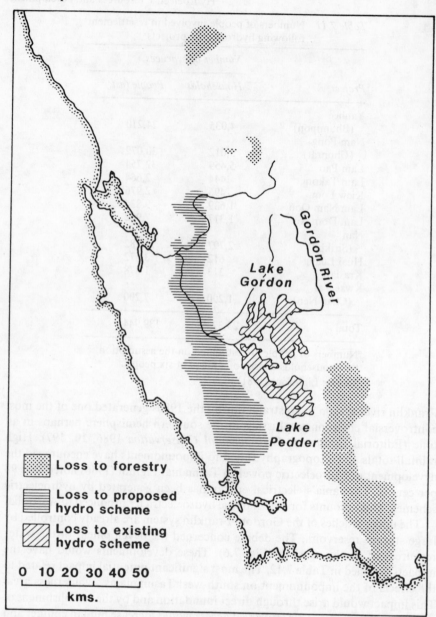

*Fig. 7.6* The Gordon–Franklin river system: storages and potential development sites

such as the Kutikina and Deena–Rena Caves would be lost. However, there is some debate about the special value of these sites which must persist in the absence of detailed archaeological inventories (Pigram 1986; Patterson 1983).

In 1983 the Australian federal government passed legislation which required

*Table 7.12* The major impacts of the development of
the lower Gordon–Franklin river system

*Direct effects*
   Inundation of main and tributary valleys
   Change from riverine to lacustrine ecology
   Loss of wild and scenic value
   Loss of recreational value
   Loss of archaeological sites
   Loss of geologically significant sites
   Loss of 30% of remaining Huon Pine stands

*Indirect effects*
   New access routes
   Power line easements     } promote fire
   Introduction of exotic species

the Tasmanian administration to cease construction. The federal government paid compensation of more than $276 million to the Tasmanian administration to cover losses accruing from works already carried out, to provide alternative employment and to encourage further hydroelectric schemes in other parts of the state. Such payments provide evidence of the growing strength and international character of the conservation lobby. It gives an indication of the value placed upon wilderness resources and the importance of international attention which derives from the designation of the area as a 'World Heritage Site'. The Gordon–Franklin debate is not unique and similar arguments have been put forward regarding other sites (Foster and Rahs 1985).

# CHAPTER 8

# River basin management

## 8.1 Background

Gilbert White (1977) has traced the modern development of water resource systems from single-purpose projects, such as the Suez Canal and the Tiza flood control scheme (Sharman 1984), which were typical of projects at the turn of the twentieth century. A decade later, the Indus barrages and the early works at Aswan were designed as multi-purpose schemes in which a single engineering structure produced a number of benefits. By the mid-1930s a group of multi-purpose projects were designed together in one basin system to produce an integrated river basin development of the type promoted by the Tennessee Valley Authority (TVA). White noted that, in the period between the early TVA developments and 1970, engineering solutions to complex problems were examined and refined. In addition, critical evaluations of existing and planned projects were made using economic criteria such as benefit–cost analysis and cost-effectiveness analysis. However, the evaluation criteria were usually characterised by a technocentric approach (Sandbach 1980), and little attention was devoted to the study of project impacts on the natural environment or society in general. In the post-1970 period, these broader issues gained in prominence and produced a climate in which:

> Heavier emphasis is placed upon research which cuts across conventional disciplinary lines of engineering and the physical, social and biological sciences to find answers to newly phrased questions relating to the environmental effects of human interventions in the hydrological cycle. (White 1977:2)

Saha (1981:25) has distinguished between the water resource management perspective, which in White's analysis characterised the period preceding 1970, and the more modern river basin planning approach, as follows:

> Water resource management is ... a set of well co-ordinated but technocratic interventions in the hydrological cycle undertaken to augment

and better regulate the existing water supplies for meeting human needs more effectively. River basin planning situates these interventions in a broader set of interrelationships which transcend both environmental and social systems. It goes a long way to internalising many of the externalities of water resource management. River basin planning is a very broad megasystem, water resource management relates to the boundary functions between some of its subsystems.

This definition suggests a more holistic and ecocentric model for river basin planning than the historically, technocentric approach of the water resource manager. Saha (1981) viewed this dichotomy as evidence that river basin planning was a discipline in the process of paradigm transition of the type outlined by Kuhn (1962). Elliot (1981) suggests that this change will be brought about by environmental managers who have the necessary powers of integration to operate at the 'megasystem' scale as illustrated in Fig. 8.1.

Much of the modern interest in river basin planning stems from the United Nations' initiatives commencing with the Economic and Social Council's resolution which requested the Secretary General to establish an expert panel to examine the social, economic and administrative implications of river basin developments. The seven-member panel was chaired by Gilbert White and its recommendations were published in 1958, and as a revised edition in 1970 (United Nations 1970). This report suggests four essential stages for integrated river basin planning.

*United Nations river basin planning stages*

STAGE 1

A preliminary stage, when the planner is likely to be acting in response to an immediate problem such as erosion or flooding. The appreciation of the broader implications of the problem is the first step in defining the bounds of the basin megasystem.

STAGE 2

The existing physical, socio-economic and administrative system is studied in detail and a development strategy formulated.

STAGE 3

Small-scale pilot projects are implemented to investigate the likely success of the large strategies proposed in Stage 2 above.

STAGE 4

Completion of the project physical structures and management of the overall scheme.

Saha (1981) has criticised the UN planning approach on two grounds. The first is the lack of any post-audit system within the four-stage structure. He suggested that this produces a bias in favour of the construction industry and its associated professional groups. This point was stressed by Wolman (1981) who attributed the sparsity of post-audit studies to the *natural* unwillingness of

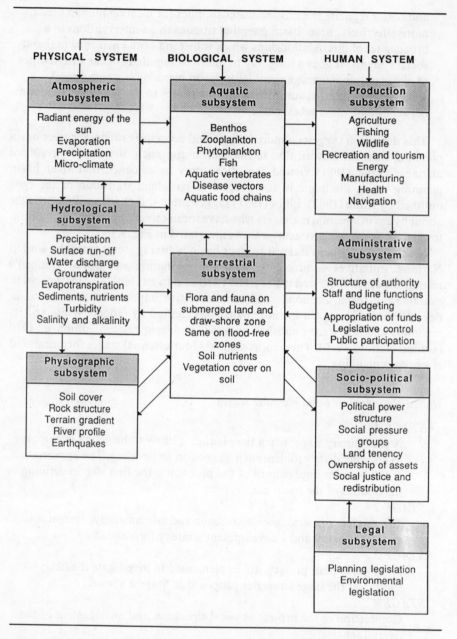

**PHYSICAL SYSTEM**   **BIOLOGICAL SYSTEM**   **HUMAN SYSTEM**

**Atmospheric subsystem**

Radiant energy of the sun
Evaporation
Precipitation
Micro-climate

**Aquatic subsystem**

Benthos
Zooplankton
Phytoplankton
Fish
Aquatic vertebrates
Disease vectors
Aquatic food chains

**Production subsystem**

Agriculture
Fishing
Wildlife
Recreation and tourism
Energy
Manufacturing
Health
Navigation

**Hydrological subsystem**

Precipitation
Surface run-off
Water discharge
Groundwater
Evapotranspiration
Sediments, nutrients
Turbidity
Salinity and alkalinity

**Terrestrial subsystem**

Flora and fauna on
submerged land and
draw-shore zone
Same on flood-free
zones
Soil nutrients
Vegetation cover on
soil

**Administrative subsystem**

Structure of authority
Staff and line functions
Budgeting
Appropriation of funds
Legislative control
Public participation

**Physiographic subsystem**

Soil cover
Rock structure
Terrain gradient
River profile
Earthquakes

**Socio-political subsystem**

Political power
structure
Social pressure
groups
Land tenency
Ownership of assets
Social justice and
redistribution

**Legal subsystem**

Planning legislation
Environmental
legislation

*Fig. 8.1* The socio-economic megasystem of river basin planning. *Source*: Saha and Barrow (1981)

professional project staff to disclose errors in plan, design and operation. White (1977) later suggested that useful post-audits had been completed for several projects including the Uncompahgre and Sabi Valley irrigation projects, the

Indus project and the Lower Rio Grande development (Shiklomanov 1985; Russell *et al.* 1970; Roder 1965; Michel 1959; Beyer 1957). However, on the general status of post-audit studies, White (1977:11) stated that:

> A conspicuous aspect of water management has been the lack of careful post-audits of the social, economic and environmental consequences of previous works.

Saha's second major criticism is the lack of attention to the beneficiary groups of any scheme. This has the effect of precluding any quantitative assessment of the income redistribution produced by a project.

More recent reviews of river basin management (Goldsmith and Hildyard 1986a; WRI 1986; Falkenmark 1985; Mitchell and Gardiner 1983; Pantulu 1983; Jenkins 1981; Saha and Barrow 1981; Falkenmark 1981; OECD 1972; United Nations 1978c; White 1977) contain many individual case studies from both the developed and the developing world. The issues addressed in these contributions include: the management of data acquisition for project design; water quality assessment and control; mathematical modelling for quantity and quality management; hydroelectric power developments; irrigation and rural development; water as disease vector; resettlement of displaced peoples; conservation of soils and natural habitats; management of international (or trans-boundary) waters; the environmental problems of inter-basin transfers; fisheries management; and, finally, channel modification. This literature contains many examples of planning errors and the resultant environmental problems. The objective of this chapter is to examine a variety of project types and to identify the significant problems produced by both the regional setting and the planning framework adopted. Many classic examples of river basin management are not included as individual case studies. This results from space constraints rather than any wish to ignore the importance of developments on the Mekong, Colorado, Indus, Nile or other similar major basins. Some of the lessons of these developments are introduced in the concluding section to this chapter.

## 8.2  The Tennessee Valley Authority

### 8.2.1  The context of the TVA

As the best-known attempt at integrated river basin management, the TVA has provided one model for projects throughout the world (Okun 1977). Many of these projects have been promoted by ex-TVA executives who, in transferring their individual experience, have influenced project design towards the TVA model (Saha and Barrow 1981). It should be noted, however, that the TVA has never been replicated either within the USA or elsewhere. In addition, the writings of practising TVA managers have provided a framework against which to judge the goals and achievements of other project organisations (Morgan 1974; Owen 1973; Moore 1962; Clapp 1955; Lilienthal 1944). It is this preeminence of the TVA as a philosophical and organisational model which makes its historical development and structure of such interest.

Many different views have been expressed on the extent to which the TVA presents a successful model of integrated planning. Saha and Barrow (1981:2) dismiss the present organisation as:

a massive electricity generating utility, now a far cry from what was envisaged in 1933.

In a less critical evaluation, Owen (1973:10) presents an alternative interpretation when she states that the:

TVA is not just a power system, it is devoted to total regional development.

The TVA itself does not see a contradiction between its electricity supply function and its role as a regional development agency. Indeed, the two strategies are viewed as complementary solutions to the problems of the Tennessee Valley region. This policy was summarised in 1982 as follows:

TVA is committed to providing an ample supply of power at the lowest feasible prices to support high economic growth in the Tennessee Valley. (TVA 1982:4)

It is now over 50 years since the TVA was created. A major problem in any evaluation is to define the criteria on which success or failure should be judged. This definition becomes particularly elusive when the shifts in public values during the course of development are considered (Mitchell 1974). These shifts have been produced as the US economy has adapted to periods of war, followed by peace and depression, followed by relative affluence. The objective of this first case study is to provide a brief historical explanation of the role played by the modern TVA. Questions relating to the utility of the model presented by the TVA in other geographical regions will be addressed in 8.6.

### 8.2.2 A historical analysis

The TVA has its origins in the Muscle Shoals controversy which arose in 1917 following the selection by the US government of a site near Muscle Shoals for a nitrate plant to provide munitions for the war effort. The plant represented a potentially valuable asset to farmers in Tennessee and Alabama, who hoped to purchase the peace-time fertilizer production. The manufacture of nitrate fertilizer by the cynamid process required large quantities of power which were initially provided by two thermal plants. These plants were later replaced by the Wilson dam hydroelectric scheme which provided for the passage of river traffic beyond Muscle Shoals.

On completion in 1919, the nitrate plant was mothballed by the US Army and the two associated dams were not completed until 1926. The potential uses of the Muscle Shoals facility generated a heated debate throughout the 1920s and early 1930s. The plant itself was becoming increasingly outdated and expensive as the new Habor process for nitrate production became available. Many local farmers favoured the production of fertilizers as originally intended. However, this would have denied electrical energy from Wilson dam to domestic consumers because of the electricity required by the relatively inefficient cynamid process.

Many private concerns were interested in operating the idle plant and over 100 bills concerning Muscle Shoals were introduced into Congress (Schlesinger 1957). Owen (1973) suggests that Congress would have tired of the whole debate had George Norris, a senator from Nebraska, not chaired the Senate committee on agriculture to which the Muscle Shoals bills were referred. Norris favoured a public agency to operate the nitrate plant. The ideas he put forward provoked a vociferous attack from the private power utilities. The majority of their case rested on the fight against 'socialism' which they perceived in the proposals to take the Muscle Shoals facility into public ownership. In addition to defeating a series of private bills, Norris presented plans to the Senate outlining his own suggestions for an integrated development of the valley. Two of his proposals were to fail by Presidential veto in 1928 and 1931 (Norris 1961; Hubbard 1961).

The breakthrough for Norris came with the presidency of Franklin D. Roosevelt and the depression of the 1930s. Roosevelt saw a broader potential in the Tennessee Valley than the Muscle Shoals plant. In a letter to Congress, dated 10 April 1933, Roosevelt stated:

It is clear that the Muscle Shoals development is but a small part of the potential public usefulness of the entire Tennessee River. Such use, if envisioned in its entirety, transcends mere power development: it enters the wide fields of flood control, soil erosion, afforestation, elimination from agricultural use of marginal land and distribution and diversification of industry. In short this power development of war days leads logically to national planning for a complete river watershed involving many states and the future lives and welfare of millions. It touches and gives life to all forms of human concerns. (Owen 1973:21)

The act establishing the TVA contained many proposals advanced in earlier bills put forward by Norris. It defined a broad field of action for the TVA Board which was empowered:

to improve the navigability and to provide for the flood control of the Tennessee River, to provide for reforestation and proper use of marginal lands in the Tennessee Valley, to provide for the agricultural and industrial development of the said valley, to provide for the national defence by the creation of a co-operation for the operation of government properties at and near Muscle Shoals in the State of Alabama and for other purposes. (Congress 1935)

This brief did not include the provision of electrical power (Street 1981). However, the supply of affordable energy has been recognised as an element in the associated agricultural and industrial development.

The first chairman of the TVA Board was Arthur E. Morgan, a man with little formal education but a proven record of well-managed construction programmes in the Ohio Conservancy Districts (Morgan 1974). Morgan was able to participate in drafting the enabling legislation, and he was instrumental in devising the three-man Board structure which was to cause so much difficulty later when he clashed with his fellow directors, Harcourt Morgan and David Lilienthal. The basis of this schism was a personality clash between Morgan and Lilienthal. Morgan (1974) suggested that the root of this problem was Lilienthal's impatience with his welfare aims. However, Morgan's own obduracy, in refusing to co-operate when questioned by President Roosevelt on this matter, played a large part in his being removed from the chair of the three-man Board in March 1938 (Owen 1973). This early conflict between the politically naive Morgan and the ambitious, pragmatic Lilienthal encapsulates the continuing problem for the TVA Board which must balance the achievement of discrete and politically desirable goals, such as cheap electricity, against the less dramatic projects with a lower political profile, such as forest management and worker welfare schemes (OTAD 1978; Claussen 1978).

A significant feature of early TVA organisation was the 'Force Account' system (Owen 1973; Morgan 1974). This allowed for construction of projects in the valley by the TVA itself rather than imported construction companies. The effect of this policy was to begin the process of economic recovery in a direct way by the employment of indigenous labour. The welfare schemes and education programmes available to TVA employees and their families provided a further impetus for development and alleviated the rural poverty so prevalent in the valley (Morgan 1974; Robock 1967).

The construction programmes of the TVA continued throughout the Second World War as power demands increased. In post-war America, electrical power demand rose dramatically as cheap appliances became available to a mass market. In the Tennessee Valley it soon became clear that the existing hydroelectric generating facilities would not be sufficient to satisfy projected demand. The TVA response was to add to its limited thermal generating capacity at Watts Bar and Muscle Shoals with new plants at Johnsonville, Widows Creek, Kingston, Colbert, John Silver, Gallalin and Shawnee (Owen 1973). The satisfaction of growing demand by thermal supplies produced a situation by the late 1980s where the TVA had become the largest single user of coal in the USA. In 1980, 66 per cent of all TVA energy was produced by coal-powered stations, leading to considerable Canadian concern over the issues of long-range transport of acidic pollutants into Ontario and Quebec (Chapter 6 and WRI 1986). During the 1980s the TVA limited its emissions of $SO_2$ from power plants and by 1986 it had achieved a 50 per cent reduction (about 1 million tonnes of $SO_2$) in annual emission (WRI 1986) (Fig. 8.2).

The TVA function as an electrical utility is financed by bond sales and revenues. Current annual turnover exceeds $1,000 million per year. This figure dwarfs the $100 million per year allocated from federal funds to provide for agricultural assistance, fertilizer research, recreational provision and environmental conservation (Street 1981). Both these programmes have an influence on

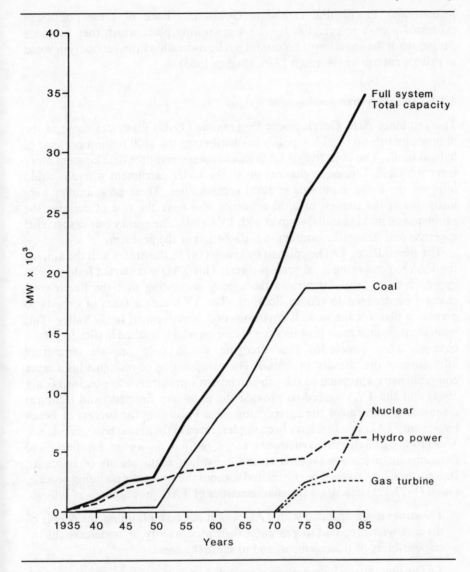

*Fig. 8.2* TVA load growth summary. *Source*: TVA (1982)

the living standards of valley dwellers. The industrial climate created by cheap power provision and the general environmental enhancement has undoubtedly produced the *primum mobile* (or initiating force) for development in the valley (Netschert 1967). This has transformed the Tennessee Valley from the 'economic and environmental disaster area' of 1933 into the productive area seen today (Norman 1976:732). In this respect, the TVA has certainly fulfilled the hopes of Norris, Roosevelt and Morgan. The degree of this success can be judged by the antagonism to this *socialist monstrosity* shown by Presidents Eisenhower and

197

Reagan and Presidential candidate Goldwater. Each of these politicians expressed a wish to privatise the TVA generating plant which they saw as a dangerous demonstration of successful public ownership in an economy devoted to private enterprise (Norman 1976; Hughes 1963).

### 8.2.3 Tributary area development

The Tributary Area Development Programme (TAD) illustrates some of the philosophy behind the TVA policy in distributing the $100 million per year of federal funds. The objective of TAD was to spread resource development away from the main Tennessee channel on to the wider catchment where it could improve the living standards of rural communities. These programmes were instigated at the request of local residents who have the role of defining the problem and making initial contact with TVA staff. The agency brings specialist expertise and financial resources to the solution of the problem.

The Beech River TAD, reported by Owen (1973), illustrates well the aims of the TVA in promoting local-scale projects. This TAD was started following an approach from local farmers to the agency requesting that the Beech river channel be dredged to reduce flooding. The TVA sent a team of experts to prepare a plan for the general environmental improvement in the valley. This team identified the main problem as soil erosion which resulted in siltation of the channel. They concluded that dredging would only provide temporary alleviation of the farmers' problems. The co-operation of residents for a more comprehensive approach to the sub-catchment's problems was obtained (Cain 1968) and the TVA agreed to provide the necessary financial and technical resources to implement the agreed proposals. Following the success of Beech river, many TAD schemes have been implemented in the areas shown in Fig. 8.3. The groups of scheme participants are organised on an *ad hoc* basis and development plans are tailored to the individual requirements of residents. Indeed, no scheme would be considered without the *bottom up* planning process. Owen (1973:125) described the characteristics of TAD programmes as follows:

> The structures associated with TAD would not be built unless the people of the area were prepared to guarantee their productivity, to undertake the responsibility of management, and to share the costs.

TAD programmes have certainly provided an impetus to economic growth and environmental improvement in the remoter, more marginal areas of the Tennessee Valley (Claussen 1978).

### 8.2.4 Assessments

Against this utopian picture of a responsive and paternal agency, fostering participation and grass-roots democracy, must be set the charges levelled at the TVA by American conservationists who have been angered by plans for nuclear power developments and pollution by stack gases from coal-fired thermal

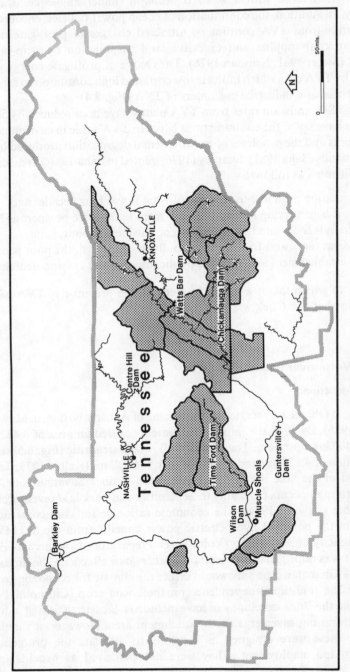

*Fig. 8.3* Tributary areas in the TVA region. *Source:* TVA (1972)

generating plant (WRI 1986). The very size of the TVA operation attracts opposition from those with a *small is beautiful* (under any circumstances) philosophy. In addition, the continuation of cheap power policies, encouraging high demands from TVA consumers, attracted charges of profligate use of Appalachian coal supplies and excessive land despoilation by strip-mining techniques (Street 1981; Norman 1976). The charge of profligate energy use is supported by TVA data which indicate low costs and high consumption rates for both residential and industrial customers of TVA (Fig. 8.4).

Although $SO_2$ emission rates from TVA plants have been reduced by 50 per cent, critics have noted the contradictions between TVA's role in environmental improvements and the problems of environmental degradation produced by the its coal demands (Saha 1981). Shapley (1976, quoted in Saha 1981:14) described the TVA dilemma as follows:

> TVA's situation is almost the reverse of what it was four decades ago,
> when ... it began trying to help the poor there build more prosperous lives.
> TVA's friends today are the establishment: business, labour, state
> government. Its newest foes are the socially handicapped, the poor people,
> the anti-establishment advocates of public interest, and environmentalists.

The extent to which this is a fair judgement on the present-day TVA will be examined further in 8.6 below.

## 8.3  The Volta river basin

### 8.3.1  Introduction

Lake Volta, in Ghana, was created by the closing of Akosombo dam in May 1964 (Graham 1986). By 1968 the impounded waters covered an area of 8,482 km² extending 402 km upstream. The lake is shallow and dendritic (Fig. 8.5) with a total shoreline of 4,828 km and a volume of $1.5 \times 10^{11}$ m³ (Kalitsi 1973; Taylor 1973). Most of the lake is contained within the Guinea Savanna zone. The maximum rainfall occurs from July to September and peak lake levels occur in early October (Lawson 1974). The economic rationale for dam construction derives from the potential hydroelectric power benefits from the 833 MW of installed capacity at Akosombo (Volta River Preparatory Commission 1956). However, it was hoped that the resultant *trickle down* effects on the industrial sector of the Ghanaian economy would create the climate for economic growth and reduce the traditional dependence on the cocoa crop (Chisholm 1982). Benefits from the Volta development have included a lacustrine fishing industry and agricultural improvements on the catchment area. However, it should be noted that these were designed as methods to alleviate the problems of resettlement and employment. They were not perceived as benefits of an integrated, multi-objective project as defined by Obeng (1980b). In many respects, the Volta provides an example of *ad hoc* river basin planning because

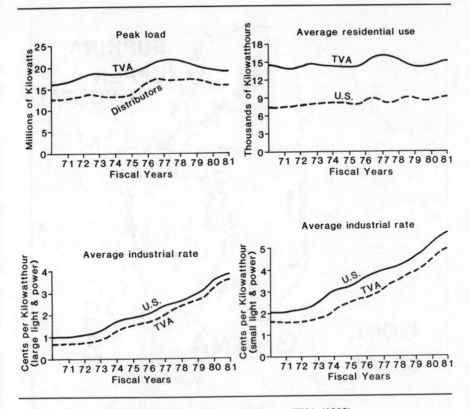

*Fig. 8.4* TVA and US power demand growth. *Source*: TVA (1982)

researchers and managers have sought to minimise the adverse effects of a single-purpose project rather than to maximise the total project benefits through an integrated planning approach (Graham 1986; Kalitsi 1973).

Two major problems encountered in the Volta scheme have been the resettlement of displaced peoples and the adverse health effects of the impoundment.

### 8.3.2 Resettlement problems

The area of inundation had a relatively low population density, containing only 1 per cent of Ghana's people on 3.6 per cent of the land area. Of the 80,000 people whose homes were flooded by Lake Volta, 2 per cent were river fishermen and the rest practised subsistence agriculture. Very few cattle were kept due to tsetse infestation (Butcher and Amarteifo 1967; unpublished data quoted by Taylor 1973). The 700 villages of the area were largely constructed of mud and thatch, and living standards were below the national average with only 35 per cent of inhabitants receiving a primary-level education (Kalitsi 1973).

The residents of the flooded area were faced with a choice between

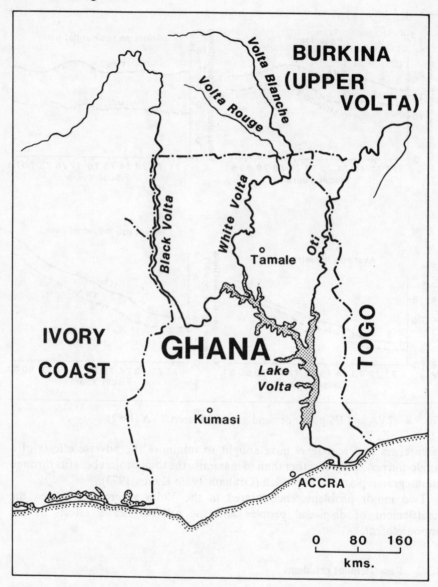

*Fig. 8.5* Lake Volta and its drainage basin

compensation for their land or property and resettlement by the Volta River Authority (VRA). Eighty-five per cent of the population chose the latter course, thus presenting an opportunity to restructure the social fabric and economy of the Volta peoples. This restructuring was to be achieved by reducing the number of settlements from 700 to 52, each having between 2,000 and 5,000 people. Care was taken in the siting of settlements to avoid friction due to traditional rivalries between the eight ethnic groups which inhabited the flooded area. This same care extended to providing units within which traditional leadership structures would operate. Housing in the new settlements consisted of core-houses which had a roof but the construction of only one room was completed. This left each family free to design and build up to three further rooms beneath their roof.

The allocation of land was perhaps the most ambitious and least successful part of the VRA resettlement programme. The aim in land allocation was to provide each family with an income slightly above the wage of the average urban dweller. To accomplish this, a four-component farming system was devised. The land uses and minimum required areas are shown below (Kalitsi 1973):

| Farming system | Area (ha) |
|---|---|
| Arable crops | 4.9 |
| Tree crops | 2.0 |
| Intensive livestock | 1.2 |
| Pastoral farming | 12.1 |

In addition, it would be essential to provide adequate mechanisation and marketing skills for the resettled peoples as well as clearing all the land required for the new agricultural ventures.

It was the lack of this essential technical support and commercial infrastructure which resulted in the failure of the resettlement scheme. By 1969 this failure of the agricultural component of the resettlement programme was evident (Afriyie 1973) and a second-best option of allocating an average of 1.2 ha of uncleared land to each family, for the purpose of subsistence farming, was commenced. The importance of this failure to the overall VRA resettlement effort can be judged by the outmigration of 42,000 (60%) of the original settlers (Taylor 1973). In a despairing review of the Volta resettlement effort, Afriyie (1973:728) stated that:

All factors considered, the agricultural programme points more to the vulnerability than to the viability of the development work now being undertaken in the settlements.

Afriyie attributed the failure of the resettlement scheme to insufficient data on soil and agricultural practices in the new areas and to the introduction of mechanisation without adequate technical support and training facilities. It is clear that insufficient planning and resources were allocated to resettlement of displaced peoples in the Volta scheme. Afriyie suggested that exaggerated expectations were created by an over-ambitious project. However, this rather harsh judgement encapsulates the dilemma of all resettlement schemes in developing countries, which must balance the potential increases in living standards against the ability of a relocated people to achieve an intensification of their agricultural system, at a time when they are faced with the many adjustments required following resettlement (Black 1975; Scudder 1973; Amarteifio 1965).

### 8.3.3 Health effects of Volta

Before the creation of Lake Volta, the disease of onchocerciasis, or river blindness, was common among the peoples living close to the river. The symptoms of this disease are caused by infection with the parasite *Onchocerca volvulus* which causes ocular lesions leading, in severe cases, to total blindness. The transmitting vector of onchocerciasis in Ghana is the fly *Simulium damnosum* which spends its sedentary larval stage as a filter feeder attached to stream-bed stones. It therefore requires flowing waters and it found excellent breeding conditions in the rapids on the pre-impoundment Volta river (Obeng 1975). The incidence of onchocerciasis has reduced as the breeding sites in the main channel have been flooded, but *S. damnosum* is evident in many of the lake feeder streams and below the dam site where the post-impoundment amelioration of extreme flows has enhanced breeding conditions for the *Simulium* vector (Edeson 1975). Eradication programmes, based upon pesticide application and flow regulation, are underway but river blindness remains a problem in the Volta river basin.

The Ghanaian population is genetically adapted to the presence of malaria in the environment. This disease is transmitted to man by the passage of *Plasmodium* parasite species which require a mosquito vector. The main danger caused by large-scale water resource developments in adapted areas is the introduction of a population without natural resistance to the malarial parasites. If the immigrant population is not protected it can initiate a malaria epidemic which will spread to the local residents. This type of epidemic is known as *malaria of tropical aggregation of labour* (MacDonald 1957). Waddy (1975) attributes the failure of early attempts at Panama Canal construction to this debilitating disease where, during the eight years of construction, 57 per cent of the 86,800 workforce were incapacitated by malaria and 5,627 workers died of the disease. In modern projects, there is no reason why malaria should cause disruption. Even following the introduction of disease-free population of workers and technicians, malaria can be controlled by spraying programmes and the distribution of prophylactic drugs such as chloroquinine. This type of action was particularly effective during dam construction at Volta (Hughes 1964).

The most significant effect of dam construction on health in the Volta region has been the increase of schistosomiasis, and in this respect the Lake Volta resembles all other major impoundment schemes in the African continent (Webbe 1972). The pathological effects of this disease are caused by the eggs of the parasitic worm (most commonly *Schistosoma haematobium*) which lodge in the tissues of an infected host and are passed out of the body in the faeces and urine. The next stage in the life-cycle of the *Schistosoma* requires that the excreted eggs should find their way into a water body. The eggs then hatch, giving rise to the larval stage, or miracidium, which must find a snail intermediate host within eight hours of hatching. After four weeks the infected snail begins to shed the circariae into the water and these are capable of entering a new human host through unbroken skin (Jordan 1975). The success of this relatively complex life-cycle depends upon the existence of a suitable environment for the molluscan intermediate host, a route for the excretal contamination of this environment and subsequent human contact with the water. Just such conditions of poor sanitation exist around all impoundments in tropical developing countries and Lake Volta is no exception.

In Lake Volta the snail *Bulinus truncatus rohlfsi* provides the intermediate host for *S. haematobium* and this species was evident in the lake in 1966 (Paperna 1970). The incidence of infection among resettled children under the age of 16 years rose from 3 to 37 per cent in the twelve months from 1967 to 1968. The distribution of infection around Lake Volta reflects the preferred habitats and population densities of the snail vectors. The shallow waters of the western margins with extreme vegetation growths provide an excellent snail breeding ground. On its eastern edge, the lake is bounded by the Volta Region Highlands and its deep waters do not favour plant and snail infestation (Obeng 1975).

Schistosomiasis eradication requires either control of the aquatic stages in the parasite life-cycle or prevention of excretal contamination of waters. The latter method is practically impossible in an LDC where children live in close association with a tropical impoundment. The former depends largely on molluscicides. In localised areas this can be effective. However, the very size of an impoundment such as Lake Volta prevents the universal application of molluscicides. There is today no effective technology for the control of schistosomiasis over large geographical areas and Jordan (1975) estimated that over 300 million people suffer from the disease worldwide.

### 8.3.4 Volta and the Ghanaian economy

The primary objective of the Volta river project was increased industrialisation of the economy promoted by electrification. This was to have effected the scale and distributions of incomes within the country as well as the structure of Ghana's exports. To a great extent, these aims failed to materialise. Up to the mid-1970s there had been no significant change in the structure of Ghana's export earnings. The export of cocoa and raw materials including bauxite continued to dominate. Cheap electricity from the Volta river has had little effect on the export economy. Hart (1977:82) suggested that a preliminary assessment

indicates a zero or negligible influence on Ghana's industrialisation. The aim ... to achieve a significant measure of industrialisation ... does not seem to have occurred.

The creation of jobs has proved expensive. The total number of industrial and associated jobs created in the Volta aluminium industry is around 9,000, but the cost per workplace averages approximately $75,000 (1977 base). Workplace costs in the Electricity Corporation of Ghana and the VRP averages $37,000. The average workplace cost in the US in 1970 was $18,000.

There has been little beneficial influence on the economies of Ghanaian regions. Indeed, it could be argued that the project has accentuated regional income and opportunity disparities. Electricity has, thus far, been supplied mainly to the richest eastern areas of Ghana. In general, the views of Graham (1986:131) that

> from the very beginning, the Volta scheme was conceived, constructed and finally coopted by the international aluminium companies and the international banks for their own profit maximization

seem justified.

## 8.4 The Senegal river valley

### 8.4.1 Background

The Senegal river drains a catchment area of 290,000 km$^2$ including parts of Mali, Guinea, Mauritania and Senegal (Mounier 1986). The southern headwaters in Mali and Guinea provide the majority of the river's flow and very little additional water is added from Senegalese and Mauritanian catchments north of Bakel (Fig. 8.6). Annual rainfall in the basin varies from 250 mm in the northern area to 2,000 mm in the south.

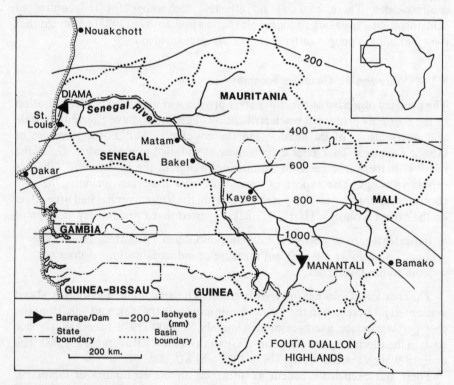

*Fig. 8.6* The Senegal valley

There is a marked summer maximum due to the advance of the inter-tropical convergence zone (ITCZ) (Nicholson 1979). This causes river levels at Bakel to rise from a minimum mean monthly discharge of 10 $m^3\ s^{-1}$ in May to a maximum mean monthly September discharge of 3,500 $m^3\ s^{-1}$ (Gould 1981). In early summer, the ITCZ moves north with greater velocity than the flow of the Senegal river. Rainfall, therefore, commences in the semi-arid northern lands before the flood waters, produced by rainfall over the southern Fouta Djallon Highlands, have arrived at Bakel (Bradley *et al.* 1977).

Figure 8.7 shows the discharge hydrograph of the Senegal river at Bakel. At a discharge of 2,000 $m^3\ s^{-1}$ floodplain inundation occurs. The total area submerged varies with the maximum flood level. A high flood (1954) will cause 5,000 $km^2$ of inundation and a low flood (1944) about 800 $km^2$ (Watt 1981; MAS 1960). The degree of flooding is extremely variable (Fig. 8.8), a product of the interaction of rainfall totals and the relative velocities of the ITCZ and the flood waters. Since 1904 the river has failed on five occasions to reach the discharge necessary for floodplain inundation.

There are three main agricultural systems in the lower valley:

1. Rain fed or *dieri* agriculture which is a type of dry land farming practised as a shifting cultivation away from the main river channel.
2. Irrigated agriculture, which is sited on the more fertile alluvial lands. The water is fed by diesel pumps and provision is organised on a village scale in the upper valley and on a larger scale in the delta region. These irrigated areas are called *perimeters*.
3. Flood recession agriculture is practised on the *walo* (or oualo) lands. This requires 30 days of inundation to allow sufficient soaking for crop maturation and it is heavily dependent upon the magnitude and timing of the flood wave. This type of cultivation is possible on approximately half of the good alluvial land (Bradley *et al.* 1977).

The walo land yields approximately 430 $kg \cdot ha^{-1}$ and the dieri land yields 400 $kg \cdot ha^{-1}$. Both figures are subject to broad oscillation due to flood-level changes in the former and uncertain soil fertility and rainfall in the case of the latter. It is this uncertainty and risk of crop failure which leads many of the young men to migrate to the towns and abroad in search of work. This *haemorrhage of the young* (Watt 1981) accounts for half the annual population growth of 2.6 per cent and causes social distortions in the remaining communities which result in an over-conservative attitude to change and a declining agricultural productivity. However, the emigrants provide a significant income for the rural community in the form of remittances.

### 8.4.2 Development proposals

The Senegal river transfers water from a surplus area in the Fouta Djallon Highlands, thus allowing agriculture in a semi-arid deficit area north of Bakel. The objective of the development proposals is to enhance the value of this

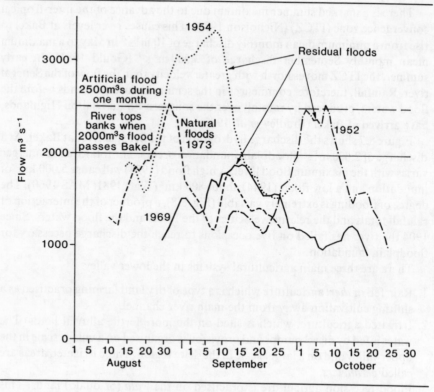

*Fig. 8.7* Discharge hydrograph of the Senegal river at Bakel. *Source*: Watt (1981)

resource by increasing its reliability and quantity. It is hoped to develop a further 255,000 ha of irrigated perimeters by 2028 which will allow double cropping of rice, tomatoes, maize, millet, sorghum and sugar cane.

The Senegal valley has a long history of development plans. An early Chinese scheme favoured the construction of a number of small headwater impoundments to provide a reliable and predictable annual flood. This scheme certainly fits the social and economic *need structures* of the present walo farmers who would not be required to change their current practices. However, the Chinese proposal was not attempted due to problems of international agreement and funding. The drought which affected the Sahelian region from the late 1960s to 1980 (Todorov 1985; Gregory 1983, 1982; Gould 1981), however, gave the impetus required to overcome these difficulties. This period re-emphasised the need for integrated river basin development in the Senegal valley and, in 1972, Senegal, Mali and Mauritania jointly formed OMVS (Organisation pour la Mise Valeur du Fleuve Senegal) to co-ordinate water resource developments. The work of OMVS has been assisted by technical support from USAID (United States Agency for International Development).

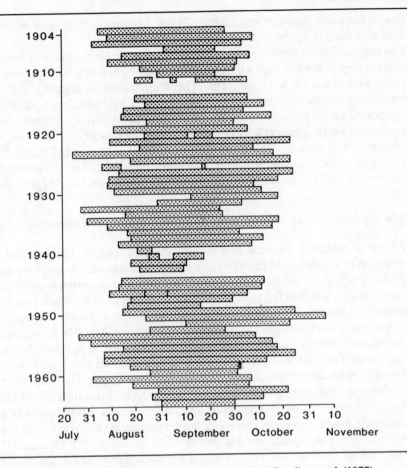

*Fig. 8.8* Flooding of the Senegal river at Bakel. *Source*: Bradley *et al.* (1977)

The requirements of the OMVS scheme are that:

1. They should allow year-round navigation to be maintained to Mali;
2. They provide sufficient water for irrigation of additional alluvial land for increased food production;
3. They prevent salt incursions into the lower reaches during low-flow conditions; and
4. They provide for hydroelectric power production (OMVS 1978).

This scheme uses two dams, one at Manantali on the Bafing river in the Mali headwaters. The second dam, or barrage, is under construction at Diama and will prevent salt incursions in the lower 200 km of the Senegal river during periods of low flow (Mounier 1986). The upper impoundment will allow for flow regulation, thus preventing the annual flood but allowing sufficient water down the channel for navigation to Kayes. In addition, 91 MW of power will be generated for use in Bamako, the capital of Mali. Sufficient irrigation water will be available for 375,000 ha of land in the lower valley.

The impoundment produced by the rockfill dam at Manantali will have a maximum depth of 60 m with an average depth of 24 m and a surface area of 480 km² extending 123 km upstream. The 8 km³ storage capacity will be adequate to provide a minimum flow of 300 $m^3 \cdot s^{-1}$ at Bakel, sufficient to allow for navigation as well as providing capacity for irrigation abstractions. There is some disagreement on the likely effects of a minimum river flow of 300 $m^3 \cdot s^{-1}$ on the salt wedge which causes problems in the lowest 200 km of channel during low flows. Watt (1981) suggested that a minimum flow of 100 $m^3 \cdot s^{-1}$ would be sufficient to prevent saline water in the lower channel, whereas Gould (1981:468) stated:

flow regulation at 300 $m^3 \cdot s^{-1}$ is not sufficient to prevent salt intrusion.

Whatever the likely outcome, OMVS have decided upon the construction of Diama dam at a location 45 km upstream of the river mouth. This will create a long, shallow impoundment, 0.65 m above mean high tide, extending 300 km upstream with a width of 0.3 to 5.0 km and a mean depth of less than 1 m. The benefits of the Diama scheme include water supply to Dakar, a road over the dam structure, and sufficient water for 100,000 ha of irrigation. It will be necessary to provide a lock for barge traffic and seven 20 m sluice gates to pass the 100-year design flood. The dam will prevent upstream migration of fish species which comprise a significant proportion of the diet of valley dwellers. The final trophic state of this shallow tropical impoundment has received little attention. In view of the potential for weed and snail infestation which could provide an intermediate host for the *schistosoma*, a deeper consideration of the impound-ment limnology would seem sensible (Bradley 1977; Jordan 1975; Obeng 1973).

The OMVS scheme will require considerable adaptation on the part of farmers who currently practice flood recession agriculture on the walo lands. In previous schemes where irrigation has been introduced to rural communities, failures have occurred because of high water taxes, distribution of land holdings and conservatism among farmers (Watt 1981; SONADER 1977). However, past successes are recorded by Fresson (1979) who studied four perimeters provided with irrigation under SAED (Senegal Rural Development Agency) and SATEC (Societe D'Aide Technique et du Co-operation, Paris) development programmes. Fresson attributed the success of their developments to the level of participation by farmers and the tailoring of projects to particular needs. She concluded with three main points:

1. The project aims must be determined in relation to the aims of the socio-economic system of farming.
2. The production model defined by the project must be flexible. For example, it might come about that by imposing on the farmers a system of organisation incompatible with their traditional social structures the whole project would come to a dead end.

3. Delegation to the farmers of some decision making powers is facilitated by decentralised organisation and non-compulsory methods. (Fresson 1979:10)

OMVS plans for the introduction of irrigation into the valley reflect the desire to learn from past failures. A five-year transitional period is planned from the closing of Manantali dam when a flood wave will be released down the valley to facilitate flood recession agriculture. During this time, *support centres* and *support perimeters* will be set up to provide advice, logistical support and a working model for surrounding farmers. From these centres an:

organic, responsive, accountable and decentralised bureaucracy

will assist with implementation of irrigation schemes at the village level (Watt 1981:181). This could result in high yields of up to 10 t·ha$^{-1}$ which will then be sold to provide an income for the village.

This utopian model is not without its potential pitfalls. The most insoluble problem is presented by land ownership of the intensively used alluvial areas. Much of this area has long-established land ownership patterns and families jealously defend their rights to the land in their possession. In many areas it is unlikely that the equitable seed and land distribution observed by Fresson will be replicated. The resultant strains could be exacerbated as farmers begin to receive cash payments for their increased crop and move away from the traditional subsistence and barter economy. Indeed, Fresson (1979) attributed part of the success of the perimeters she studied to the fact that farmers were not providing for an external market but satisfying their own needs.

A major problem ahead for USAID, OMVS and SAED will be to bring benefits of the development scheme to all in the valley while maintaining an efficient production system to allow for import substitution and an increase in living standards.

## 8.5  Regional water authorities in England and Wales

### 8.5.1  Background

Sharpe (1978:405) defined the three objectives of river basin management in the United Kingdom as follows:

(a) to make available water of sufficient quantity and reliability, and standard of consistency of quality to meet requirements in homes and for commerce and industry;
(b) at the same time to make adequate provision for *in situ* requirements for water and water space for such purposes as the ecology generally, including fisheries, dilution of effluents, recreation and conservation of the environment;
(c) to treat and dispose of resulting effluents in a manner, at a location, and

to a standard that is appropriate and acceptable having regard to the interests of other abstractors and water users; that also takes into consideration the needs of the ecology and environment as well as the essential requirement to safeguard public health.

Achieving these objectives in England and Wales is the responsibility of ten regional water authorities (RWAs) shown in Fig. 8.9.

*Fig. 8.9* The regional water authorities of England and Wales. *Source*: HMSO (1986)

These multifunctional resource agencies were established on 1 April 1974 by the 1973 Water Act (Wisdom and Skeet 1981; Okun 1977; Water Act 1973). The RWAs replaced over 1,400 (Andrews 1979) single-purpose agencies including: 1,393 local authority sewage treatment departments; 29 river authorities; and 157 statutory water supply undertakings. Establishment of these multifunctional units on a catchment basis allows control over nearly all aspects of the hydrological cycle and provides the potential for integration between the water supply and effluent disposal functions of the water authorities (Chapter 3). In addition, the provision of recreational facilities can be organised to prevent conflicts with the primary resource functions of water supply and sewage disposal.

There is undoubtedly a strong case for the present system of catchment-based administrative units with a multifunctional role. These authorities are forced to internalise many of the externalities created by previous single-purpose management units (Parker and Penning-Rowsell 1980). Some of the benefits of this structure can be seen in the improvements in lowland river water quality achieved as a result of the same agency being responsible for upstream effluent disposal, downstream abstraction and fisheries management. This *control at source* has been further aided by the better-equipped scientific arms of the large regional authorities, which have provided a firmer base for effective research into demand management and prediction (Clarke 1980; Stott 1980).

The arguments against catchment-based administrative units have been outlined by Parker and Penning-Rowsell (1980) who suggest two main objections to the RWA system. First, the removal of water planning from the local authority system prevents complete integration of water, housing, transportation and industrial planning. Second, the spatial distribution of demand need not follow catchment-defined areal units. A further argument was explored by Chilver (1974:136) who suggested that councillor representatives on RWAs would not provide an efficient channel of local democracy because:

> they will not be chosen because they have got something to contribute to the task in hand. They will be chosen because they are councillors and because they are not wanted for the housing committee, the finance committee or the general purposes committee on the authority which they serve. I am not saying that they will not be able, but they are not chosen because they are particularly well suited to serve on a RWA.

### 8.5.2 Examples

The benefits of this integrated catchment-based approach adopted by the reorganised British water industry have been outlined by Sharpe (1980) who illustrated his argument with reference to the River Severn and the River Dove/River Derwent systems.

The Dove/Derwent system provides a clean tributary to the River Trent and is used for potable abstractions and effluent disposal (Fig. 8.10). The problems

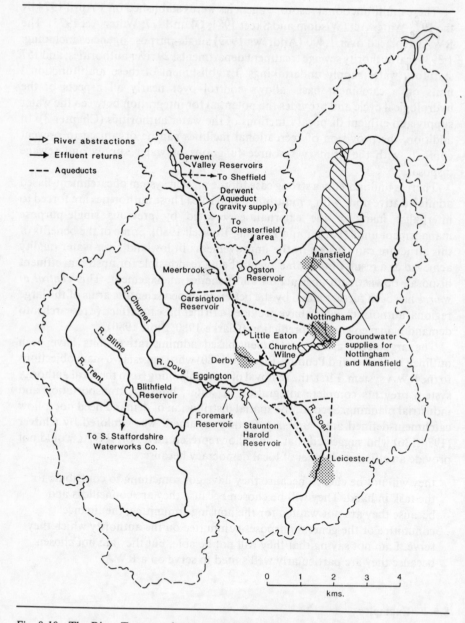

*Fig. 8.10* The River Trent catchment and the Dove/Derwent system. *Source*: Sharpe (1978)

facing the Severn Trent Water Authority in this sub-catchment include the allocation of various sources (upland supplies, river abstraction and groundwater supplies) between centres of demand which have differing population growth rates and available supply/demand margins. This problem is made more complex by the changing costs of alternative potable supplies produced by variable energy costs which are reflected in treatment and pumping charges. As a further complication, the provision of new supplies from two pump-filled reservoirs at Foremark and Carsington have to be allocated between areas of potential surplus such as Leicester and relatively deficient areas such as Nottingham and Derby. A resource-demand model has been used to allocate resources and it allows alternative strategies to be investigated with a range of growth-rate assumptions built into the programme (IWE 1972). Using such an approach can allow management to produce long-term plans which provide a balance between supply reliability and minimum cost criteria. In addition, the effects of individual plans can be judged in the light of the total catchment resource needs.

The River Severn catchment presents a different set of problems and management options from those of the Dove/Derwent system outlined above. These arise because of the nature of the catchment which is considerably larger with a lower concentration of industry (Fig. 8.11). The main resource allocation

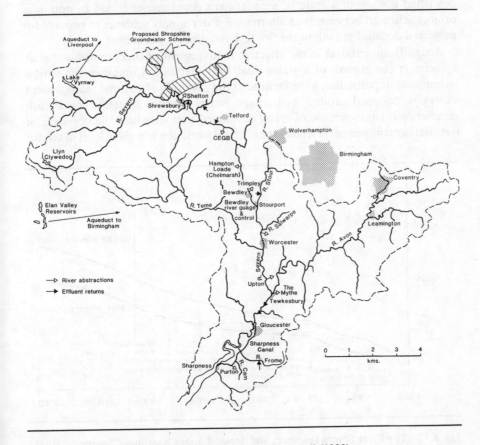

*Fig. 8.11* The River Severn catchment. *Source*: Tattersall (1980)

problem in the Severn catchment results from the increasing demand for abstractions from the channel. In 1976, these abstractions were 475 Ml·d$^{-1}$ and by 2001 the projected figure is 1,010 Ml·d$^{-1}$ (Sharpe 1978).

Figure 8.12 shows the projected resource availability of the Severn system above Sharpness. This type of supply/demand calculation can be accomplished without the complex modelling techniques required when quality becomes an important factor. Tattersall (1980) provided a simple method of constructing a residual flow diagram (Fig. 8.13) which can be used to judge the impact of proposed abstractions and additions to a river's flow (Glover 1980).

Further examples of integrated river basin development by RWAs are presented by Lambert (1981) and Pearson and Walsh (1981). In the former study, Lambert illustrated the application of on-line hydrological simulation to the management of the River Dee system to provide for multiple objectives, including: (i) hydroelectric power generation at Llyn Celyn; (ii) abstractions for potable and industrial use; (iii) flood reduction; (iv) fisheries enhancement; and (v) recreational use of the regulating impoundments. Pearson and Walsh (1981) described the use of a suite of management programmes to aid in optimum project selection between four alternative water supply schemes to provide for projected demand growth in the South Lancashire conurbation.

A significant catalyst in the effective management of these multifunctional agencies is the growth of systems analytical methods. Computer simulation techniques, in particular, have facilitated the planning of optimal management strategies designed around a drainage basin resource system. The British experience is characteristic of many developed nations where the objective of river basin management is seen as the efficient provision of a given level of service

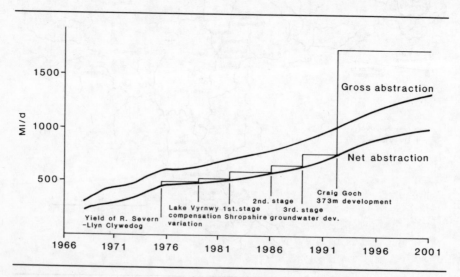

*Fig. 8.12* The River Severn resources and demand above Sharpness. *Source*: Sharpe (1978)

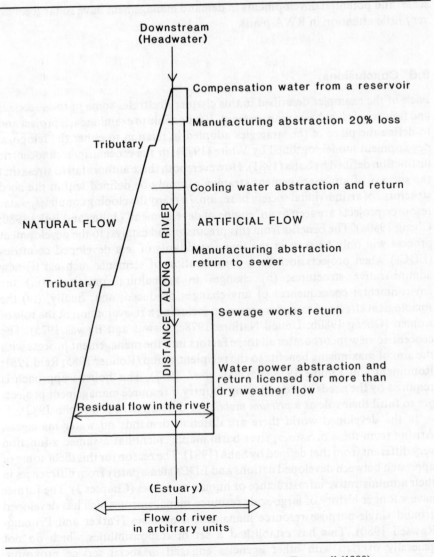

*Fig. 8.13* A hypothetical residual flow diagram. *Source*: Tattersall (1980)

(Gershon *et al.* 1982; Grigg and Fleming 1981; Jenkins 1981; Lester 1981). The nature of the services provided and their future levels are determined by the characteristics and growth of the particular economy. The function of the river basin manager is to prevent any break in future economic development by providing for the demanded level of resource availability. Used in this way, the present river basin management systems are following the classical *supply fix* approach to resource provision (Parker and Penning-Rowsell 1980; Rees 1976; Herrington 1976). The efficiency so far achieved has resulted from the increase in

217

scale, and potential developments in demand management have so far received very little attention in RWA plans.

## 8.6 Conclusions

Each of the examples described in this chapter illustrates some of the successes and failures of river basin management. It is possible to examine each project and to define the place of the strategies adopted in relation to either the temporal development model, outlined by White (1977), or the ecocentric/technocentric distinction defined by Saha (1981). However, both these authors fail to stress that the success of any management strategy can only be defined within the need structures of an individual society or region. In many developing countries, water resource projects are seen as an 'engine of development' (Julius and Buky 1980; Obeng 1980a). The benefits from this precursor and catalyst to the development process will only be seen in the living standards of less developed countries (LDCs) when projects include a consideration of elements such as: (i) new administrative structures; (ii) changes in agricultural practices; (iii) the environmental consequences of any changes produced; and, finally, (iv) the sociological effects of resource provision including a re-evaluation of the role of women (Obeng 1980b; United Nations 1978c; Biswas and Biswas 1975). The ecocentric view incorporates all these factors into the management process with the aim of maximising benefits to the recipient group (Ronner 1985; Reid 1981; Rondinelli and Ruddle 1978; Farinan et al. 1977). This holistic approach is required by the needs of a developing country if resource management projects are to fulfil their role as a *primum mobile* for development (Chisholm 1982).

In the developed world there are different demands on water managers. Arising from these pressures, river basin management has assumed a function very different from that defined by Saha (1981). The reason for this dichotomy of approach between developed nations and LDCs stems partly from differences in their administrative infrastructure or human resources (Chapter 3). The former have a longer history of large-scale resource management which has developed around single-purpose resource management agencies (Parker and Penning-Rowsell 1980). This has established a set of responsibilities which do not generally overlap with other agencies engaged in social service provision, although co-operation between groups of agencies in a river basin is evident in some cases. Hence river basin managers in the developed countries take a more technocentric view. This stance is not surprising from resource management agencies usually dominated by the engineering profession (Parker and Penning-Rowsell 1980:12).

In the British water industry, integration of these technocentric functions has been facilitated by the creation of the catchment-based regional water authorities (Kromm 1985; Musgrave 1979) and in the United States by the river basin commissions (since terminated by President Reagan). These management units all utilise techniques of systems analysis and simulation modelling which

218

presuppose a holistic perspective of the multi-purpose resource system (Fleckseder 1981; French and Krenkel 1981; Jenkins 1981; Pearson and Walsh 1981; Berezner and Ereshko 1980; IWE 1972). However, the majority of the agencies' efforts are limited to the efficient provision of the water resources required by society, and the role of the agency is to predict future demand levels and then to manage the resource to meet those demands (Clarke 1980). In this framework the river basin planners are avoiding brakes on future economic development, rather than acting as a *primum mobile* for development itself.

Evidence for this interpretation can be found in the examples outlined in this chapter. The modern TVA illustrates the technocentric organisation in which 90 per cent of its budget is devoted to electrical energy provision. This dominance of the agency's electrical supply function has led Saha and Barrow (1981) to suggest that, after 50 years, the TVA is little more than a non-profit-making electrical supply utility. The early struggles between Arthur Morgan and David Lilienthal illustrate the conflict between the ecocentric ideal of the self-taught water resources expert and the technocentric pragmatism of the engineer. In this instance, the technocentric view prevailed, and some would interpret this as evidence of a lost opportunity for integrated resource management. However, it is possible to view these events as merely the rational development of the TVA's goals as the needs of society progressed. Initially, concern centred on rural development and the alleviation of extreme poverty. The later phase was dominated by industrial growth requiring cheap and plentiful power. In reality, the development of the Tennessee valley can be placed somewhere between these two extremes.

The early TVA, which Roosevelt intended would *reclaim land and human beings*, certainly approached the concept of an integrated development as defined by Saha (1981). Central to this success was the *force account* system which ensured that local labour was used for all major construction projects. The Tributary Area Development Programme continued the process of providing direct benefits to the people of the Tennessee valley. The *bottom up* planning process, required by TAD projects, ensured that planning actions were suited to perceived need structures of a community. However, the success of this strategy depends largely on a representative and responsive leadership at the local level. The agency communicates with and through this leadership, and this has led Tugwell and Banfield (1950) to suggest a *grass tops* rather than a *grass roots* type of communication is more common in dealings with TVA. Selznick (1949) attributed the failure of TVA to fulfil many of Roosevelt's aspirations to the agency's unwillingness to accommodate the wishes of the most powerful local organisations, and in particular the American Farm Bureau Federation.

The TVA shows that project design for maximum local benefits will require efficient communication with the recipient groups. However, it is essential that communication is with a truly representative group, and that powerful sectional interests are not allowed to detract from plans which provide the maximum net benefit to the full community. This problem is of particular relevance to a resource development agency created outside the recipient region which must be

219

responsive to local interests and communicate with local people. In this instance, it is the powerful and well-organised groups that are able to provide the articulate and *high-profile* communication required by the resource agency. Tugwell and Banfield (1950) suggested that the TVA had effectively chosen to manage this type of input to the planning process by the mechanism of co-opting protesting groups which then become part of the system against which they were originally protesting. However, the agency must be able to resist pressure to change its plans where such alteration would cause an overall strategy to be reduced in effectiveness.

River basin developments in developing nations often have problems of communication because of cultural and language differences between the agency staff and the indigenous population. Saha and Barrow (1981) suggested that this problem is exacerbated by the narrow range of the UN consultancy circuit. However, Lightfoot (1981) has itemised failures of resettlement efforts by the government of Thailand which are not subject to external control. These developments in the upper Mekong basin have been characterised by a lack of communication which Lightfoot (1981:13) described as follows:

> Neither has there been any institutional channel for the participation of evacuees in formulating the resettlement strategy.

Similar breakdowns in communication can be identified in the Volta scheme. Resettlement failures were compounded by insufficient resources allocated to the provision of new settlements and the preparation of land. Initial indications from the Senegal river development indicate a desire to consult with the local community and tailor plans for agricultural development to the existing organisational structures at the village level.

The Rattvik conference (Johnels 1983) identified river basin management as a major environmental research and management priority for the late 1980s. At that conference, Pantulu (1983:109, 111) identified the international political dimension as the major obstacle to river basin management:

> Very little information exists that could provide a basis for the formulation of universally acceptable principles or arrangements for international river basin management, or for the sharing of waters. The formulation of such general principles, or the creation of model institutions for the management of river basins are not, in themselves, difficult. But their universal acceptance is almost impossible to achieve in view of the political considerations involved ... on the political level the problems are particularly complicated in international river basins. There is very little that could be done at present beyond providing for the exchange of information, with emphasis on benefits of regional co-operation among international river organisations.

The techniques of simulation modelling and multi-objective planning are well understood, but the political problems of implementation both at the international and village scales present the most insoluble problems for the planning agencies. An encouraging trend towards hydrologically defined basin authorities in developing nations, such as those in Burkino Faso (Volta basin) and Nigeria (Sokoto river), has been identified by WRI (1986).

Very few projects encapsulate true 'river basin planning' which Saha (1981) defines as a discipline combining land and water resource management. More often the management structures established are not designed to take such an holistic view of their role. In both developing and developed nations, river basin management is most often seen as the more efficient allocation of water resources to facilitate irrigation and water supply. The basin management agency does not often become involved in regional economic development generated by the operation of the basin mega-system outlined in Fig. 8.1.

There are some isolated examples of agencies which attempt to combine land and water management within a basin authority. The Ontario conservation authorities provide one example of such agencies. There are 38 conservation authorities in Ontario which receive funding from both local and provincial sources. The major function of these agencies is to limit flood damage. Related activities, such as pollution control and water supply, are usually managed by other agencies (Mitchell 1981). Each conservation authority is a partnership between the provincial and local, or municipal, authorities and they were formed in response to local demand. The funding levels of these authorities are very small when compared with the more formal and comprehensive agencies discussed in this chapter. Figure 8.14 illustrates the distribution of funding between the 38 conservation authorities. A disproportionate share of these provincial resources goes to two of the authorities, Metropolitan Toronto and the Grand River Conservation Authority (GRCA) which receive $7.1 million and $6.5 million respectively (1986). The total provincial allocation to the 38 authorities is only $41.3 million (Ontario Ministry of Natural Resources 1987).

The allocation to Metropolitan Toronto takes account of the high population in this authority. The relatively generous allocation to the GRCA is justified because this area was chosen in the late 1970s for comprehensive study leading to a basin management plan (Grand River Implementation Committee 1982a, b). This has broadened the role of the GRCA which has placed increased emphasis on problems of water quality, soil conservation and afforestation in addition to its flood control responsibilities (GRCA 1983a, b, 1984). However, with a total revenue of only $14 million per annum (1984), almost half of which is devoted to capital works for water and land management, the GRCA is far from the basin mega-system management agency envisaged by Saha (1981). In fact, this agency operates in the role of adviser and integrator, providing the expertise and research capacity to oil the wheels of integration. This offers a potentially useful model for other regions where co-operation between existing agencies to effect basin-wide integration is needed. Perhaps the key to the success of the GRCA and the other conservation authorities derives from the local, or 'grass-roots', element in their inception and present financial structure.

Often, the parameters of basin management are defined by the terms of an international agreement rather than a formal agency with a clearly defined role.

221

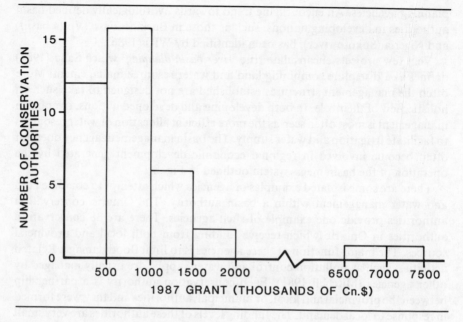

*Fig. 8.14* Funding levels of the 38 Ontario conservation authorities

Integration might be needed in such a situation but political realities often preclude such desirable developments. Mageed (1985) studied the Nile basin. He attributed the failure of the riparian states to develop 'integration' to the post-colonial legacy of weak administrations, underdevelopment and post-colonial crisis management.

Similar examples of poorly integrated river basin management can be identified in the developed nations. Water allocation within the Colorado basin is founded on a series of international and interstate treaties and compacts which define the permissible abstractions and minimum acceptable flows. Rapid population growth in the lower basin and increasing demands for irrigation waters are straining this rigid pattern of resource allocation (Gaylord 1985). In the absence of a powerful international basin management organisation, the political structure of this basin prevents even responsive adjustments to demographic changes through resource re-allocations. There is little sign therefore of true multi-functional integration of land and water management.

The weaker management structures of the Colorado and Nile basins are more typical than the stronger, integrated developments that have formed the main examples of this chapter. While such strong integrated agencies may form the 'ideal' when measured in terms of efficiency and/or equity (Williams 1985), the examination of sub-optimal administrative structures offers perhaps the most fruitful future research avenue. We would agree with the views of Crow

(1985:262) who, after a study of the failure of transnational planning efforts on the Ganges, stated that:

> legal tools, geographical concepts and engineering technology are insufficient to control either rivers or governments. People control both, but the way in which they do so, through their collective institutions and their differences as classes and nations in conflict, require careful analysis.

# CHAPTER 9

# Issues and strategies

In the first part of this chapter we identify the major issues that have to be addressed in water resource management in the future. In subsequent sections we consider some strategies that might be of help in addressing these issues.

## 9.1 Issues

Three key issues are addressed. The first concerns scale, not simply as a physical attribute but as impacts of differing magnitude. The second reviews the need to develop technologies and standards that are relevant to the societies in which they are to be applied. Finally, the need to integrate management both within water resources and among all resources is examined.

### 9.1.1 Scale

Issues of scale are central to understanding the problems of water resource management. Scale can be considered in two dimensions:

1. the physical size of the project;
2. the societal impact of the project.

#### 9.1.1.1 System size and management

Scale is an issue when the size of a physical system makes effective management difficult or impossible. For example, the global water balance, discussed in Chapter 2, is increasingly seen as a vital resource system which is affected by human activity. Eagleson (1986:6, 14) has suggested that:

> Hydrologists are now being forced to consider the atmosphere and the land surface as an interactive coupled system. ... Because of humanity's sheer numbers and its increasing capacity to affect large regions, the hydrological

cycle is being altered on a global scale with consequences for the human life support system that are often counterintuitive.

No effective management control of the hydrological cycle exists at the global scale.

The smallest scale resource systems discussed in earlier chapters are the village water supply systems in the developing world. Here, too, management is often ineffective because the agencies are structured at a national or even international scale. In responding to the needs of the client nations, a growing body of evidence indicates that the responses must be made at a small (group, tribe, village) scale. It is difficult for these personnel to operate at both of these scales simultaneously.

Different sets of problems can arise in the management of large-scale water resource projects in countries at a broadly similar level of technical and social development. These can be explained by the differences in the scales of administrative complexity which are encountered. In the USSR inter-basin transfers, the administration is relatively simple and centralised and some of these schemes are being implemented. In North America, on the other hand, inter-basin transfers such as the NAWAPA scheme encounter complex administrative frameworks in which differences in jurisdiction and approach at provincial, state, federal and international scales act to hinder implementation. Such difficulties are not restricted to inter-basin transfers. In the USA, Kusler (1985) has identified the problems of integrating regional programmes with national policy in the context of floodplain management.

### 9.1.1.2 Impact

Studies to date have often failed to pay due regard to either societal or environmental considerations. In the less developed countries, projects have impacted on the health of the society and the quality of life of the population. The water-related mortality rates outlined in Chapter 6 almost exclusively focus upon developing nations (WRI 1986; WHO 1986). By comparison, the societal impacts of water projects in the developed countries are less severe and are generally measured in terms of inconvenience, not mortality. Insufficient development of water resources acts as a mild brake on economic growth or as a short-term need to be supplied from stand-pipes.

Environmental impacts range greatly in scale. At one extreme is the possible modification in global climatic regime and sea levels associated with the diversions of waters flowing to the Arctic (Chapter 4). At the other is the minor modification of a river's thermal regime following upstream impoundment (Welsh Water 1984). The differences in severity of these environmental impacts are a significant issue because, in the case of the former, the impacts fall outside the nation that generates them and potentially involve several resource agencies. The latter involves a single river system and fewer agencies, indeed in many cases one nation and one agency. The complexity of solutions that would have to be sought are commensurately different.

### 9.1.2 Appropriateness and transfer

#### 9.1.2.1 Appropriate technology

The concept of appropriateness has received most attention in respect to technology transfer from the developed world to the developing nations. Chapter 8 illustrated how large-scale capital projects initiated by developed *donor* agencies and governments may be inappropriate to the needs of a developing nation where the political and social structure may not exist to allocate the benefits derived from the scheme. It would be wrong, however, to conclude that small-scale or very simple technology is always appropriate to the needs of developing nations. In Chapter 4 the requirement for appropriate technology in the provision of rural water supply systems was discussed (Table 4.3). Inappropriate technology should not be confused with the level of technological input. Even low-level 'hand-pump' technology may be inappropriate to many developing nations. The breakdown rates reported by Mathur (1986) for the Indonesian programme and by ITDG (1978) for the Indian programme indicate an imported technology which has been inappropriate to the societies in which it is being applied.

#### 9.1.2.2 Appropriate standards

The concept of appropriateness goes beyond the area of technology. Table 6.2 presented levels of drinking water quality commonly found in the developing world. Strict application of drinking water quality standards, which may be firmly based on good epidemiological evidence, could result in the closure of many affected supplies in such areas. This would be unacceptable. Hence the global criteria would be inappropriate to the vast majority of water supplies in the rural areas of the developing world (WHO 1984).

Even within the developed nations, engineering solutions to water resource management problems have often been applied which have been inappropriate. Goldsmith and Hildyard (1984) examined the effects of building large impoundments. They concluded that the majority of schemes produced few net benefits to the societies concerned. In the context of developed nations, the inappropriateness will follow from (i) poor demand forecasts or (ii) a simplistic understanding of the ecological environment on which the resource system depends. The latter leads to management conflicts and ecological degradation.

#### 9.1.2.3 Transfer

Many errors could have been avoided if detailed attention had been paid to the appropriateness of project proposals at an early stage in planning. This may sound obvious and elementary. However, there are real difficulties in designing appropriate projects for the developing world. The main difficulty derives from the education and training of the cadre of experts and engineers responsible for

226

project design. This group takes a primarily technocentric view of resource planning. They are seldom asked to view a project as a development scheme in which the net benefits are viewed in the regional or national scale and due account is taken of ecological and environmental impacts.

The developed nations are formalising such considerations within the planning of large projects (Maclaren and Whitney 1985; NRC 1986; Pearse *et al.* 1985; Westmann 1985; NEPA 1969). However, this stage in the project design is expensive and often requires large amounts of information on cultural and ecological impacts which are difficult to quantify. This information may not be understood by the engineering profession and the weighting of these elements becomes a 'political' process. It may be convenient therefore to ignore or downgrade these 'complexities' in order not to delay the task in hand of building the physical structures required. Legislation is the best means to ensure due consideration of these elements. However, such consideration could be achieved, but with less certainty, through policy, regulation and funding.

In developing nations, the checks and balances which derive from adequate control agencies and environmental legislation may not exist. The developer is able to implement a project in a much less restrained manner leading to the types of problems illustrated by Lake Volta. Technology and expertise transfer is essential for water resource management in the developing world. The very size of the problem created by water-borne disease, outlined in Chapter 4, makes inaction unacceptable. Future projects must incorporate a consideration of impacts at an early stage through a much more integrated planning approach.

### 9.1.3 A place for integration

#### 9.1.3.1 Within the water resource domain

Integration is a strategy that is frequently advocated in the water resource management literature. At several points in this text, integration, or more often the lack of it, has been discussed. A number of questions should be raised at this point. What is the nature of the experience base related to integrated management of water resources? Is the experience base from a wide range of natural and cultural environments? Have these been successful experiences? Are there lessons to be gained from an analysis of any past work?

There have been few real attempts to provide integrated management information and even fewer evaluative studies of the policy and management of integration within the water resource field. In the UK, the regional water authorities provide an integrating structure but this operates at the regional scale *only*; nationwide integration is conspicuously absent. Within each water authority the requirement to conduct inventory work and to develop management plans has usually been conducted on the separate facets of water management. Furthermore, no more than lip service has been paid to the possibilities of integration between water and other resource areas. In 1972 the Scottish Development Department (SDD) initiated a study of the water resources of central Scotland (SDD 1973). This study was limited to the provision of water for supply. It ignored the integration of water resources into the overall planning of the region. The most important omissions, in the Scottish context, were water quality management, flooding and fisheries.

Royal Commissions, and the equivalent analyses conducted in other countries, are very often charged with the examination of a particular, narrow and clearly defined issue that has degenerated into a problem. The Commissions are responsible for the provision of a plan or recommendations to alleviate the problem; they are not charged with the creation of a plan for integrated management. There is a need to design terms of reference that permit such investigations to adopt a holistic perspective.

At the international or the global level, integration for management does not exist. The proceedings of the many international meetings and initiatives indicate that the recommendations are usually simple statements of intent which would be difficult, if not impossible, to use as guides to be implemented at a national level (Johnels 1983; United Nations 1978c).

In Canada, an inquiry into federal water policy was conducted in the mid-1980s. This was a unique exercise conducted not in response to some emergency but in:

> ... response to a growing environmental consciousness and concern about the management of Canada's freshwater resources. Water is a special resource demanding visionary policies for its management. (Pearse *et al.* 1985:3)

The inquiry findings recommended that the management structure for water should have a number of key features which stress integration and the need for comprehensive management:

> a watershed plan *sufficiently comprehensive* to take into account *all* uses of the water system and *other activities that affect water flow and quality characteristics* to provide a reference for management;
> information about the watershed's *full* hydrological regime;
> an analytical system, or model, capable of *revealing the full range of impacts* that would be produced by particular uses and developments in the watershed;
> specified management objectives for the watershed, with criteria for assessing management alternatives in an objective and unbiased way;
> *participation of all relevant regulatory agencies;*
> provisions for public participation in determining objectives and in management decisions. (Pearse *et al.* 1985:96 – authors' italics)

Pearse and his colleagues noted that these were the elements of an ideal framework and that for some of the less populated and unstressed watersheds in Canada it would be unrealistic to expect such plans to be developed. In much of Europe, the need for such a framework is beyond doubt: population density is high and the rivers often highly stressed. The acceptance of the above framework with its focus on integration is the most viable basis for water resource management. However, implementation delays may be inevitable because of competing demands from other sectors of society (Chapter 3).

### 9.1.3.2 Inter-resource integration

In the last section it became clear that there have been few examples of integrated water resource management despite a growing number of calls for such a management philosophy. Integration between resources is, by comparison, at a most embryonic stage. The extent and the importance of the links between resources has only recently become recognised:

> The connectedness of nature is more pervasive and the context for water policy more expansive than has previously been believed. (Pearse *et al.* 1985:7)

At a small scale, say a catchment of less than 100 km², management of the land can have a significant effect on water resources. Management of forests, for example, can modify snowmelt timings; the introduction of a new forest cover can modify water yields from the catchment; the introduction of drainage or of vegetation burning as a land improvement measure can modify catchment chemistries and alter water quality. All of these practices are instigated by managers who are not involved with water management.

At a larger scale, the Great Lakes furnish evidence of the need for a more integrated inter-resource management strategy. The findings of the Pollution from Land Use Activities Research Group (PLUARG 1983) have indicated that restoration of environmental quality in the Great Lakes cannot be tackled solely from the control of industrial and municipal point sources. Much of the deterioration comes from non-point sources. Improvement, therefore, relies on the general introduction by land managers of good management practices that will in the long term benefit the water quality of the Great Lakes. At the present time there are few mechanisms by which these improved practices can be demanded, encouraged, compensated or rewarded. Inter-resource integration is needed but is not common.

At the largest scale, the need for integration, or at the very least co-operation, between resource groups and countries is self-evident. Acidic depositions impact upon crops, forests and water resources both in the source country and in neighbouring areas. These arguments could be paralleled in an analysis of the impacts of radioactive fallout, associated with energy policy, on the water, forests, soils and livestock of several countries as was observed and still remains to be resolved from the Chernobyl incident in 1986.

In Table 3.2 the international agencies with an interest in water resource management were identified. At the national level, organisations exist that claim to have a role in inter-resource and international integration. These bodies or, if necessary, newly established bodies with a broader remit should seek

- to establish the validity of the claimed impacts from all forms of resource management;

229

- to represent and to receive the views of all management agencies; to commission research on problems of a cross-disciplinary or transnational character;
- to identify priorities (according to scale) for the use of land or the implementation of remedies.

Elements of these tasks are attempted by various organisations at present. The results, as measured by effects, are not adequate when judged against the seriousness of environmental problems. Once again, at the heart of this difficulty is the common property nature of the problems and the degree to which short-term national and political self-interest interdicts to block good resource management.

## 9.2 Strategies

In reviewing possible developments within the field of water resource management, a clear distinction must be made between those strategies that are applicable to the developed world and those that relate to the developing world.

### 9.2.1 The developed world

#### 9.2.1.1 Information and complexity

Ever-increasing volumes of data are becoming available to the water resource manager, but the size and complexity of the data base presents problems. The manager must be able to assess the quality of the information and cope with its complexity.

*Information assessment*

The implication of the greater amount of information and the broader spectrum of sources is that decision-makers will be faced with information that comes from unfamiliar disciplines. These people will therefore not have the body of knowledge, from training or experience, with which to form a judgement on the value of the information. In part, this problem stems from the different groups of experts involved in this field. On the one hand, there are the scientists in both the natural and social science fields who provide the data and, on the other, the policy makers and implementers who use the data. The problems of information transfer between these two groups have been summarised by MacGill (1985:583) as follows:

At the interface of these two realms is the transfer of knowledge from various academic disciplines to various planning contexts in order to inform the minds of policy makers and planners, so that better decisions and greater good can be sought. Observers of this interface ... should be well aware of the many blockages in the way of securing the successful transfer of knowledge leading to good planning decisions.

One strategy that might aid in the problem of cross-discipline information transfer is the 'accreditation of data', a system through which the quality of the information might be identified. Progress in this area has been made by Funtowicz and Ravetz (1986) who have identified a framework for communicating the quality of quantitative information to the user. Their framework consists of five parts: **N:U:S:A:P.**

The **N** and **U** are the most basic characteristics of the information, its numeric value and unit. In the context of water resources, one might consider the need for additional irrigation water at an appropriate village level in the sub-Sahel region. The rainfall regime might be characterised as follows. The **N** might have the value 22 and the **U** a characteristic of $cm \cdot yr^{-1}$. The usefulness of the notational framework lies in the **S:A:P** values. The spread in the data is given in the term **S** which in the sub-Sahel example could be crucial to the viability of the proposed scheme, so simple rainfall information might have an added **S** of $\pm 16$. In effect, the 16 is a technical, statistical assessment of possible error ranges. An assessment of the reliability of the data is given by **A**. There may be concern over the record length or the operator reliability or the effects of high evaporative losses in an infrequently read or remotely sited raingauge. The final characteristic of the notation is **P**, which stands for the 'pedigree' of the information. This is the least developed phase of the notation and involves the grading of the information under four headings for each of which five levels of pedigree are identified. Thus the quality of the data input can be graded according to its source from highly controlled experimental data (4) to uneducated guess (0) through categories of (uncontrolled) field data (3), calculated data (2), and educated guess (1). The work of categorising data to give the user a guide to the amount of credence that can be placed on it is at a very early stage of development. However, as a strategy to be refined and applied in the future, it deserves careful consideration (MacGill 1985).

*Recognition of complexity*

There are a variety of ways of coping with complex phenomena. One is to make a number of assumptions in order to simplify reality. The decisions based on such a simplification depend for their validity on the nature of the assumptions. As more disciplines are involved, the likelihood of the user not appreciating the assumptions increases. For example, much of the debate regarding surface water acidification in Europe has concentrated on air pollution levels. The importance of catchment characteristics on acidic susceptibility has been ignored in much of the political debate. This complexity is demonstrated by the field investigations outlined in Chapter 6 and should be recognised and incorporated into policy formulation.

### 9.2.1.2 Expert systems

Expert systems have potential in water management because:

> their ability to use fuzzy data of highly interrelated character is particularly appealing for the modelling of social and behavioural systems. (Unwin and Dawson 1985:231)

Expert systems are defined as:

> Computer programs that undertake the solution of difficult tasks by using the knowledge of and mimicking the solution methods of human experts in a problem domain. (Davis *et al.* 1987:6)

> An intelligent computer program that uses expert knowledge and inference procedures to solve problems that are difficult enough to require significant human expertise for their solution. (Mooneyhan 1983; quoted in Davis and Nanninga 1985:378)

Such systems have gained widespread use in many fields, for example, chemistry (Linsay *et al.* 1980), computer design (McDermott 1983), medicine (Szolovitz 1981) and mineral exploration (Gasching 1982). Environmental applications have been documented in weather forecasting (Mackenzie 1984), agriculture (Tou and Cheng 1983) and flood protection (Cuena 1983). Water and land resources management applications have been reported by Starfield and Bleloch (1983), Pereira *et al.* (1982) and Gasching *et al.* (1981). Developments in the use of expert systems for Australian fire management have been reported by Davis *et al.* (1987) and Davis and Nanninga (1985).

Expert systems allow for 'professional' judgements which may be initiated by inexperienced and untrained personnel. They seem likely to have a place in the developed world, but perhaps the most exciting potential development of them is that they provide a mechanism for technology and knowledge transfer to the developing nations. Technology from the developed nations has often been dismissed as inappropriate because insufficient expert backup was available in the recipient nation. Expert systems offer the potential for providing knowledge support in parallel with the technology transferred.

This view may be unrealistic. Very simple technology, such as the hand water pump, may be unreliable or inappropriate to many less developed nations. The skills required to operate a prepared expert system are not widely available in the developing nations and the dependence on imported computers is a significant weakness in this form of technology transfer. The most likely applications for expert systems in the medium term is within developed nation management agencies where the basic educational standards of operatives are high and the infrastructure exists to service and maintain the hardware required.

### 9.2.1.3 Networks and performance indicators

Water resource systems are increasingly complex. This complexity arises because of the developments of the interlinkages in the physical systems and because of the needs of management to interface with the 'engineering' system. In 9.2.1.1, it was suggested that the minimum stance that could be adopted in the face of this increase in complexity was its recognition. In this section, some ways of handling the system complexity are presented.

Since 1970 the main elements of the water resource system have evolved from a linear structure (a single source supplying a single demand) to a network structure (a system of multiple demands supplied from multiple sources). An example of this evolution in the Yorkshire Water Authority (UK) area is provided in Fig. 9.1. This shows the growth in the main elements of the water supply network since 1975.

The real system is more complex, having, for example, some 350 sources and not the nine identified in Fig. 9.1. Even were it static, the real system cannot be optimised easily. However, the real world is dynamic with short-term changes in demand associated with climate and industrial activity, and long-term changes associated with population growth and redistribution. Source availability also changes in the short and long term through such factors as drought and system failures.

To aid in the management of such complex systems, several workers have been advocating the use of coupled network models. There are several elements to such models:

1. the articulation of the network;
2. the characterisation of the network;
3. the coupling of cost information;
4. the analysis of the performance of the system.

The network can be regarded as a set of nodes and links (Wilson 1981; de Neufville 1974; Bishop and Hendricks 1974). Wilson *et al.* (1986) identify three types of node termed source, value added and final node. The nature of the source and final nodes depends on the characteristics of the water resource network being modelled. The value-added nodes are associated with treatment, valving, branching or pumping works. Here, a cost input to the system is made which must be identified if the economic and engineering evaluation of the systems is to be effectively coupled to form a management tool.

The hydraulic behaviour of the system is based upon physical principles and is relatively straightforward, but depends crucially upon an accurate and complete articulation of the network. Herein lies the first value of such an approach – the potential to verify the integrity of the interlinkages in the system. In many water resource systems, for example the Victorian water supply systems of the UK, the present structure has been developed over a long time period. Managers may not be fully aware of the physical structure of their system and may not have an accurate network model.

The definition of the system involves the input of information on the physical location, size, capacity, phase of maintenance, age, responsible section etc. for every node and link. At this stage of development the system could be used to

233

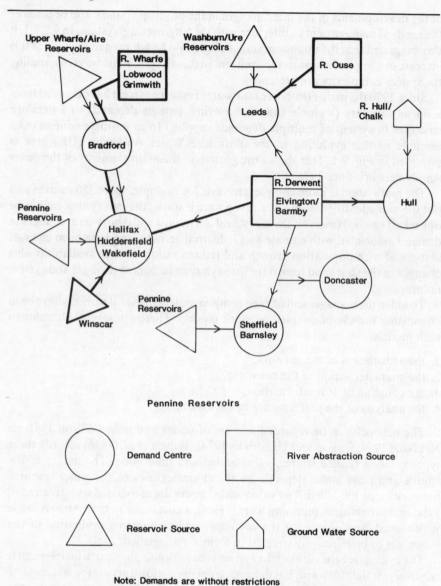

Upper Wharfe/Aire
Reservoirs

R. Wharfe
Lobwood
Grimwith

Washburn/Ure
Reservoirs

R. Ouse

R. Hull/
Chalk

Leeds

Bradford

Pennine
Reservoirs

Halifax
Huddersfield
Wakefield

R. Derwent
Elvington/
Barmby

Hull

Doncaster

Winscar

Pennine
Reservoirs

Sheffield
Barnsley

Pennine Reservoirs

| | |
|---|---|
| ◯ Demand Centre | ⬛ River Abstraction Source |
| △ Reservoir Source | ⬠ Ground Water Source |

Note: Demands are without restrictions

*Fig. 9.1* The network of water sources and distribution areas in Yorkshire, U.K. Additions to the network are shown in bold.

provide information on the actions to be taken in the event of a major system failure. Such failure is not an unusual occurrence. Remaining with the Yorkshire Water Authority case, failures in the system have occurred, for example:

1. Following a major pollution incident on the River Derwent which supplies the major abstraction plant at Elvington (1984);

234

2. Following the closure of all three trip valves on a major link supplying Bradford (1986); and

3. Following the rupture of two of the three trunk mains supplying north Leeds in 1985 (Plate 9.1).

Thus such models have a role in the management of risk inherent in such complex systems. The full value of such models is not realised until costs are allocated to each component of the system. Costs are easy to identify but more difficult to quantify. Capital costs are difficult to assign especially in a system that has developed over a long period of time. Old reservoirs will have no capital costs while the newer impoundments will attract high capital repayment charges. Should these costs be allocated directly or pooled over all the impoundments regardless of age? Costs associated with manpower cannot simply be allocated to a single plant, node or link.

Such models can be viewed as water accounting systems using flow monitoring information from various points in the system to identify zones of leakage (an important consideration in view of the high leakage rates in older supply systems). They can also be viewed as a financial accounting system, routing water over the most cost-efficient network. The most valuable application of these systems lies in the provision of management information and decision support rather than cost minimisation alone.

Pearse *et al.* (1985) have suggested that watershed plans should contain a set of criteria and an assessment framework (section 9.1.3.1). Wilson *et al.* (1986) would term these criteria 'performance indicators' (PI). Performance indicators could be generated for each administrative unit. They could be routinely generated over time to identify cost and efficiency trends and could be used to evaluate new configurations for the system. The same modelling strategy could be applied to operations and planning.

### 9.2.2 Developing world

#### 9.2.2.1 Education and training

Education and training of water resource managers and operatives is the most essential element in improving the resource provision in developing nations. Considerable effort is now being devoted to make technology appropriate. This effort, although essential, often produces solutions that are sub-optimal. For example, hand pumps operated by means of a 'T' bar on the main vertical shaft are simpler than those with a fulcrum mechanism. The T bar removes the requirement for a bearing at the fulcrum and reduces both maintenance and failure risk (Arlosoroff *et al.* 1984). This simpler, and more appropriate, design does not incorporate the useful lever mechanism which facilitates easy operation and higher lift. Basic education of pump operatives, and a good supply of spare parts, would allow most of the required maintenance tasks to be completed immediately. Only with such education will the more efficient and productive technologies be available to the rural population of the developing nations.

235

*Plate 9.1*   Military water tankers supply householders during the emergency in the city
of Leeds in 1985 following the failure of two arterial supply pipes

In the longer term, developing nations will seek to increase the living standards of their people through economic growth. Significant checks on a nation's economic development would be inevitable if a group of educated and innovative resource managers were not available.

### 9.2.2.2 *Management structures*

Studies of water industry administrative structures have proliferated in the developed nations (Sewell *et al.* 1985; Mitchell and Gardiner 1983; Okun 1977; OECD 1972). Such studies are rare in the context of the developing world where implementation failures are common.

Political stability and legitimacy form the pre-requisites for successful resource planning. However, many Third World nations do not possess these attributes. WRI (1986:191) summarised this problem as follows:

> A government's ability to move from understanding the condition of its resources to the creation of a policy, and from there to the execution of that policy, depends principally on its stability and political legitimacy and on the availability of funds and adequate technical and human resources.

Institutional structures and policy implementation in the developing world have received little research attention and are poorly understood. Future management strategies should ensure that a responsive, effective and adequately funded management structure is established in parallel with any resource development. The objectives must be defined, and here lessons from the early years of the TVA (section 8.2) may be useful. It might be that a successful agency will result if its goals are defined more widely to encompass regional development as a whole. The specific water resource project would be seen as an important element and the potential *primum mobile*, but the success of the managers should be judged on the basis of the development goals achieved. To some extent, trans-national organisations such as the OMVS in the Senegal river catchment (section 8.4) present a useful model for development agencies. However, in the case of the Senegal river catchment, serious criticisms have been levelled at the project's 'apparent contempt for the local population' (Mounier 1986:109). These problems and lessons require more attention.

### 9.2.2.3 *Shifting priorities*

In the developing nations, the need for more integrated and ecocentric water resource planning is now recognised. Writers such as Eagleson (1986), Falkenmark (1986a), Goldsmith and Hildyard (1986a, 1984), and WRI (1986) have stressed the interconnectedness of the environment and pointed the way towards more rational resource planning. Errors associated with large-scale water projects such as the Volta scheme (Graham 1986) or Aswan high dam (Lavergne 1986) are now more likely to be recognised at an early stage in project design.

237

The overriding priority of the developing nations must still be the reduction of water-related disease. This is undoubtedly the major water resource problem facing humanity. Some improvement in water supply and sanitation provision is evident from the WHO (1986) data presented in Figs 4.13 and 4.14. However, the Drinking Water Supply and Sanitation Decade targets are not being met. The urban centres present a particularly difficult problem because the rapid population growth rates cannot be matched by new supply and sanitation provision.

In the developed nations a significant move away from single-purpose resource agencies to integrated, basin-wide, management units is evident (Kromm 1985; Pearse *et al.* 1985). Large-scale projects have diminished in importance in the Western world due to the recent economic recession and awareness of environmental implications. Management agencies are placing more emphasis on resource conservation through demand management (Consumers' Association 1986; Pearse *et al.* 1985). The days of water being considered a free good in the developed world are numbered. Even in water-rich Canada (Tables 4.1 and 4.2), metering and pricing are already being used in some cities as means of reducing demand and the consequent environmental pressures which derive from unrestricted water use. Pearse *et al.* (1985:99) have recommended that the Canadian federal government should:

> encourage water conservation and demand management practices by
> explicitly endorsing the principle that beneficiaries should pay for water
> and wastewater services by means of appropriate prices.

Water quality priorities in the developed world have shown a marked shift from parameters of *sanitary* significance to those of carcinogenic and genetic importance. The research priority in the latter area is to define the epidemiological effects of such substances on the population. These effects derive from synergistic mixtures of toxins in the environment, only some of which will be ingested with water. The effects may be chronic and sub-lethal. The exact degree to which the observed symptom attack rates can be attributed to the water resource system will be very difficult, if not impossible, to ascertain. This will present a problem for the policy-makers and resource managers who have shown a reluctance to implement stringent water quality standards until quantified health damage has been demonstrated.

# CHAPTER 10

# Lessons for the future

Water resource management is not an exact science and the 'perfectly successful' project has not, to date, been identified. The objective of this final chapter is to draw out some of the lessons from the examples discussed earlier and to define broad principles of good practice which are transferable across a range of water resource management problems.

## 10.1 Integration

### 10.1.1 At the global scale

#### 10.1.1.1 The global resource perspective

The need for more holistic management of water resources at the global scale is being stressed (Eagleson 1986; Falkenmark 1986a; Stumm 1986). In this approach, water resources are treated as one element in the global ecosystem. This ecocentric perspective on resource management is gaining credence among the 'observers' of the water resource system. However, it is less certain that this philosophy will be translated into firm action by the 'actors' in water resource management and development – the largely national management agencies that continue to regard water in a more technocentric manner. Falkenmark (1986a:192) offered a useful insight into the present status of water as a resource when she stated:

> The traditional approach to natural resources and global development is basically anthropocentric and strongly influenced by conditions in water rich countries. This approach takes as its starting point demographic trends in birth rate and mortality. The resources and systems needed to support these populations are generally discussed in a fragmented fashion; human settlements, food and agriculture, forests and rangelands, ocean fishing are

239

generally treated as non-related sectors. In such studies water is seen as a technical commodity only and is placed far down the list.

This compartmentalisation of the resource base causes severe environmental problems and prevents a comprehensive assessment of the range of impacts caused by human activities which can often be additive, synergistic or even counterintuitive.

### 10.1.1.2 Water quality standards

The most obvious area requiring an ecological perspective is water quality. The emerging water quality problems derive from the application of pesticides and fertilizers which can produce contamination over very wide areas. They derive from non-point sources which are difficult to control (OECD 1986). The epidemiological effects of these pollutants are different from the dramatic and visible enteric diseases that swept through the conurbations of nineteenth-century Europe. Often the effects are sub-clinical and do not become evident until many years of ingestion have taken place. This lack of a clear cause and effect relationship makes integrated pollution control measures more difficult to achieve, especially in a situation where trans-national policies are essential.

An emergent issue is the use of pesticides in the developing world. Relatively little is known of the ecological pathways by which persistent organochlorine residues are cycled through tropical ecosystems (Perfect 1980). Some evidence suggests that serious problems of operator competence and education exist in the developing nations. For example, Atuma and Okor (1985:341) have noted that in Nigeria:

Applicators wear little or no protective clothing due to ignorance in the hot and sometimes humid climate.
Information from the rural areas reveals a gross misuse and abuse of pesticides in the environment, in human food and in health measures.

In the case of Nigeria, the government is guided in its environmental policy by the recommendations of the WHO and FAO. However, the implementation of these standards may not be possible in many less developed nations because of infrastructure and educational constraints. The implementation of global water quality standards will create many problems.

The agencies that exist to effect this integration have few powers to compel the relevant national authorities to implement integrated policies. Even where such authority does exist, as in the European Community, national governments can often circumvent the trans-national legislation by manipulation of the criteria and rules applied within their borders. One example of such circumvention was the UK's attempts to nullify the effects of the EEC Bathing Waters Directive by the designation of only 27 bathing waters around the UK coastline (see section 6.2.2 and Kay and McDonald 1986b). Perhaps the highest level of trans-national integration that can be expected in the pollution control area derives from agencies such as the WHO, OECD and EEC which can suggest standards and commission research to validate their advisory role. This form of 'moral' pressure is evident in the recent OECD report on water pollution by nitrates and pesticides which defines a clear set of management recommendations and research needs (OECD 1986).

### 10.1.2 Regional scale

The concepts of river basin planning, outlined in Chapter 8, offer the best models of resource integration. In this respect, the basin megasystem depicted in Fig. 8.1 provides a first attempt to define the parameters of the management task. There is a need for the type of manager who can comprehend and apply the skills and perspectives, required in the analysis of the management task, into a practical and feasible policy that is likely to solve the problem. To date, little attention has been devoted to training this cadre of 'integrators' who should be able to avoid the glaring mistakes of the past. The work of Goldsmith and Hildyard (1984, 1986a, b) and Saha and Barrow (1981) suggested that we are currently at the stage of identifying past errors in river basin planning. Isolated examples exist of successful integration between land use and water resources but the overwhelming evidence is of technocentric planning with little regard for sound ecological principles. A central reason for these errors in system management and design has been the inappropriate transfer of management models from the developed to the developing nations.

### 10.1.3 Small-scale integration

There is some evidence of integrated water resource management at the local scale in both the developed and developing world.

In Britain, the 30 years of upland catchment research, outlined in Chapters 2 and 6, are now being used in the formulation of integrated catchment use policy. The first steps have involved examinations of both water quality and quantity effects (Hornung and Newson 1986). The recent growth in collaborative, interdisciplinary and inter-agency research into the problems of acidification in the British uplands has done much to accelerate the pace of this integration. The next approach should include the modelling of catchment land-use water management interactions. Here the work of Bennett and Thomas (1982) on the Murray river catchment in Australia might offer a useful starting point. Tentative steps towards the development of expert systems as catchment management tools are being made and these offer scope for formalising the now considerable knowledge base into an integrated management model (Hornung pers. comm. 1986).

In the developing world, there has not been the same sustained collection of process information on which to build integrated management systems. In this less favoured environment, integration can be identified more in the attempts to make the control agencies relevant within the social need structures that exist in the recipient countries. The presence of organisations such as OMVS in the Senegal valley suggests a serious attempt to produce an integration of water management and rural development at the village scale (Watt 1981). However, there will seldom be unanimity on the characteristics of a 'successful' management agency in the context of a Third World state and the OMVS agency has attracted some criticism (Mounier 1986).

## 10.2 Appropriateness

The concept of appropriateness is central to the failure of water resource management systems. A project must be appropriate in the fields of:

1. technology transfer;
2. environmental standards;
3. hazard mitigation; and
4. the distribution of project benefits.

Appropriate design might range in scale from the indigenous technology hand pumps discussed by Arlosoroff *et al.* (1984) to the continental-scale water-transfer proposals such as the NAWAPA plan outlined in Chapter 4. Too often, inappropriate models have been applied in the developing world. It is for the governments of these developing nations to take greater control of the project design and implementation stages. There is little evidence that the governments of the developing nations have the will or the ability to effect such control. Even in a powerful developing nation, such as India, inappropriate large-scale water resource projects have failed on economic (Bandyopadhyay 1986), agricultural (Mishra 1986), environmental (Rao 1986) and organisational (Vriksh 1986) criteria. Dogra (1986:207, 208) suggested that the large-scale projects are inappropriate and that the

> experience with large dams has been disastrous. Yet that experience is ignored by the government, which continues to approve new dam projects despite the lessons of the past.

Dogra suggested that the Indian government's continued backing for such projects is explained by the vested interests of construction companies, senior officials and politicians. In his words:

> For politicians the 'Big Dam' brings votes and international kudos: for local contractors and foreign engineers, it means money; and for those involved in planning and implementing the project, it frequently means 'kick backs'.

India presents a host of examples where the importation of large-scale technology has led to project failure in both the colonial era and the post-1947 period. There is some evidence that external recognition of the past Indian problems has encouraged the World Bank to take a more interventionist role.

However, truly appropriate design will only result from the explicit definition of project aims which must include the requirements of the populations in the regions receiving such investment. The Centre for Science and Environment (1982:69) has commented:

> Why have the environmental costs of large dams been ignored so far? One reason is that our planners and engineers are mainly rooted in urban India. Their lives are far removed from a direct dependence on natural resources. The negative impact of such projects is mostly borne by tribals, peasants and the hill folk, whose daily lives depend closely on their immediate environment. Dr Madhav Gadgil suggests that the interests of these weaker sections of our society should be used to determine whether a project is environmentally sound and whether it will promote a balanced development process. 'If these interests are given serious consideration, we will orient ourselves towards planning for true sustainable development.'

Even defining 'these interests' can present severe difficulties to the water resource manager. With whom does he or she communicate? Tribal leaders might not always represent the views of their peoples, and they can use the powers that information about a project bestows to further their own sectional interests within the community (Centre for Science and Environment 1982:68).

The Indian example has been used here to illustrate that the reasons for project failure may not always be rooted in an inappropriate level of technology. More often, the projects are inappropriate to the social and political structure of the recipient nation. It is difficult to design a project to be appropriate for a specific culture. This suggests that the designer of appropriate projects should devote resources to studies in the fields of anthropology, sociology and political science and that this work should come before design of any physical structures.

## 10.3 Knowledge transfer

A recurring theme throughout this book has been the transfer of Western approaches and experiences from the developed north to the developing south. This problem goes to the heart of the 'appropriateness' issue since often the Western engineer is incapable of understanding the requirements of the society he is serving. Even well-intentioned, intermediate hand-pump technology may not work in the rural areas of developing nations because the designers of an installation scheme do not understand the social structure and local skill within which the simple technology must operate (Chapter 4). These problems will not be overcome by the donation of skills, time, and money from the rich north. They will only be solved when the design skill is truly indigenous and the engineers themselves come from the societies they are serving. Although a utopian model offering little immediate problem alleviation for those facing famine or drought, the training and local retention of indigenous water resource managers must be among the highest priorities for the developing nations.

It is now realised that the direct transfer of Western technology often has not worked. The establishment of the local cadre of experts in the developing nations will generate a separate body of knowledge and solutions applicable within those nations and appropriate to their needs.

## 10.4 Water resource principles

In this section the main principles of water resource management are identified. The first six principles are global and should be applied in both the developed and developing world. In addition, four further principles are presented for both nation groups.

### Global principles

1. Every water project is unique and should be treated as such. Direct transfer of experience can take place only where the project and the social and physical settings are identical. Transferability of knowledge must be tempered by a recognition of the differences in environments and the likely implications of those differences.
2. Project design should take place only after a full definition of the need structures (Chapter 8) of the recipient society.
3. The project design group should be broadly based and not drawn solely from the engineering profession. Central to the design process should be public participation.
4. Every project should be managed as a component of both the total ecological and socio-economic systems.
5. A post-audit study should be an integral part of every project. The lessons of the post-audit study should be widely distributed.
6. The sharing of project benefits both within and between groups must be agreed at the project's design stage. The allocation of benefits must be made on the basis of efficiency and equity criteria.

### Principles in the developed world

7. Water management agencies must be independently policed and must be politically and financially accountable.
8. Planning should cease to be crisis driven. Planning must be pro-active or anticipatory.
9. The comfortable alliance between the water industry and government must end. The political nature of water resource developments often encourages an uncritical attitude from governments. Failings in water resource planning must be explicitly acknowledged.

10. Circumspection must be exercised in the interpretation of water demand forecasts where this involves the commitment of finance and manpower well in advance of the expected needs.

## Developing world principles

11. The principles, techniques and skills of the Western world are not automatically applicable in the Third World.
12. The scale of the problems addressed by water managers in the developing world are orders of magnitude different from those in the developed nations and must be so recognised.
13. The priority afforded to water resource development must be increased. Effective industrial or rural development should proceed from a strong water resource base.
14. Control of project design and implementation must be taken by the developing nations.

Perhaps the best description of the use of the hydrological cycle comes from the words of the Holy Qu'ran:

> We send down pure water from the sky,
> That with it we may give
> life to a dead land,
> and slake the thirst
> of things We have created,
> cattle and men in great numbers.
>
> And We have distributed
> The (water) amongst them, in order
> that they may celebrate
> (Our) praises, but most men
> Are averse (to aught) but
> (Rank) ingratitude.
>
> (The Holy Qu'ran Sura xxv.48–50)

Societies' use and misuse of resources create the issues that this book has addressed. We would concur with Beck (1985:92) on the main issue in resource management that:

> The real issue is who is deciding what the issues are to be.

# References

Aagaard, K. and Coachman, L. K. (1975) Toward an ice-free Arctic ocean, *Transactions of the American Geophysical Union* **56**, 484–6.

Abrams, L. W. and Barr, J. L. (1974) Corrective taxes for pollution control: an application of the environmental pricing and standards systems to agriculture, *Journal of Environmental Economics and Management* **1**, 12–19.

Ackerman, W. C. (1966) *Guidelines for Research on Hydrology of Small Watersheds*, United States Department of the Interior, Office of Water Resources Research No. 26.

Afriyie, E. K. (1973) Resettlement agriculture: an experiment in innovation, in Ackerman, W. C., White, G. F. and Worthington, E. F. (eds) *Man-made Lakes: Their Problems and Environmental Effects*, American Geophysical Union, Washington, DC, pp. 726–9.

Airey, D. and Jones, P. D. (1982) Mercury in the Mersey, *Water Research* **17**, 565–77.

Akintola, F. O., Areola, O. and Faniran, A. (1980) The elements of quality and social costs in rural water supply and utilisation, *Water Supply and Management* **4**, 275–82.

Albrecht, F. (1960) Jahreskarten des Warme- und Wasserhaushaltes der Ozeane, *Ber. Dt. Wd.* 9. Nr 66. 19S. Offenbach.

Amarteifio, G. (1965) *Proceedings of the Volta Resettlement Symposium*, Volta River Authority, Accra, Ghana, pp. 38–85.

Ames, B. N., McCann, J. and Yamasaki, E. (1975) Methods of detecting carcinogens and mutagens with the Salmonella/Mammalian-microsome mutagenicity test, *Mutation Research* **31**, 347–64.

Amivan, R. (1975) The water supply to Israelite Jerusalem, in *Jerusalem Revealed, Archaeology in the Holy City 1968–1974*, The Israel Exploration Society and Shikoma Publishing Company, pp. 75–8.

Andrews, C. D. (1979) The mosaic that turned into a unified industry, *Water* **25**, 24–8.

Anglian Water (1986) *Annual Report and Accounts 1985/6*, Anglian Water Authority, Huntingdon, 44 pp.

Anon (1980) The UK nitrates 'timebomb' – fact or fiction, *World Water*, Dec., 21–5.

Anon (1985) Anglian Water Authority counts cost of nitrate reduction, *Water Bulletin* **170** (August), 5.

APHA (American Public Health Association) (1975) *Standard Methods for the Examination of Water and Wastewater*, 14th edn, APHA, Washington, DC, 964pp.

Appu, P. S. (1974) The bamboo tubewell a low cost device for exploiting ground water, *Economic and Political Weekly* **9**, 63–5.

Arlosoroff, S., Grey, D., Journey, W., Karp, A., Langenbenegger, O., Rosenhall, L. and Tschannerl, G. (1984) *Rural Water Supply Hand Pumps Project*, Technical Paper No. 29, World Bank, Washington, DC, 399pp.

Arnell, N. W. (1984) Flood hazard management in the United States and the National Flood Insurance Program, *Geoforum* **15(4)**, 525–42.

Atkinson, B. W. (1974) The atmosphere, in Bowen, D. Q. (ed.) *A Concise Physical Geography*, Hulton, London, pp. 1–76.

Atuma, S. S. and Okor, D. I. (1985) Pesticide usage in Nigeria, *Ambio* **14(6)**, 340–1.

Auer, P. (1981) *Energy and the Developing Nations*, Pergamon, London.

Baird, R. J., Gute, C., Jacks, R., Jenkins, L., Neisess, B., Scheybeler, R. and Yanko, W. (1980) Health effects of water reuse: a combination of toxicological and chemical methods for assessment, in Jolley, R. L., Brungs, W. A. and Cumming, R. B. (eds), *Water Chlorination: Environmental Impact and Health Effects*, Ann Arbor Science Publishers, Michigan, pp. 925–35.

Baker, A. (1985a) Water tests at beaches under fire, *Toronto Globe and Mail*, 27 May 1985.

Baker, A. (1985b) Pollution warnings posted on beaches, *Toronto Globe and Mail*, 19 July 1985.

Baker, K. M. (1983) Fish farming in the Senegal river region, *Geography* **68(4)**, 350–3.

Baker, R. A. (1983) Taste and odour in water, in Greeson, P. E. (ed.) *Organic Substances in Water*, United States Geological Survey Circular 848–6, pp. 5–10.

Bandyopadhyay, J. (1986) The economics of large dams in India, in Goldsmith, E. E. and Hildyard, N. (eds) *The Social and Environmental Effects of Large Dams*, Wadebridge Ecological Centre, UK, pp. 209–13.

Barabas, S. (1986) Monitoring natural waters for drinking water quality, *World Health Statistics Quarterly* **39(1)**, 32–45.

Barrow, G. I. (1981) Microbial pollution of waste and estuaries: the public health implications, *Water Pollution Control* **80(2)**, 221–30.

Bates, C. G. and Henry, A. J. (1928) Forest and streamflow experiment at Wagon Wheel Gap, Colo. Final report on the completion of the second phase of the experiment, *Monthly Weather Review Supplement* **30**, 79pp.

Batterbee, R. W., Flower, R. J., Stevenson, A. C. and Rippey, B. (1985) [210] Dating of Scottish lake sediments, afforestation and accelerated eutrophication, *Nature* **314**, 350–2.

Baumgartner, A. and Reichel, E. (1975) *The World Water Balance*, Elsevier, Munich, 179pp.

Beamish, R. J. (1976) Acidification of lakes in Canada by acid precipitation and the resulting effects on fisheries, *Water Air and Soil Pollution* **6**, 501–14.

Beamish, R. J. and Harvey, H. H. (1972) Acidification of the La Cloche mountain lakes, Ontario, and resulting fish mortalities, *Journal of the Fish Resources Board of Canada* **29**, 1131–43.

Beaumont, P. (1978) Man's impact on river systems: a world view, *Area* **10**, 38–41.

Beaumont, P. (1985) Irrigated agriculture and groundwater mining on the high plains of Texas, *Environmental Conservation* **5(12)**, 119–30.

Beck, M. B. (1985) *Water Quality Management: a Review of the Development of Mathematical Models*, Springer-Verlag, New York, 120pp.

Bennett, D. and Thomas, J. F. (eds) (1982) *On Rational Grounds: Systems Analysis in Catchment Land Use Planning*. Elsevier Scientific Publishing Company, Amsterdam, 362pp.

Bennet, G. (1970) Bristol floods 1968, controlled survey of effects on health of local community disaster, *British Medical Journal* **3**, 454–8.

Bennett, W. J. and Mitchell, B. (1983) Floodplain management: land acquisition versus preservation of historic buildings in Cambridge, Ontario, Canada, *Environmental Management* **7(4)**, 327–37.

Berezner, A. A. and Ereshko, F. I. (1980) Co-ordination of models in software systems for large scale water resource projects, *Water Supply and Management* **4**, 253–62.

Berger, B. P. and Divorsky, P. (1977) Water pollution control, *EOS* **58**, 16–28.

Beyer, J. L. (1957) *Integration of Grazing and Crop Agriculture: Resource Management*

References

*Problems in the Uncompahgre Valley Irrigation Project*, University of Chicago Department of Geography.

Binns, W. O. and Redfern, D. B. (1983) *Acid Rain and Forest Decline in West Germany*, Forestry Commission Research and Development Paper No. 131, Edinburgh.

Bishop, A. B. and Hendricks, D. W. (1974) Analysis of water re-use alternatives in an integrated urban and agricultural area, in de Neufville, R. and Marks, D. H. (eds) *Systems Planning and Design*, Prentice Hall, Englewood Cliffs, pp. 169–89.

Biswas, A. K. (1972) *A History of Hydrology*, North Holland, Amsterdam.

Biswas, A. K. (ed.) (1978) *Water Development, Supply and Management Vol. 2*, United Nations Water Conference Summary and Main Documents, Pergamon, London, 217pp.

Biswas, M. R. and Biswas, A. K. (1975) Environmental impacts of increasing the world's food production, *Agriculture and Environment* 2, 281–309.

Black, R. H. (1975) Human ecological factors of significance, in Stanley, N. F. and Alpers, M. P. (eds) *Man Made Lakes and Human Health*, Academic Press, London, pp. 363–73.

Blackie, J. R. and Newson, M. D. (1985) *The Effects of Forestry on the Quantity and Quality of Runoff in Upland Britain*, Paper No. 26, WRC/WHO conference on the effects of land use on fresh waters, Stirling University, July 1985.

Bland, A. (1985) *Peak Demand Forecasting*, mimeographed paper presented at the Water Demand Forecasting Workshop, 12 July 1985, University of Leicester, UK, 6pp.

Blum, D. and Feachem, R. G. (1983) Measuring the impact of water supply and sanitation investments on diarrhoeal diseases: problems, *International Journal of Epidemiology* 12(13), 357–64.

Boulton, P. (1986) Mozambique's Cabora Bassa Project on environmental assessment, in Goldsmith, E. and Hildyard, N. (eds) *The Social and Environmental Effects of Large Dams*, Vol. 2, Wadebridge Ecological Centre, UK, pp. 156–67.

Bowden, C. (1971) *Killing the Hidden Waters*, University of Texas Press, 174pp.

Bourne, P. (1980) Improving the quality of life, *Water* (Nov.), 2–4.

Bradley, D. J. (1977) The health implications of irrigation schemes and man-made lakes in tropical environments, in Feachem, R., McGarry and Mara, D. (eds) *Water Wastes and Health in Hot Climates*, Wiley, London, pp. 18–29.

Bradley, P., Raynault, C. and Torrealba, J. (1977) *The Guidimaka Region of Mauritania*, War on Want, UK, 151pp.

Braekke, F. H. (ed.) (1976) *Impact of Acid Precipitation on Forest and Freshwater Ecosystems in Norway*, Research Report No. 6, SNSF project, Oslo, Norway, 111pp.

Briscoe, J. (1984a) Intervention studies and the definition of dominant transmission routes, *American Journal of Epidemiology* 120(3), 449–55.

Briscoe, J. (1984b) Water supply and health in developing countries: selective primary health care revisited, *American Journal of Public Health* 74(9), 1009–13.

Brown, L. (1985) *State of the World*, W. W. Norton and Co., New York, 301pp.

Buchanan, B. G. (1982) New research on expert systems, *Machine Intelligence* 10, 269–99.

Budyko, M. I. (1963) *Atlas of Heat Balance of the Earth. Vol. 5*, Moscow.

Budyko, M. I. (1970) *The Water Balance of the Oceans*, International Association for Scientific Hydrology, Publication No. 92, pp. 24–33.

Bumstead, J. C. (1979) The politics of regionalization: a public perspective, *Journal of the American Water Works Association* 71(12), 708–12.

Burby, R. J., Kaiser, E. J., Miller, T. L. and Moreau, D. H. (1983) *Drinking Water Supplies: Protection Through Watershed Management*, Ann Arbor Science, Michigan, 273pp.

Burk, D. (1980) *Cancer Mortality Linked with Artificial Fluoridation in Birmingham, England*, Paper presented at the 4th International Symposium on the Prevention and Detection of Cancer, Wembley, England, July 1980.

Burke, W. (1963) Drainage of Blanket Peat on Glen Amoy. *Proceedings of the 2nd International Peat Congress. Leningrad.*

248

Burton, I. and Kates, R. W. (1965) *Readings in Resource Management and Conservation*. Chicago University Press, Chicago.

Burton, I. (1970) Flood damage reduction in Canada, in Nelson, J. G. and Chambers, M. J. (eds) *Water*. Methuen, London.

Busenberg, E. and Langway, S. C. (1979) Levels of ammonia, sulphate, chloride, calcium and sodium in snow and ice from Southern Greenland, *Journal of Geophysical Research C84*, 1705–8.

Cabelli, V. J. (1977) Indicators of recreational water quality, in Hoadley, A. W. and Dutka, B. J. (eds) *Bacterial Indicators/Health Hazards Associated with Water*, American Society for Testing and Materials, pp. 222–38.

Cabelli, V. J. (1979) Evaluation of recreational water quality: the E.P.A. approach, in James, A. and Evison, L. (eds) *Biological Indicators of Water Quality*, Wiley, Chichester, Chapter 14.

Cabelli, V. J. (1980) *Health Effects Criteria for Marine Recreational Waters*, Report E.P.A.-600/1-80-031, Environmental Protection Agency, Cincinnati, Ohio.

Cabelli, V. J., Dufour, A. P., McCabe, L. J. and Levin, M. A. (1982) Swimming associated gastroenteritis and water quality, *American Journal of Epidemiology* **115(4)**, 606–16.

Cabelli, V. J., Dufour, A. P., McCabe, L. J. and Levin, M. A. (1983) A marine recreational water quality criterion consistent with indicator concepts and risk analysis, *Journal of the Water Pollution Control Federation* **55**, 1306–14.

Cabelli, V. J., Levin, M. A., Dufour, A. P. and McCabe, L. J. (1975) The development of criteria for recreational waters, in Gameson, A. L. H. (ed.) *Discharge of Sewage from Sea Outfalls*, Pergamon, Oxford, pp. 63–74.

Cain, H. C. (1968) *A Soil-Erosion–Reforestation Study of the Beach River Watershed. Henderson County, Tennessee*, Beach River Watershed Development Authority and Tennessee Valley Authority, 16pp.

Cairncross, S., Carruthers, I., Curtis, D., Feachem, R., Bradley, D. and Baldwin, G. (1980) *Evaluation for Village Water Supply Planning*, John Wiley, Chichester, 179pp.

Cairo, P. R., Lee, R. G., Aptowiez, B. S. and Blankenship, W. M. (1979) Is your chlorine safe to drink, *Journal of the American Water Works Association* **71**, 450–4.

Calder, I. R. (1979) Do trees use more water than grass, *Water Services* **83**, 11–14.

Calder, I. R. and Newson, M. D. (1979) Land use and upland water resources in Britain – a strategic look, *Water Resources Bulletin* **15(6)**, 1628–39.

Calder, I. R., Newson, M. D. and Walsh, P. D. (1982) *The Application of Catchment, Lysimeter and Hydrometeorological Studies of Coniferous Afforestation in Britain to Land Use Planning and Water Management*, International Association of Scientific Hydrology, Berne Symposium, 22 September, Vol. 3, pp. 853–63.

Canadian Forestry Service (1985) *The Potential Impact of the Long Range Transport of Air Pollutants on Canadian Forests*, Information report E-X-36, Economics Branch, Canadian Forest Service, 43pp.

Canadian Government (1981) *Still Waters*, a report by the House of Commons sub-committee on acid rain, House of Commons, Ottawa, Canada.

Canadian Government (1985) *Time Lost: a Demand for Action on Acid Rain*, a report by the House of Commons sub-committee on acid rain, House of Commons, Ottawa, Canada.

Canadian Government (1986) House of Commons Issue No. 7, *Minutes of Proceedings and Evidence of the Special Committee on Acid Rain*, Canadian Government Publishing Centre, Ottawa, Canada.

Cano, G. J. (1985) Legal and administrative tools for river basin development, in Lundqvist, J., Lohm, U. and Falkenmark, M. (eds) *Strategies for River Basin Management: Environmental Integration of Land and Water in a River Basin*, D. Reidel Publishing Company, Lancaster, pp. 189–200.

CAS (Centre for Agricultural Strategy) (1980) *Strategy for the U.K. Forest Industry*, CAS Report No. 6, Reading, UK.

249

# References

Casey, H. and Clarke, R. T. (1979) Statistical analysis of nitrate concentrations from the river Frome (Dorset) for the period 1965–76, *Freshwater Biology* **9**, 91–7.

Centre for Science and Environment (1982) *The State of India's Environment 1982: a Citizen's Report*, Centre for Science and Environment, New Delhi, 192pp.

Chadwick, M. J. (1983) Acid deposition and the environment, *Ambio* **12(2)**, 80–3.

Chilver, R. C. (1974) Forms of organisation, in Funnel, B. M. and Hey, R. D. (eds) *The Management of Water Resources in England and Wales*, Saxon House, Farnborough, UK, pp. 133–57.

Chisholm, M. (1982) *Modern World Development: a Geographical Perspective*, Hutchinson University Library, 216pp.

Chow, V. T. (1956) *Hydrologic Studies of Floods in the United States*, International Association for Scientific Hydrology Publication 42, pp. 134–70.

Churchill, R. K. and Hutchins, D. W. (1984) Flood hazards in Ratnapura, Sri Lanka – individual attitudes vs collective action, *Geoforum* **15(4)**, 517–24.

Clapp, G. R. (1955) *The T.V.A.: an Approach to the Development of a Region*, Chicago University Press, Chicago, 206pp.

Clarke, K. F. (1980) Forecasting methods and forecasts in England and Wales, in ICE, *Water Resources a Changing Strategy*, Institution of Civil Engineers, London, pp. 41–7.

Clarke, R. T. and Newson, M. D. (1978) Some detailed water balance studies of research catchments, *Proceedings of the Royal Society, London, Series A 363*, 21–42.

Claussen, P. (1978) From O.A.T.D.'s director, *T.V.A. Tributary Area Development Newsletter* **2(3)**, 15.

Clay, E. J. (1980) The economics of the bamboo tubewell, *Ceres* **13(3)**, 43–7.

Clay, E. J. (1982) Technical innovation and public policy: agricultural development in the Kosi region, Bihar, India, *Agricultural Administration* **9**, 189–210.

Coltruvo, J. A., Simmon, V. F. and Spanggord, R. J. (1978) Investigation of mutagenic effects of products of ozonation reactions in water, *Annals of the New York Academy of Sciences* **298**, 124–40.

Comly, H. R. (1945) Cyanosis in infants caused by nitrates in well waters, *Journal of the American Medical Association* **129**, 112–16.

Commoner, B. (1977) Cost–risk–benefit analysis of nitrogen fertilization: a case history, *Ambio* **6**, 157–61.

Congress (1935) *Act of Congress*, Publication No. 17–73D, US Government Printing Office, Washington, DC.

Consumers' Association (1986) Troubled waters, *Which* (Nov), 494–7.

Conway, V. and Miller, A. (1960) The hydrology of some small peat covered catchments in the Northern Pennines, *Journal of the Institute of Water Engineers* **14**, 415–24.

Cook-Mozaffari, P., Bulusus, L. and Doll, R. (1981) Fluoridation of water supplies and cancer mortality. I A search for an effect in the U.K. on risk of death from cancer, *Journal of Epidemiology and Community Health* **35**, 227–32.

Cook-Mozaffari, P. and Doll, R. (1981) Fluoridation of water supplies and cancer mortality. II Mortality trends after fluoridation, *Journal of Epidemiology and Community Health* **35**, 233–8.

Cooper, E. M. (1973) Iceberg farming: a new supply of fresh water, *Ocean Industry* **8(3)**, 28–9.

Coulston, F. and Mrak, E. (eds) (1977) *Water Quality*, Academic Press, London, 295pp.

Courtney, R. G. (1976) A multinomial analysis of water demand, *Building and Environment* **11**, 203–9.

Craine, L. E. (1969) *Water Management Innovations in England and Wales*, John Hopkins Press, Baltimore.

Crawford, C. (1982) Manager of Power Information, TVA, Personal communication, 14 October 1982.

Crow, B. (1985) The making and breaking of agreement on the Ganges, in Lundqvist, J.,

Luhm, U. and Falkenmark, M. (eds) *Strategies for River Basin Management: Environmental Integration of Land and Water in a River Basin*, D. Reidel Publishing Company, Lancaster, pp. 255–64.

Cuena, J. (1983) The use of simulation models and human advice to build an expert system for the defence and control of river floods, in Bundy, A. (ed.) *Proceedings of the Eighth International Joint Conference on Artificial Intelligence*, Karlruhe, West Germany, pp. 246–9.

Cvjetanovic, B. (1986) Health effects and impacts of water supply and sanitation, *World Health Statistics Quarterly* **39(1)**, 105–17.

Daglish, J. (1979) Third world energy strategies, *Atom* **274**, 207–10.

Dahlberg, P. (1981) *Beyond the Green Revolution*, Cambridge University Press.

d'Arge, R. C. and Kneese, A. V. (1980) State liability for international environmental degradation. Economic perspective. *Natural Resources Journal* **26**, 427–50.

David, L. (1985) River basin development strategies in the Tisza valley, in Lundqvist, J., Lohm, U. and Falkenmark, M. (eds) *Strategies for River Basin Management: Environmental Integration of Land and Water in a River Basin*, D. Reidel Publishing Company, Lancaster, pp. 19–30.

Davidson, D. A. (1978) *Science for Physical Geographers*, Edward Arnold, 187pp.

Davis, J. R. and Nanninga, P. M. (1985) GEOMYCIN: towards a geographic expert system for resource management, *Journal of Environmental Management* **21**, 377–90.

Davis, J. R., Hoare, J. R. L. and Nanninga, P. M. (1987) Developing a fire management expert system for Kakadu National Park, *Journal of Environmental Management* (in press).

Day, J. C. (1978) International aquifer management: the Hueco Bolson on the Rio Grande River, *Natural Resources Journal* **18**, 163–80.

Deck, F. L. O. (1986) Community water supplies and sanitation in developing countries 1970–1990, an evaluation of the levels and trends of service, *World Health Statistics* **39(1)**, 2–31.

D'itri, F. M. (ed.) (1982) *Acid Precipitation: Effects on Ecological Systems*, Ann Arbor Science, Michigan, 506pp.

DoE (Department of the Environment) (1985a) Survey of U.K. coastal bathing waters, *Environment News Release* No. 625, 18.12.85, 13pp.

DoE (Department of the Environment) (1985b) Survey of South West coastal bathing waters, *Environment News Release* No. SW 143, 23.12.85, 4pp.

Dogra, B. (1986) The Indian experience with large dams, in Goldsmith, E. E. and Hildyard, N. (eds) *The Social and Environmental Effects of Large Dams*, Wadebridge Ecological Centre, UK, pp. 201–8.

Dommen, A. J. (1975) The bamboo tubewell: a note on an example of indigenous technology, *Cultural Change* **23**, 483–9.

Douglas, I. and Crabb, P. (1972) Conservation of water resources in upland Britain, *Biological Conservation* **4(2)**, 109–16.

Doviak, R. J. (1983) A survey of radar rain measurement techniques, *Journal of Climate and Applied Meteorology* **22(5)**, 832–49.

Downs, A. (1972) Up and down with ecology – the 'issue attention cycle', *Public Interest* **28**, 38–50.

Drablos, D. and Tollan, A. (eds) (1980) *Ecological Impact of Acid Precipitation*, SNSF Project, Oslo, 383pp.

Dragun, A. K. (1983) Hydro-electric development and wilderness conflict in South West Tasmania, *Environmental Conservation* **10(3)**, 197–204.

Drosdov, O. A. (1964) *Siche*, Atlas Mira.

Dufour, A. P. (1982) *Fresh Recreational Water Quality and Swimming Associated Illness*, Second National Symposium on Municipal Wastewater Disinfection, Orlando, Florida, 26–28 January, 21pp.

Dufour, A. P. (1982) Disease outbreaks caused by drinking water, *Journal of the Water*

References

*Pollution Control Federation* (June), 980–3.

Dufour, A. P. (1984) Bacterial indicators of recreational water quality, *Canadian Journal of Public Health* **75**, 49–56.

Eagleson, A. (1986) The emergence of global scale hydrology, *Water Resources Research* **22(9)**, 6–14.

Edeson, J. F. B. (1975) Filariasis, in Stanley, N. F. and Alpers, M. D. (eds) *Man Made Lakes and Human Health*, Pergamon, London, pp. 51–6.

Edmunds, W. M. and Walton, N. R. G. (1982) The Lincolnshire limestone: hydrogeochemical evolution over a ten year period, *Journal of Hydrology* **61**, 201–11.

Edwards, A. M. C. (1987) Some problems of catchment management experienced in Yorkshire Water Authority, in Kay, D. and McDonald, A. T. (eds) *British Upland Catchment Research*, mimeographed, 156pp.

Edwards, K. A. and Rodda, J. C. (1972) A preliminary study of the water balance of a small clay catchment, *Symposium of Wellington: Results of Research on Representative and Experimental Basins*, IASH Publication No. 97, pp. 187–99.

EEC (European Economic Community) (1975) Council directive of 16.6.75 concerning the quality of water intended for abstraction of drinking water in the member states, *Official Journal of the European Communities* L194/26.

EEC (European Economic Community) (1976) Council directive of 8.12.75 concerning the quality of bathing waters, *Official Journal of the European Communities* 31/1–31/7.

EEC (European Economic Community) (1978) Council directive of 18.7.78 on the quality of fresh waters needing protection or improvement in order to support fish life, *Official Journal of the European Communities* L222/1.

El Ashray, M. T. (1980) Groundwater salinity problems related to irrigation in the Colorado river basin, *Groundwater* **18(1)**, 37–45.

El-Hinnawi, E. E. (1980) The state of the Nile environment: an overview, in Kassas, M. and Ghabbour, S. I. (eds) *The Nile and its Environment*, Pergamon, London, pp. 1–12.

Elliot, C. M. (1981) Forward, in Saha, S. K. and Barrow, C. J. (eds) *River Basin Planning*, Wiley, London, 258pp.

Ellsworth, S. (1984) *Acid Rain*, Pluto Books, London, 154pp.

Environment Canada (1984a) *Acid Rain: the Canadian Perspective*, Environment Canada, Ottawa, 15pp.

Environment Canada (1984b) *Acid Rain Milestones*, Environment Canada, Ottawa, 6pp.

Esrey, S. A. (1985) Interventions in the control of diarrhoeal diseases among children: improving water supplies and excreta disposal facilities, *Bulletin of the World Health Organization* **63(4)**, 757–72.

Evans, D. (1978) *Western Energy Policy*, Macmillan Press, London.

Evison, L. M. (1985) Bacterial pollution of coastal waters in the U.K. and Mediterranean, *Society for Applied Bacteriology Seminar Series No. 14*, 81–94.

Falkenmark, M. (1981) Integrated view of land and water: the new cornerstone of integrated planning, *Geographiska Annaler* **63A**, 3–4.

Falkenmark, M. (ed.) (1982) *Rural Water Supply and Health*, Scandinavian Institute for African Studies, Uppsala, 118pp.

Falkenmark, M. (1984) New ecological approach to the water cycle: ticket to the future, *Ambio* **13(3)**, 152–60.

Falkenmark, M. (1985) Integration in the river basin context, *Ambio* **14(2)**, 118–20.

Falkenmark, M. (1986a) Freshwater: a time for a modified approach, *Ambio* **15(4)**, 192–200.

Falkenmark, M. (1986b) Global resources and international conflict, in Westing, A. (ed.) Stockholm International Peace Research Institute, Stockholm.

Falkenmark, M. and Lindh, G. (1974) How can we cope with the water resource situation in the year 2015?, *Ambio* **3(4)**, 114–22.

Falkenmark, M. and Lundqvist, J. (eds) (1984) *Water for All: Coordination, Education, Participation*, Tema V Report 9, University of Linkoping, Department of Water in

Environment and Society, Sweden, 279pp.

Farinan, A., Akintola, F. O. and Okechukwv, G. C. (1977) Water resources development process and design: case study of the Oshun river catchment, in Farinan, A. and Mabogunje, A. L. (eds) *Regional Planning and National Development in Tropical Africa*, Ibidan University Press, Ibidan, pp. 202–11.

Feachem, R. G. (1976) An improved role for faecal coliform to faecal streptococci ratio in the differentiation between human and non-human pollution sources, *Water Research* **9**, 689–90.

Feachem, R. G. (1977) Infectious disease related to water supply and excreta disposal facilities, *Ambio* **6(1)**, 55–8.

Feachem, R. G. (1978) Domestic water supplies, health and poverty: a brief review, in Biswas, A. K. (ed.) *Water Development Supply and Management Vol. 7 Water and Society Conflicts in Development*, Pergamon, London, pp. 351–62.

Feachem, R. G. (1980) Bacterial standards for drinking water quality in developing countries, *The Lancet* (2 August), 225–56.

Feachem, R. G. (1984) Intervention for the control of diarrhoel diseases among young children: promotion of personal hygiene, *Bulletin of the World Health Organization* **62(3)**, 467–76.

Fleckseder, H. (1981) Multi-objective decision making in water management, *Water Science and Technology* **13(3)**, 115–28.

Fleuret, P. (1985) The social organisation of water control in the Taita Hills, Kenya, *American Ethnology* **12(1)**, 103–18.

Forbes, R. J. (1956) Power in Singer, C., Holmyard, E., Hall, A. and Williams, T. (eds) *A History of Technology Vol. II*, Oxford University Press, pp. 589–622.

Forestry Commission (1977) *The Wood Production Outlook for Britain*, Forestry Commission, Edinburgh, UK.

Forkasiewicz, J. and Margat, J. (1980) *Tableau mondial de données nationales d'économie de l'eau. Resources et Utilisations*, Département Hydrologéologie, 79 SGN 784 HYD, Orleans, France.

Foster, S. S. D. and Crease, R. I. (1974) Nitrate pollution of chalk groundwater in East Yorkshire – a hydrogeological appraisal, *Journal of the Institute of Water Engineers and Scientists* **28**, 178–94.

Foster, B. R. and Rahs, E. Y. (1985) A study of canyon dwelling goats in relation to a proposed hydroelectric development in Northern British Columbia, Canada. *Biological Conservation* **33**, 209–28.

Foulton, G., Maurin, J., Quoi, N. N. and Martin-Bouyer, G. (1983) Etude de la morbidity humaine en relation avec la pollution bacteriologique des aux de baignade en mer, *Revue Francaise des Sciences de l'Eau* **2(2)**, 121–43.

Frank, N. and Husain, S. A. (1971) The deadliest cyclone in history, *Bulletin of the American Meteorological Society* **52(6)**, 438–44.

French, R. H. and Krenkel, P. A. (1981) Effectiveness of river models, *Water Science and Technology* **13(3)**, 99–114.

Fresson, S. (1979) Public participation on village-level irrigation perimeters in the Malam region of Senegal, in Miller, D. (ed.) *Self-help and Popular Participation in Rural Water Supplies*, OECD, Paris, 149pp.

Frissel, M. J. (1977) Application of nitrogen fertilizers: present trends and projections, *Ambio* **6(2–3)**, 152–61.

Funnell, B. M. and Hey, R. D. (1978) *The Management of Water Resources in England and Wales*, Saxon House, Farnborough, UK, 162pp.

Funtowicz, S. O. and Ravetz, J. R. (1986) Policy related research: a notational framework for the expression of quantitative technical information, *Journal of the Operational Research Society* **37(3)**, 1–5.

Gallopin, G., Lee, T. R. and Nelson, M. (1980) The environmental dimension in water management: the case of the dam at Salo Grande, *Water Supply and Management* **4**,

References

224–41.

Galnoor, I. (1978) Water policy making in Israel. *Policy Analysis* **4(3)**, 339–67.

Gameson, A. L. H., Barrett, M. J. and Shewbridge, J. S. (1972) The aerobic Thames estuary, in Jenkins, S. H. (ed.) *Advances in Water Pollution Research*, Pergamon, London.

Gameson, A. L. H., Agg, A. R., Stanfield, G. and Gould, D. T. (1978) *Investigations of Sewage Discharges to Some British Coastal Waters*, Water Research Centre Reports Nos. TR67, TR68, TR193, Medmenham, Bucks, UK.

Gardiner, V. (1986) The Kielder water scheme – financial and environmental implications of demand forecasting, in Gardiner, V. and Herrington, P. (eds) *Water Demand Forecasting*, Geo Books, Norwich, pp. 119–24.

Gardiner, V. and Herrington, P. (1986) The basis and practice of water demand forecasting, in Gardiner, V. and Herrington, P. (eds) *Water Demand Forecasting*, Geo Books, Norwich, pp. 7–16.

Garvey, G. (1972) *Energy Ecology Economy*, Macmillan, London.

Gasching, J. (1982) PROSPECTOR: an expert system for mineral exploitation, in Michie, D. (ed.) *Introductory Readings in Expert Systems*, Gordon and Breach, New York, pp. 47–64.

Gasching, J., Reboth, R. and Reiter, J. (1981) *Development of a Knowledge Based Expert System for Water Resource Problems*, Stanford Research Institute, California.

Gash, J. H. C. and Stewart, J. B. (1977) Evaporation from Thetford forest during 1975, *Journal of Hydrology* **35**, 38596.

Gates, J. (1975) *Quality and Availability of Water in Westernmost Texas*, USGS Open File Report.

Gaylord, S. V. (1985) Problems of water reallocation in Colorado – America's most fully utilised river, in Lundqvist, J., Lohm, U. and Falkenmark, M. (eds) *Strategies for River Basin Management Environmental Integration of Land and Water in a River Basin*, D. Reidel Publishing Company, Lancaster, pp. 219–28.

Gee, A. and Stoner, J. H. (1985) *The Effects of Seasonal and Episodic Variations in Water Quality on the Ecology of Upland Waters in Wales*, Welsh Water Authority, Brecon, UK.

Geldreich, E. E. (1976) *Faecal Coliform and Faecal Streptococcus Density Relationships in Waste Discharges and Receiving Waters*, CRC Critical Reviews in Environmental Control, pp. 349–68.

Geldreich, E. E. and Kenner, B. A. (1969) Concepts of faecal streptococci in stream pollution, *Water Pollution Control Federation Journal* **41**, R336–R352.

Gershon, M., Duckstein, L. and McAniff, R. (1982) Multiobjective river basin planning with qualitative criteria, *Water Resources Research* **18(2)**, 193–202.

Gilbert, J. B. (1978) The California drought – out of disaster better water management, *Journal of the American Water Works Association* **70**, 79–81.

Gilli, G., Corrao, G. and Favilli, S. (1984) Concentrations of nitrates in drinking water and incidence of gastric carcinogens, *Science of the Total Environment* **34**, 35–48.

Gleser, G. C., Green, B. and Winget, C. (1981) *Prolonged Psycho-Social Effects of Disaster: a Study of Buffalo Creek*, Academic Press, New York.

Glover, H. A. (1980) Comment on Tattersall 1980, *Journal of the Institution of Water Engineers and Scientists* **34(5)**, 468–9.

Goddard, J. E. (1973) *An Evaluation of Urban Flood Plains*, American Society of Civil Engineers, Technical Memorandum No. 19, Urban Water Resources Research Program, 38pp.

Goldsmith, E. and Hildyard, N. (eds) (1984) *The Social and Environmental Effects of Large Dams Vol. I 'OVERVIEW'*, Wadebridge Ecological Centre, Cornwall, UK.

Goldsmith, E. and Hildyard, N. (eds) (1986a) *The Social and Environmental Effects of Large Dams Vol. II 'CASE STUDIES'*, Wadebridge Ecological Centre, Cornwall, UK.

Goldsmith, E. and Hildyard, N. (eds) (1986b) *The Social and Environmental Effects of*

*Large Dams Vol. III 'BIBLIOGRAPHY'*, Wadebridge Ecological Centre, Cornwall, UK.

Golubev, G. N. (1984) Economic activity, water resources and the environment: a challenge for hydrology, *Hydrological Sciences Journal* **28(1)**, 57–75.

Golubev, G. N. and Biswas, A. K. (eds) (1979) *Interregional Water Transfers: Projects and Problems*, International Institute for Applied Systems Analysis, Laxenburg, Austria, 211pp.

Gordon, D. J. and Berry, G. T. (1982) *Report to the International Joint Commission Re: Ross Dam* 2 April, 48pp.

Gordon, S. I. (1985) *Computer Modelling in Environmental Planning*, Van Nostrand, Reinhold, 222pp.

Goudie, A. (1981) *The Human Impact Man's Role in Environmental Change*, Basil Blackwell, Oxford, 316pp.

Gould, M. S. (1981) A water quality assessment of development in the Senegal river basin, *Water Resources Bulletin* **17(3)**, 466–73.

Graham, R. (1986) Ghana's Volta resettlement scheme, in Goldsmith, E. and Hildyard, N. (eds) *The Social and Environmental Effects of Large Dams Vol. II*, Wadebridge Ecological Centre, Cornwall, UK, pp. 131–9.

Grand River Implementation Committee (1982a) *Grand River Basin Water Management Study*, Grand River Implementation Committee, Ontario, 168pp.

Grand River Implementation Committee (1982b) *Grand River Basin Water Management Study: Summary and Recommendations*, Grand River Implementation Committee, Ontario, 13pp.

GRCA (Grand River Conservation Authority) (1983a) *Interim Resource Management Plan for the Grand River Watershed*, GRCA, Ontario, 120pp.

GRCA (Grand River Conservation Authority) (1983b) *Annual Report*, GRCA, Ontario, 43pp.

GRCA (Grand River Conservation Authority) (1984) *Annual Report*, GRCA, Ontario, 51pp.

Greene, L. A. (1978) Nitrates in water supply abstractions in the Anglian region: current trends and remedies under investigation, *Water Pollution Control* **77**, 478–91.

Greeson, P. E. (ed.) (1983) *Organic Substances in Water*, United States Geological Survey Circular 848-C, 19pp.

Gregory, S. (1982) Spatial analysis of Sahelian annual rainfall 1961–1980, *Arch. Met. Geoph. Boikl.* Ser. **B.** (31), 276–86.

Gregory, S. (1983) A note on mean seasonal rainfall in the Sahel, 1931–60 and 1961–80, *Geography* **68(1)**, 31–6.

Grigg, N. S. and Fleming, G. H. (1981) Water quality management in river basins: U.S. national perspective, *Water Science and Technology* **13(3)**, 31–42.

Grima, A. P. (1981) Institutional instruments for water pollution control, *GeoJournal* **5(5)**, 505–11.

Gu Heng-Yue (1986) Personal communication.

Hafele, W. (1981) *Energy in a Finite World*, Ballinger, Massachusetts.

Handmer, J. W. and Smith, D. I. (1983) Health hazards of floods: hospital admissions for Lismore, *Australian Geographical Studies* **21**, 221–30.

Hanke, S. H. (1972) Flood losses. Will they ever stop? *Journal of Soil and Water Science* **27**, 242–43.

Hardin, G. (1969) The tragedy of the commons. *Science* **162**, 1243–48.

Hare, F. K. (1983) *Climate and Desertification: a Revised Analysis*, World Climate Program Report, WCP 44, UNEP, Geneva.

Harmeson, R. H., Sollo, F. W. and Larson, T. E. (1971) The nitrate situation in Illinois, *Journal of the American Water Works Association* **63**, 303–10.

Harriman, R. (1978) Nutrient loading from fertilized forest watersheds, *Journal of Applied Ecology* **15**, 933–42.

Harriman, R. and Morrison, B. R. S. (1982) Ecology of streams draining forested and non-forested catchments in an area of central Scotland subject to acid precipitation, *Hydrobiologia* **88**, 251–63.

Harrold, T. W., English, E. J. and Nicholas, C. A. (1973) The Dee weather radar project, *Weather* **28**, 332–8.

Harrold, T. W., English, E. J. and Nicholas, C. A. (1974) The accuracy of radar derived rainfall measurements in hilly terrain, *Quarterly Journal of the Royal Meteorology Society* **100**, 331–50.

Hart, D. (1977) *The Volta River Project*, Edinburgh University Press, Edinburgh.

Hauser, D. and Amaynec, P. (1983) Exponential size of raindrops and vertical air motions deduced from vertically pointing doppler radar data using a new method, *Journal of Climate and Applied Meteorology* **22(3)**, 407–18.

Havas, M., Hutchinson, T. C. and Lickens, G. E. (1984) Red herrings in acid rain research, *Environmental Science and Technology* **18(6)**, 176–86.

Henriksen, A., Skogheim, O. K. and Rossel, B. O. (1984) Episodic changes in pH and aluminium speciation kills fish in a Norwegian salmon river, *Vatten* **40**, 255–60.

Herbert, J. R. (1985) Effects of components of sanitation on nutritional status: findings from south Indian settlements, *International Journal of Epidemiology* **14(1)**, 143–52.

Herrington, P. R. (1976) The economics of water supply and demand, *Economics* **12(2)**, 67–84.

Hill, A. R. (1978) Factors affecting the export of nitrate–nitrogen from drainage basins in Southern Ontario, *Water Research* **12**, 1045–57.

Hill, A. R. (1981) Nitrate nitrogen flux and utilization in a stream ecosystem during low summer flows, *Canadian Geographer* **15(3)**, 225–39.

Hill, A. R. (1982) Nitrate nitrogen rain balance for two Ontario rivers, in Fontaine, T. D. (ed.) *Dynamics of Lotic Ecosystems*, Ann Arbor Science, Michigan, pp. 457–77.

Hill, M. J., Hawksworth, G. and Tattersall, G. (1973) Bacteria nitrosamines and cancer of the stomach, *British Journal of Cancer* **28**, 562–7.

Hirsch, A. M. (1959) Water legislation in the Middle East, *American Journal of Comparative Law* **8**, 168.

HMSO (1948) Ministry of Health Report of the Gathering Grounds Committee, *Public Access to Gathering Grounds. Afforestation and Agriculture on Gathering Grounds*, HMSO, London.

HMSO (1969) *The Bacteriological Examination of Water Supplies*, Reports on Public Health and Medical Subjects No. 71, HMSO, London, 51pp.

HMSO (1982) *The Bacteriological Examination of Water Supplies 1982*, Reports on Public Health and Medical Subjects No. 71, HMSO, London, 111pp.

HMSO (1983) House of Lords select committee on science and technology, session 1982–3 1st report, *The Water Industry (Vol. I Report) (Vol. II Evidence)*, HMSO, London.

HMSO (1984) *Royal Commission on Environmental Pollution Tenth Annual Report*, HMSO, London.

HMSO (1985a) *Coastal Sewage Pollution in Wales Minutes of Evidence 5.12.84, Minutes of Evidence 16.1.85, Appendices to the Minutes of Evidence 30.10.85*, Committee on Welsh Affairs, House of Commons, UK, HMSO, London.

HMSO (1985b) First report from the Committee on Welsh Affairs, *Coastal Sewage Pollution in Wales Vol. I*, HMSO, London, xxviipp.

HMSO (1986) *Privatization of the Water Authorities in England and Wales*, Command Paper 9734, HMSO, London.

Hoadley, A. W. (1967) On the significance of *Pseudomonas aeruginosa* in surface water, *Journal of the New England Water Works Association*, **82**, 99–111.

Hoinkes, H. (1968) Das eis der erde, *Umschau* **68**, 301–6.

Hollobon, J. (1983) Sunnyside bathers are being warned water is polluted, *Ontario Globe and Mail* 22 July, p. 5.

Hood, A. E. M. (1982) Fertilizer trends in relation to biological productivity within the U.K., *Philosophical Transactions of the Royal Society London* **B296**, 315–28.

Hoover, R. N., McKay, F. W. and Franklin, J. F. (1976) Fluoridated drinking water and the occurrence of cancer, *Journal of the National Cancer Institute* 57, 757.

Horgan, D. (1983) Beach closings complete probe, *Ontario Globe and Mail* 24 August, p. 5.

Hornung, M. and Newson, M. D. (1986) Upland afforestation: influences on stream hydrology and chemistry, *Soil Use and Management* 2(2), 61–5.

Howard, K. W. F. (1985) Denitrification in a major limestone aquifer, *Journal of Hydrology* 76, 265–80.

Hubbard, P. J. (1961) *Origins of the T.V.A.: The Muscle Shoals Controversy, 1920–1932*, Vanderbelt University Press, Nashville, Tennessee.

Hughes, E. J. (1963) *The Ordeal of Power: A Political Memoir of the Eisenhower Years*, Atheneum, New York.

Hughes, J. P. (1964) *Industry and Tropical Health V*, proceedings of the fifth conference of the Industrial Council for Tropical Health, Boston, pp. 43–52.

Hulm, P. (1983) A dark decade ahead for acid rain, *Ambio* 12(2), 131.

Hunt, D. A. and Springer, J. (1974) *Preliminary Report on a Comparison of Total Coliform and Faecal Coliform Values in Shellfish Growing Areas and a Proposed Faecal Coliform Growing Area Standard*, paper presented at the 8th National Shellfish Sanitation Workshop Food and Drug Administration, Washington, DC.

Hurd, M. (1979) Regionalization opportunities and obstacles: a case study, *Journal of the American Water Works Association* 71(12), 713–19.

Hutchinson, T. C. (1974) *Heavy Metal Toxicity and Synergism to Floating Aquatics*, XIXth Congress of the International Association for Limnology, Winnipeg, Canada, 22–29 August.

Hutchinson, T. C. and Havas, M. (eds) (1980) *Effects of Acid Precipitation on Terrestrial Ecosystems*, Nato Conference Series I Ecology, Plenum Press, New York, 654pp.

ICE (Institution of Civil Engineers) (1981) *Water Resources a Changing Strategy*, Institution of Civil Engineers, London, 214pp.

ICF (International Canoe Federation) (1978) *Policy Statement on Recreational Water Quality for Competitive Canoeing*, ICF, Rome.

IOH (Institute of Hydrology) (1986) *An Interim Report on the Llyn Brianne Project*, October 1986, Institute of Hydrology, Wallingford, UK.

Ion, D. C. (1980) *Availability of World Energy Resources*, Graham and Trotman, London.

ITDG (Intermediate Technology Development Group) (1978) Water for the thousand million, in United Nations, *Proceedings of the United Nations Water Conference*, Pergamon, London, pp. 1105–67.

ITDG (Intermediate Technology Development Group) (1980) Guidelines on planning and management of rural water supplies in developing countries, *Appropriate Technology* 7(3), 17–20.

Ivanov, V. V. and Nikiforov, E. G. (1976) Means of estimating the possible changes in the hydrologic regime of the Kara Sea owing to interbasin river diversion [in Russian], *Tr. Arkt. Antarkt. Nauchno-Issled. Inst.* 314, 176–82.

IWE (Institute of Water Engineers) (1972) *Symposium on Advanced Techniques in River Basin Management: the Trent Model Research Programme*, Institution of Water Engineers, London, 213pp.

Jacobs, W. C. (1951) Large scale aspects of energy transformation over the ocean, *Association of Pacific Coast Geography Yearbook* 30, 63–78.

Jagerstad, M. (1977) Dietary intake of nitrate and nitrite using the duplicate-sampling portion technique, *Ambio* 6(5), 276–7.

Jayal, N. D. (1985) Destruction of water resources – the most critical ecological crisis in East Asia, *Ambio* 14(2), 95–8.

Jayaraman, T. K. (1981) A case for professionalisation of water management in irrigation projects in India, *Public Administration and Development* 1(3), 235–44.

Jenkins, A., Kirby, M. J., Naden, P., McDonald, A. T. and Kay, D. (1983) A process

References

based model of faecal bacterial levels in upland catchments, *Water Science and Technology* **16**, 453–62.

Jenkins, S. H. (ed.) (1981) New developments in river basin management, *Water Science and Technology* **13(3)**, 2–313.

Johnels, A. (1983) Conference on environmental research and management priorities for the 1980's, *Ambio* **12(12)**, 58–9.

Johnston, R. H. and Brown, G. M. (1976) *Cleaning up Europe's Waters: Economics Management and Policies*, Praeger Press, New York.

Jones, F. and White, W. R. (1984) Health and amenity aspects of surface waters, *Water Pollution Control* **83(2)**, 215–25.

Jones, F. O. (1954) Tukiangyien: China's ancient irrigation system, *Geographical Review* **44**, 543–59.

Jones, V. J., Stevenson, A. C. and Baterbee, R. W. (1986) Lake acidification and the land use hypothesis: a mid-post-glacial analogue, *Nature* **322(6075)**, 157–8.

Jordan, P. (1975) Schistosomiasis – epidemiology, clinical manifestations and control, in Stanley, N. F. and Alpers, M. P. (eds) *Man Made Lakes and Human Health*, Academic Press, London, pp. 35–50.

Julius, D. S. and Buky, J. B. (1980) Assessment of the economic contribution of water resources to national development, in ICE, *Water Resources: a Changing Strategy*, ICE, London, pp. 15–19.

Kalinin, G. P. and Bykov, V. D. (1969) The world's water resources, present and future, *Impact of Science on Society (UNESCO)* **19**, 135–50.

Kalitsi, E. A. (1973) Lake Volta in relation to human population and some issues in economics and management, in Ackermann, W. C., White, G. F. and Worthington, E. B., *Man Made Lakes: their Problems and Environmental Effects*, American Geophysical Union, Washington, DC, pp. 77–85.

Kay, D. and McDonald, A. T. (1980) Reduction of coliform bacteria in two upland reservoirs: the significance of distance decay relationships, *Water Research* **14**, 305–18.

Kay, D. and McDonald, A. T. (1982a) Management of trans-boundary water resources and implications for federal/provincial conflicts in Canada, in Cook, D. D. (ed.) *The Political Dimension of Geography*, Kingston Polytechnic, London, pp. 40–52.

Kay, D. and McDonald, A. T. (1982b) New problems with upland waters, *Water Services* **86**, 29–31.

Kay, D. and McDonald, A. T. (1983a) Predicting coliform concentrations in upland impoundments: the design and calibration of a multivariate model, *Applied and Environmental Microbiology* **46**, 611–18.

Kay, D. and McDonald, A. T. (1983b) Enteric bacterial entrainment in a recreational channel used for competitive canoeing, *Cambria* **9(2)**, 61–8.

Kay, D. and McDonald, A. T. (1985) Water resource management issues on the Great Lakes: some issues for the 1980s, in Atkinson, K. and McDonald, A. T. (eds) *Planning and the Physical Environment in Canada*, Regional Canadian Studies Centre, Leeds University School of Geography, Leeds, UK, pp. 47–72.

Kay, D. and McDonald, A. T. (1986a) Bathing water quality: the relevance of epidemiological research in the U.K. context, *European Water and Sewage Journal* **90(1085)**, 321–8.

Kay, D. and McDonald, A. T. (1986b) Bathing water quality: the significance of the 1985 Commons Welsh Affairs Committee investigation, *Journal of Shoreline Management* **1(2)**, 259–83.

Keevin, T. M. (1982) The Corp of Engineers planning process as it relates to the assessment of the environmental impacts of low head hydro-power development, in Yuan, S. W. (ed.) *Energy Resources and Environment*, Pergamon, London.

Kiely, J. R. (1981) Long term value of hydro-electric energy for developing nations, in Auer, P. (ed.) *Energy and the Developing Nations*, Pergamon, London, pp. 64–83.

Kierans, T. W. (1980) Thinking big in North America; the Grand Canal concept, *The*

*Futurist* **14(6)**, 29–32.

Kinlen, L. and Doll, R. (1981) Fluoridation of water supplies and cancer mortality. III A re-examination of mortality in cities in the U.S.A., *Journal of Epidemiology and Community Health* **35**, 239–44.

Kittredge, J. (1948) *Forest Influences*, McGraw Hill, New York.

Klepper, R. (1978) Nitrogen fertilizer and nitrate concentrations in tributaries of the upper Sagamon river, Illinois, *Journal of Environmental Quality* **7(1)**, 13–22.

Knoch, K. (1961) *Niederschlag und Temperatur (weltkarten) Welt-Suchen Atlas II 5s.*, 3K, Hamburg.

Kohl, D. H., Shearer, G. B. and Commoner, B. (1971) Fertilizer nitrogen: contribution to nitrate in surface water in a corn belt watershed, *Science* **174**, 1331–4.

Korzoun, V. I. and Sokolov, A. A. (1978) World water balance and water resources of the earth, in United Nations, *Water Development and Management Proceedings of the United Nations Water Conference, Mar del Plata, Argentina, March, 1977*, Pergamon, London, pp. 2199–215.

Kraybill, H. F. (1981) Carcinogenesis of synthetic organic chemicals in drinking water, *Journal of the American Water Works Association* **73(7)**, 370–2.

Krenkel, P. A. (1973) Mercury in the environment, *Critical Review of Environmental Control* **3(3)**, 303–73.

Krenkel, P. A. and Novotny, V. (1980) *Water Quality Management*, Academic Press, London, 671pp.

Kromm, D. (1985) Regional water management: an assessment of institutions in England and Wales, *Professional Geographer* **37(2)**, 183–91.

Krutilla, J. V. (1967) *The Columbia River Treaty: the Economics of an International River Basin Development*, John Hopkins Press, Baltimore, 211pp.

Kucera, V. (1976) Effects of sulphur dioxide and acid precipitation on metals and anti-rust painted steel, *Ambio* **5**, 243–8.

Kudo, A., Miyahara, S. and Miller, D. R. (1981) Movement of mercury from Minamata Bay into Yatsushiro Sea, *Progress in Water Technology* **12**, 509–24.

Kuhn, T. S. (1962) *The Structure of Scientific Revolutions*, International Encyclopaedia of Unified Science, University of Chicago Press.

Kunreuter, H. (1978) *Disaster Insurance Protection: Public Policy Lessons*, Wiley, New York.

Kusler, J. A. (1985) Management of flood prone areas in the United States two roles along the river – regional programmes meet national policy, *Environment* **27(7)**, 18.

La Bounty, J. F. (1982) Assessment of the environmental effects of constructing the Three Gorges Project on the Yangtze River, in Yuan, S. W. (ed.) *Energy Resources and the Environment*, Pergamon, London.

Lamb, H. H. and Morth, H. T. (1978) Arctic ice, atmospheric circulation and world climate, *Geographical Journal* **144**, 1–22.

Lambert, A. O. (1981) The River Dee regulation scheme: operation experience of on-line hydrological simulation, in Askew, A. J., Greco, F. and Kindler, J. (eds) *Logistics and Benefits of Using Mathematical Models of Hydrologic and Water Resource Systems*, Pergamon Press, Oxford, pp. 75–98.

Lang, D. R., Kurzepa, H., Cole, M. S. and Loper, J. C. (1981) Malignant transformation of BALB/BTB cells by residue organic mixtures from drinking waters, *Journal of Pathology and Experimental Toxicology* **23**, 114–120.

Lavergne, M. (1986) The seven deadly sins of Egypt's Aswan High Dam, in Goldsmith, E. E. and Hildyard, N. (eds) *The Social and Environmental Effects of Large Dams*, Wadebridge Ecological Centre, Cornwall, UK, pp. 181–3.

Law, F. (1956) The affects of afforestation upon the yield of water catchment areas, *Journal of the British Waterworks Association* **38**, 484–94.

Law, F. (1957) Measurements of rainfall, interception, and evaporation losses in a plantation of sitka spruce trees, *Proceedings of the International Association of Scientific Hydrology Conference*, Toronto, pp. 397–411.

References

Lawson, G. W. (1974) Lessons of the Volta – a new man-made lake in tropical Africa, *Biological Conservation* **2(2)**, 90–6.

Lean, G. (1983) Children near Windscale have high cancer levels, *Observer 10025* 30 August, 1.

Lear, J. (1965) The crisis in water. What brought it on? Perhaps it was man's abuse of nature and his lack of foresight, *Saturday Review* **23**, 24–80.

Lee, R. (1980) *Forest Hydrology*, Columbia University Press, New York, 349pp.

Lester, W. F. (1981) River basin management by economic measures of regulatory sanctions – national experiences, England, *Water Science and Technology* **13(3)**, 7–22.

Lewis, W. (1985) The significance of water management in relation to public and environmental health, *Journal of Applied Bacteriology Symposium Supplement No. 14*, 1S–13S.

Lightfoot, R. P. (1981) Problems of resettlement in the development of river basins in Thailand, in Saha, S. K. and Barrow, C. J. (eds) *River Basin Planning*, Wiley, Chichester, pp. 93–114.

Lilienthal, D. E. (1944) *Democracy on the March*, Harper and Brothers, New York.

Linsay, R. K., Buchanan, B. G., Feigenbaum, E. A. and Lederberg, J. (1980) *Applications of Artificial Intelligence for Organic Chemistry: the DENDRAL Project*, McGraw Hill, New York.

Lippy, E. C. (1981) Waterborne disease: occurrence is on the upswing, *Journal of the American Water Works Association* **73(1)**, 57–62.

Lippy, E. C. and Waltrip, S. C. (1984) Waterborne disease outbreaks – 1946–1980: a thirty year perspective, *Journal of the American Water Works Association* **76**, 60–7.

Lloyd, D. (1950) Discussion on Lynmouth, *Journal of the British Association* **7**, 567–9.

Loper, J. C. (1980) Mutagenic effects of organic compounds in drinking water, *Mutation Research* **76**, 241–68.

Lowe, P. D. (1975a) Science and government: the case of pollution, *Public Administration* **54**, 287–98.

Lowe, P. D. (1975b) The environmental lobby: a survey, *Built Environment Quarterly* **1**, 73–6.

Lowe, P. D. (1977) Amenity and equity: a review of local environmental pressure groups in Britain, *Environment and Planning* **B 9**, 35–58.

Lowe, P. D., Cox, G., Macewan, M., O'Riordan, T. and Winter, M. (1986) *Countryside Conflicts the Politics of Farming Forestry and Conservation*, Gower/Maurice Temple Smith, Aldershot, UK, 380pp.

Lucas, S. (1980) Charging households for water, *Water* **35**, 24–5.

Luckin, B. (1986) *Pollution and Control: a Social History of the Thames in the Nineteenth Century*, Adam Hilger, Bristol, 198pp.

Lundqvist, J., Lohm, U. and Falkenmark, M. (eds) (1985) *Strategies for River Basin Management: Environmental Integration of Land and Water in a River Basin*, D. Reidel Publishing Company, Lancaster, 346pp.

L'Vovich, M. I. (1974) *Global Water Resources and the Future*, Moscow.

L'Vovich, M. I. (1977) World water resources present and future, *Ambio* **6(1)**, 13–21.

Maass, A. (1982) *Design of Water Resource Systems*, Harvard University Press, Cambridge, Ma.

MacDonald, C. (1957) *The Epidemiology and Control of Malaria*, Oxford University Press.

MacGill, S. M. (1985) Qualifying imperfect products of science, *Environment and Planning* **A 17**, 582–4.

Mackenzie, H. G. (1984) *Expert Systems – a Case Study*, Technical Report No. 11, CSIRO, Division of Computing Science, Canberra, Australia.

MacLaren, V. W. and Whitney, J. B. (1985) *New Directions in Environmental Impact Assessment in Canada*, Methuen, Toronto, 245pp.

MacMullan, J. T., Morgan, R. and Murray, R. B. (1983) *Energy Resources*, Arnold, London.

Mageed, Y. A. (1985) Integrated river basin management: The challenges of the Nile basin countries, in Lundqvist, J., Lohm, U. and Falkenmark, M. (eds) *Strategies for River Basin Management: Environmental Integration of Land and Water in a River Basin*, D. Reidel Publishing Company, Lancaster, pp. 151–60.

McBain, H. (1985) Towards a viable water utility in Jamaica, *Social Economics* **34(1)**, 77–96.

McDermott, J. (1983) Extracting knowledge from expert systems, in Bundy, A. (ed.) *Proceedings of the Eighth International Joint Conference on Artificial Intelligence*, Karlsruhe, West Germany, pp. 100–7.

McDonald, A. T. (1973) Some views on the effects of peat drainage, *Scottish Forestry* **27(4)**, 315–27.

McDonald, A. T. (1974) *Administrative Arrangements for Water Resources in some E.E.C. Countries*, School of Geography, University of Leeds, UK, Working Paper No. 45.

McDonald, A. T. (1982) Rivers and drainage of the U.S.S.R. in *An Encyclopaedia of Russia and the U.S.S.R.*, Oxford University Press.

McDonald, A. T. and Kay, D. (1981) Enteric bacterial concentrations in reservoir feeder streams: baseflow characteristics and response to hydrograph events, *Water Research* **15**, 961–8.

McDonald, A. T. and Kay, D. (1982) *Forest Expansion and Water Resources: the Case for the Forest Industry*, Leeds University School of Geography Working Paper No. 317, 15pp.

McDonald, A. T. and Kay, D. (1984) Beach closures and water quality, *Environments* **16(1)**, 43–6.

McDonald, A. T., Kay, D. and Jenkins, A. (1982) Generation of faecal and total coliform surges by streamflow manipulation in the absence of normal hydrometeorological stimuli, *Applied and Environmental Microbiology* **44**, 292–300.

McDonald, A. T. and Ledger, D. (1981) Flood area modelling from an elementary data base, *Journal of Hydrology* **53**, 85–94.

McDonald, M. E. (1985) Acid deposition and drinking water, *Environmental Science and Technology* **19(9)**, 772–7.

McFee, W. W. (1983) Sensitivity rating of soils to acid deposition: a review, *Environmental and Experimental Botany* **23(3)**, 203–10.

Magnuson, J. J. (1982) *A Critical Assessment of Effects of Acidification on Fisheries in North America*, The Royal Society, London. A meeting for discussion. Ecological effects of deposited sulphur and nitrogen compounds, 5–7 September 1983.

Mallard, G. E. (1982) Micro-organisms in stormwater, in USGS Circular 848-E, *Microbiology of the Aquatic Environment*, pp. 23–33.

Magee, P. N. (1982) Nitrogen as a potential health hazard, *Philosophical Transactions of the Royal Society London* **B296**, 543–50.

Margat, J. and Saad, K. F. (1984) Deep lying aquifers: water mines under the desert, *Nature and Resources* **2**, 7–13.

Marsh, J. J. (1980) Towards a nitrate balance for England and Wales, *Water Services* (October.) 601–6.

Marshall, J. S. (1981) Combined effects of cadmium and zinc on a Lake Michigan zooplankton community, *Journal of Great Lakes Research* **7**, 215–20.

Martinez, P. Z. (1979) Meeting future water demands in Monterrey, Mexico, *Journal of the American Water Works Association* **71(10)**, 546–7.

MAS (Mission d'Aménagement du Fleuve Senégal) (1960) *La vallée du fleuve, Tome II*, Centre Et. Equipem. Outremer., Paris, mimeographed.

Mathur, S. P. (1986) The application of appropriate technology in the field of rural water supplies in Indonesia, *World Health Statistics Quarterly* **39(1)**, 71–80.

Mazal, A. (1975) The aqueducts of Jerusalem, in The Israeli Exploration Society, *Jerusalem Revealed: Archaeology and the Holy City 1968–1974*, Shikoma Publishing Co.

References

Meinardus, W. (1928) *Uber den Kreislauf des Wassers*,. Festrede Univ., Göttingen. Dietric'sche Univ., Buchdr.

Mendoza, A. S. (1979) Potable water in Mexico: history and problems, *Journal of the American Water Works Association* **71(19)**, 540–1.

Meyer, W. (1976) *Digital Model for Simulating Effects of Groundwater Pumping in the Hueco Bolson, El Paso Area, Texas, New Mexico, U.S.*, Geological Survey Water Resources Investigations, pp. 58–75.

Michel, A. A. (1959) *The Kabul, Kunduz and Helmand Valleys and the National Economy of Afghanistan*, National Academy of Sciences – National Research Council.

Micklin, P. P. (1977) N.A.W.A.P.A. and two Siberian water diversion proposals, *Soviet Geography: Review and Translation* **XVIII(2)**, 81–99.

Micklin, P. P. (1981) A preliminary systems analysis of impacts of proposed Soviet diversions on Arctic sea ice, *Transactions of the American Geophysical Union* **62(9)**, 489–93.

Micklin, P. P. (1984) Recent developments in large scale water transfers in the U.S.S.R., *Soviet Geography* **25(4)**, 261–3.

Micklin, P. P. (1986) Soviet river diversion plans: their possible environmental impact, in Goldsmith, E. and Hildyard, N. (eds) *The Social and Environmental Effects of Large Dams. Vol. II Case Studies*, Wadebridge Ecological Centre, Cornwall, UK, pp. 91–108.

Miettinen, J. K. (1977) Inorganic trace elements as water pollutants their implications to the health of man and aquatic biota, in Coulston, F. and Mark, E. (eds) *Water Quality*, Academic Press, London, pp. 13–136.

Mikhalov, N. I., Nikolayev, V. A. and Timashev, I. Ye. (1977) Environmental problems in relation to the diversion of the flow of Siberian rivers, *Soviet Hydrology: Selected Papers* **16(3)**, 232–5.

Miles, J. (1981) *Vegetation Dynamics*, Chapman Hall, London.

Miller, M. J. (ed.) (1977) *Schistosomiasis: Proceedings of a symposium on the future of schistosomiasis control*, Tulane University Press, New York.

Miller, J. B. and Flanders, F. (1985) Technology transfer in hydrology, in Rodda, J. C. (ed.) *Facets of Hydrology Vol II*, John Wiley, Chichester, pp. 389–411.

Mishra, A. (1986) The Tawa dam: an irrigation project that has reduced farm production, in Goldsmith, E. E. and Hildyard, N. (eds) *The Social and Environmental Effects of Large Dams*, Wadebridge Ecological Centre, UK, pp. 214–16.

Mitchell, B. (1970) The institutional framework for water management in England and Wales, *Natural Resources Journal* **10**, 566–89.

Mitchell, B. (1974) Value conflicts and water supply decisions, in Leversedge, F. (ed.) *Priorities in Water Management*, Western Geographical Series vol. 8, University of Victoria, pp. 37–59.

Mitchell, B. (1981) Comprehensive river basin management: Canadian experiences, in Atkinson, K. and McDonald, A. T. (eds) *Man and Natural Resources in Canada*, Regional Canadian Studies Centre, Leeds University, UK, pp. 21–34.

Mitchell, B. and Leighton, P. H. (1977) A comparison of multivariate and trend forecasting estimates with actual water use, *Water Resources Bulletin* **13(4)**, 817–24.

Mitchell, B. and Gardiner, J. S. (eds) (1983) *River Basin Management: Canadian Experiences*, Department of Geography, University of Waterloo, Ontario, 443pp.

Moiseev, N. N., Berezner, A. S., Ereshko, F. I. and Lotov, A. V. (1980) A systems approach to the study of interbasin water transfers: the partial diversion of the U.S.S.R.'s northern rivers flow into the Volga, *Water Supply and Management* **4**, 323–37.

Morgan, A. E. (1974) *The making of the T.V.A.*, Prometheus Books, Buffalo, New York, 205pp.

Moore, B. (1975) The case against microbial standards for bathing beaches, in Gameson, A. L. H. (ed.) *Discharge of Sewage from Sea Outfalls*, Pergamon, Oxford, pp. 103–10.

Moore, B. (1977) The EEC Bathing Waters Directive, *Marine Pollution Bulletin* **8(12)**, 269–72.

Moore, J. R. (1962) *The Economic Impact of T.V.A.*, University of Tennessee Press, Knoxville, 163pp.

Moss, M. E. and Dowdy, D. R. (1980) Supply and demand and the design of surface water supplies, *Hydrological Sciences Bulletin* **25(3)**, 283–95.

Mounier, F. (1986) The Senegal river scheme: development for whom? in Goldsmith, E. and Hildyard, N. (eds) *The Social and Environmental Effects of Large Dams. Vol. II Case Studies*, Wadebridge Ecological Centre, Cornwall, UK, pp. 109–19.

Mowli, P. P. (1980) Futurology and urban requirement of water in India, *Journal of the Indian Water Works Association* **12(3)**, 249–53.

MRC Medical Research Council (1953) *Sewage Contamination of Bathing Beaches in England and Wales*, Medical Research Council Memorandum No. 37, 32 pp.

Muckleston, K. W. (1976) The evolution of approaches to flood damage reduction, *Journal of Soil and Water Conservation* **31**, 53–9.

Murthy, K. S. S. (1979) Interregional water transfers: case study of India, in Golubev, G. N. and Biswas, A. K. (eds) *Interregional Water Transfers: Projects and Problems*, International Association for Applied Systems Analysis, Laxenburg, Austria, pp. 117–26.

Musgrave, D. C. (1979) The evolution of integrated water management in the U.K., in Blackburn, A. M. (ed.) *The Thames/Potomac Seminars, the Interstate Commission on the Potomac Basin, Rockville*, pp. 16–19.

NCC (Nature Conservancy Council) (1986) *Nature Conservation in Britain*, NCC, Peterborough, UK, 108pp.

Nemec, J. and Kite, G. W. (1979) Mathematical model of the upper Nile basin, in Askew, A. J., Greco, F. and Kindler, J. (eds) *Logistics and Benefits of Using Mathematical Models of Hydrologic and Water Resource Systems*, pp. 167–78.

NEPA (National Environment Policy Act) (1969) Congress, Dec.

NERC (Natural Environment Research Council) (1975) *Flood Studies Report*, 5 vols, NERC, Wallingford, UK.

Netboy, A. (1986) The damming of the Columbia River: the failure of bioengineering, in Goldsmith, E. and Hildyard, N. (eds) *The Social and Environmental Effects of Large Dams. Vol. II Case Studies*, Wadebridge Ecological Centre, Cornwall, UK, pp. 33–48.

Netschert, B. C. (1967) Electric power and economic development, in Moore, J. R. (ed.) *The Economic Impact of T.V.A.*, University of Tennessee Press, Knoxville, pp. 1–23.

Neufville, de R. (1974) Systems analysis of large scale public facilities: New York's city water supply as a case study, in Neufville, de R. and Marks, D. H. (eds) *Systems Planning and Design*, Prentice Hall, Englewood Cliffs, pp. 30–47.

Newson, M. D. (1976) *The Physiography, Deposits and Vegetation of the Plynlimon Catchments*, Natural Environment Research Council, Institute of Hydrology Report No. 30, Wallingford, UK.

Newson, M. D. (1979) The results of ten years experimental study at Plynlimon, Mid Wales and their importance for the water industry, *Journal of the Institution of Water Engineers and Scientists* **33**, 321–33.

Newson, M. D. (1982) *Concepts of Management – Surface Water; the Example of the British Uplands*, NATO Seminar on Land and its Uses, 22 September, Edinburgh.

Newson, M. D. (1983) *Upland Reservoir Catchments – Towards Multiple Resource Planning*, Welsh Conservation Conference, Cardiff, pp. 265–72.

Nicholson (1979) Revised rainfall for the West African sub tropics, *Monthly Weather Review* **197(5)**, 620–3.

Nijhoff, P. (1979) Lake Biakal endangered by pollution, *Environmental Conservation* **6(2)**, 111–15.

Norman, C. (1976) Tennessee valley energy, *Nature* **262**, 732–4.

Norris, G. W. (1961) *Fighting Liberal: the Autobiography of George W. Norris*, Collier, New York.

References

North West Water (1986) *12th Annual Report and Accounts*, North West Water Authority, Warrington, UK, 23pp.

Norton, C. C., Mosher, F. K. and Hunton, B. (1979) A recent investigation of surface albedo variations during the recent Sahel drought, *Journal of Applied Meteorology* **18**, 1252–62.

NRC (National Research Council) (1986) *Ecological Knowledge and Environmental Problem Solving: Concepts and Case Studies*, National Academy Press, Washington, DC, 388pp.

NWC (National Water Council) (1981) *Thirsty Third World*, National Water Council, 42pp.

Obeng, L. E. (1973) Volta lake: physical and biological aspects, in Ackermann, W. C., White, G. F. and Worthington, E. B. (eds) *Man-Made Lakes their Problems and Environmental Effects*, American Geophysical Union, Washington, DC, pp. 87–98.

Obeng, L. E. (1975) Health problems of the Volta lake ecosystem, in Stanley, N. F. and Alpers, M. P., *Man-Made Lakes and Human Health*, Pergamon, London, pp. 221–30.

Obeng, L. E. (1980a) Water in the environment: the U.N.E.P. experience, *Water Supply and Management* **4**, 155–70.

Obeng, L. E. (1980b) Some environmental issues in water for development, *Water Supply and Management* **4**, 115–28.

Obeng, L. E. (1983) The control of pathogens from human wastes and their aquatic vectors, *Ambio* **12(2)**, 106–8.

O'Donnell, A. R., Mance, G. and Norton, P. (1983) *A Review of the Toxicity of Aluminium in Fresh Water*, Water Research Centre, Stevenage, 37pp.

Odum, E. P. (1971) *Fundamentals of Ecology*, 2nd edn, Saunders, Philadelphia.

OECD (Organisation for Economic Cooperation and Development) (1972) *Water Management Basic Issues*, OECD, Paris, 546pp.

OECD (Organisation for Economic Cooperation and Development) (1977) *The Long Range Transport of Air Pollutants: Measurements and Findings*, OECD, Paris.

OECD (Organisation for Economic Cooperation and Development) (1985) *Environmental Data*, OECD, Paris.

OECD (Organisation for Economic Cooperation and Development) (1986) *Water Pollution by Fertilizers and Pesticides*, OECD, Paris, 144pp.

Okun, D. A. (1977) *Regionalization of Water Management*, Applied Science Publishers, London, 377pp.

Oliver, B. G. (1978) Chlorinated non-volatile organics produced by the reaction of chlorine with humic materials, *Cancer Research* **11**, 21–2.

Oliver, J. (1967) The application of the T.V.A. experience to underdeveloped countries, in Moore, J. R. (ed.) *The Economic Impact of the T.V.A.*, University of Tennessee Press, Knoxville, 163pp.

OMVS (1978) *Hydro Agricultural Projects in the Senegal River Basin*, OMVS, Dakar, Senegal.

Ontario Ministry of Environment (1980) *The Case Against Acid Rain*, Information Services Branch, Ministry of Environment, Ottawa, 24pp.

Ontario Ministry of Natural Resources (1987) Natural resources Minister announces 1987 funding for Conservation Authorities, *News Release*, 25 February.

O'Riordan, T. (1976) *Environmentalism*, Pion, London.

Ormerod, S. and Edwards, R. W. (1985) Stream acidity in some areas of Wales in relation to historical trends in afforestation and the usage of agricultural limestone, *Journal of Environmental Management* **20**, 189–97.

OTAD (Office of Tributary Area Development) (1978) What is tributary area development?, *Tributary Area Development Newsletter* **2(3)**, 1.

Ott, H., Geiss, F. and Town, W. G. (1978) The environmental chemicals data and information network (E.C.D.I.N.) and related activities of the European Communities, in Hutzinger, O., Van Lelyveld, I. H. and Zoeteman, B. O. J. (eds) *Aquatic Pollutants:*

*Transformation and Biological Effects*, Pergamon, Oxford, pp. 33–8.

Owen, M. (1973) The Tennessee Valley Authority, Praeger Publishers, London, 275pp.

Page, T., Harris, R. H. and Epstein, S. S. (1976) Drinking water and cancer mortality in Louisiana, *Science* **193**, 55–7.

Palmer, M. D. (1985) *Eastern Beaches Study 1984*, Gorre and Storrie Ltd, Consulting Engineers, Toronto, 236pp.

Palmer, M. D., Lock, J. D. and Gowda, T. P. H. (1984) The use of bacteriological indicators for swimming water quality, *Water and Pollution Control* (June), 14–16.

Pantulu, V. R. (1983) River basin management, *Ambio* **12(2)**, 109–11.

Paperna, I. (1970) Study of an outbreak of schistosomiasis in the newly formed Volta Lake Ghana, *Zeitschrift für Tropenmedizin und Parasitologie* **21**, 411–25.

Parker, D. J. and Harding, D. M. (1979) Natural hazard evaluation. *Geography* **64(4)**, 307–16.

Parker, D. J. and Penning-Rowsell, E. C. (1980) *Water Planning in Britain*, George Allen and Unwin, London, 227pp.

Parsons, R. M. Co. (1975) *North American Water and Power Alliance. Vol. I. Engineering*, File No. 606-2943-19.

Patterson, S. (1983) Franklin Valley not so special. *Nature* **304**, 354.

Paxton, J. (ed.) (1984) *The Statesman's Yearbook 1984*, Macmillan, London, 1692pp.

Pearce, D. (1982) *Watershed: the Water Crisis in Britain*, Junction Books, London, 208pp.

Pearse, P. H., Bertrand, F. and MacLaren, J. W. (1985) *Currents of Change: Final Report Inquiry on Federal Water Policy*, Canadian Government, Ottawa, 222pp.

Pearson, D. and Walsh, P. D. (1981) The implementation and application of a suite for the simulation of complex water resources systems in evaluation and planning studies, in Askew, A. J., Greco, F. and Kindler, J. (eds) *Logistics and Benefits of Using Mathematical Models of Hydrologic and Water Resource Systems*, Pergamon, London, pp. 213–28.

Pentland, R. L. and Long, B. L. (1978) Boundary waters management, in United Nations, *Water Development and Management Proceedings of the United Nations Water Conference. Mar del Plata, Argentina, March 1977*, Pergamon, London.

Pereira, L. M., Sabatier, P. and Oliveira, E. (1982) *O.R.B.I. An Expert System for Environmental Resource Evaluation through Natural Language*, Report 3-82, Portugal, Universidade de Lisboa.

Perfect, J. (1980) The environmental effects of D.D.T. in a tropical agro-ecosystem. *Ambio* **9(1)**, 16–21.

Perrault, P. (1674) *De l'origine des fontaines*, Paris.

Peters, P. E. (1984) Struggles over water, struggles over meaning – cattle water and the state of Botswana, *Africa* **54(3)**, 29.

PHLS (Public Health Laboratory Service) (1959) Sewage contamination of coastal bathing waters in England and Wales: a bacteriological and epidemiological study, *Journal of Hygiene*, Cambridge **57(4)**, 435–72.

Pickering, R. J. (1983) Why study organic substances in water, in Greeson, P. G. (ed.) *Organic Substances in Water*, United States Geological Survey Circular 848-6, pp. 3–4.

Pigram, J. J. (1986) *Issues in the Management of Australia's Water Resources*, Longman Cheshire, Melbourne.

Pike, E. B. (1985) *Coastal Sewage Pollution in Wales*, House of Commons Welsh Affairs Committee, Minutes of Evidence, 5 December 1984, p. 11.

Platt, R. H. (1976) The National Flood Insurance Program: some mid-stream perspectives, *Journal of the American Institute of Planners* **42(2)**, 303–13.

Platt, R. H. (1982) The Jackson flood of 1979: a public policy disaster, *Journal of the American Planning Association* **48**, 219–31.

PLUARG (Pollution from Land Use Activities Research Group) (1983) *Nonpoint Source Pollution Abatement in the Great Lakes Basin: an Overview of Post-P.L.U.A.R.G. Developments*, Report to the Great Lakes Water Quality Board of the International

References

Joint Commission, Windsor, Ontario, 129pp.

Pocock, S. J., Shaper, A. G., Cook, D. G., Packham, R. F., Lacey, R. F., Powell, P. and Russell, P. F. (1980) British regional heart study geographic variations in cardiovascular mortality, and the role of water quality, *British Medical Journal* 24 May, 1243–9.

Porter, E. A. (1978) *Water Management in England and Wales*, Cambridge University Press, Cambridge.

Postel, S. (1985) Managing freshwater supplies, in Anon, *State of the World*, Norton, New York, p. 42.

Powers, F. B. and Shows, E. W. (1979) A status report on the National Flood Insurance Program – mid 1978, *The Journal of Risk and Insurance* **46(2)**, 61–76.

Price, L. (1984) Scottish customers reap nuclear benefits, *Atom* **335**, 30.

Privett, D. W. (1959) Monthly charts of evaporation from the N. Indian ocean, *Quarterly Journal of the Royal Meteorological Society* **85**, 424–8.

Privett, D. W. (1960) The exchange of heat energy between the atmosphere and oceans of the southern hemisphere, *Geophysical Memoirs* **13(104)**, 1–61.

Probst, J. L. (1985) Nitrogen and phosphorus exploration in the Garonne basin (France), *Journal of Hydrology* **76**, 281–305.

Proudman, J. (1962) *The Final Report of the Sub-Committee on the Growing Demand for Water*, HMSO, London.

Pudlis, E. (1983) Poland's plight: environment damaged from air pollution and acid rain, *Ambio* **12(12)**, 125–7.

Quigg, P. W. (1977) A water agenda to the year 2000, *Common Ground* **3(4)**, 11–16.

Radosovich, G. E. (1979) Western water law, *Water Spectrum* **11(3)**, 1–9.

Ramsey, C. L., Reggia, J. A., Nau, D. S. and Ferrentio, A. (1986) A comparative analysis of methods for expert systems, *International Journal of Man Machine Studies* **24(5)**, 475–99.

Rao, S. K. (1986) The Rajghay dam: an environmental assessment, in Goldsmith, E. E. and Hildyard, N. (eds) *The Social and Environmental Effects of Large Dams*, Wadebridge Ecological Centre, UK, pp. 217–23.

Rees, J. A. (1976) Rethinking our approach to water supply provision, *Geography* **61**, 232–45.

Reid, G. W. (1981) Model for the selection of appropriate technology for a water resource system, in Askew, A. J., Greco, F. and Kinder, J. (eds) *Logistics and Benefits of Using Mathematical Models of Hydrologic and Water Resource Systems*, Pergamon, London, pp. 115–28.

Renne, R. R. (1967) Research guidelines to sound watershed management, *Journal of the Irrigation and Drainage Division, American Society of Civil Engineers* **93**, 53–8.

Renshaw, E. F. (1982) Conserving water through pricing, *Journal of the American Water Works Association* **74(1)**, 2–5.

Robie, R. B. (1980) The impact of federal water policy on state planning: a cautionary example, *Journal of the American Water Works Association* **72(2)**, 70–3.

Robinson, J. F. (1984) *A Review of Land Use Farming and Fisheries in the Esk and Duddon Valleys*, North West Water Authority, Rivers Division, Water Quality North, October, 22pp.

Robinson, M. (1981) Initiating and promoting activities of chemicals isolated from drinking waters in the Sencar mouse: a five city survey, in Sandhu, S. S. (ed.) *Application of Short-Term Bioassays in the Analysis of Complex Environmental Mixtures. Vol. II*, Plenum, New York.

Robock, S. H. (1967) An unfinished task: a socio-economic evaluation of the T.V.A. experiment, in Moore, J. R. (ed.) *The Economic Impact of T.V.A.*, University of Tennessee Press, Knoxville, pp. 106–20.

Rodda, J. C. (1974) Data collection systems and their impact on the future development of hydrology, in United Nations, *Three Centuries of Scientific Hydrology*, UNESCO–WMO/OMM–IAHS/AISH, Paris, pp. 80–8.

Rodda, J. C. (1976) Basin studies, in Rodda, J. C. (ed.) *Facets of Hydrology*, Wiley, London, pp. 257–97.

Rodda, J. C., Downing, R. A. and Law, F. M. (1976) *Systematic Hydrology*, Newnes Butterworth, London, 399pp.

Roder, W. (1965) *The Sabi Valley Irrigation Projects*, University of Chicago, Department of Geography, Chicago.

Rondinelli, D. A. and Ruddle, K. (1978) Coping with poverty in international assistance policy: an evaluation of spatially integrated investment strategies, *World Development* **6**, 479–97.

Ronner, U. (1985) Nitrogen transformations in the Baltic proper: denitrification counteracts eutrophication, *Ambio* **14(3)**, 134–38.

Rosenqvist, I. (1981) Alternative sources for acidification of river water in Norway. *Science of the Total Environment* **10**, 39–49.

Rostvedt, J. O. *et al.* (1968) *A Summary of Floods in the United States during 1983*, USGS Water Supply Paper 1830-B.

Rothschild (1979) Risk, *Atom* **268**, 30–5.

Royal Society (1983) *The Nitrogen Cycle in the United Kingdom*, The Royal Society, London, 263pp.

Russell, C., Arey, D. and Kates, R. W. (1970) *Drought and Water Supply*, John Hopkins Press, New York.

Russell, D. B. (1976) Water and man, *Alternatives* **5**, 4–14.

Rutter, A. J. (1963) Studies in the water relations of *Pinus sylvestris* in plantation conditions, *Journal of Ecology* **51**, 191–203.

Rutter, A. J., Kershaw, K. A., Robins, P. C. and Morton, A. J. (1971) A predictive model of rainfall interception in forests. I Derivation of the model from observations in a plantation of Corsican pine, *Agricultural Meteorology* **9**, 367–84.

Rutter, A. J., Morton, A. J. and Robins, P. C. (1975) A predictive model of rainfall interception in forests. II Generalisation of the model and comparison with observations in some coniferous and hardwood stands, *Journal of Applied Ecology* **12**, 367–80.

Rutter, A. J. and Morton, A. J. (1977) A predictive model of rainfall interception in forests. III Sensitivity of the model to stand parameters and meteorological variables, *Journal of Applied Ecology* **14**, 567–88.

Sabato, J. A. and Ramesh, J. (1979) *Third World Energy Strategies*, Royal Society Forum, London.

Saha, S. K. (1981) River basin planning as a field of study: design of a course structure for practitioners, in Saha, S. K. and Barrow, C. J. (eds) *River Basin Planning: Theory and Practice*, Wiley, London, pp. 9–40.

Saha, S. K. and Barrow, C. J. (eds) (1981) *River Basin Planning: Theory and Practice*, Wiley, London, 357pp.

Saha, S. K. and Barrow, C. J. (1981) Introduction, in Saha, S. K. and Barrow, C. J. (eds) *River Basin Planning: Theory and Practice*, Wiley, London, pp. 1–8.

Salanetz, L. W. (1965) Correlation of coliform and faecal streptococci indices with the presence of Salmonella and enteric viruses in seawater and shellfish, *Advances in Water Pollution Research* **3**, 17.

Samuels, T. A. and Kerr, G. C. (1980) Forecasting techniques in developing countries, in ICE, *Water Resources a Changing Strategy*, Institution of Civil Engineers, London, pp. 49–59.

Sandbach, F. (1980) *Environment, Ideology and Policy*, Basil Blackwell, Oxford, 254pp.

Saunders, R. J. and Warford, J. J. (1976) *Village Water Supply: Economics and Policy in the Developing World*, The John Hopkins University Press, Baltimore, 279pp.

Schlesinger, A. M. (1957) *The Coming of the New Deal*, Houghton Mifflin, Boston.

References

Schumacher, E. F. (1973) *Small is Beautiful: a Study of Economics as if People Mattered*, Bland and Briggs, London.

Schumacher, E. F. and McRobie, G. (1969) Intermediate technology and its administrative implications, *Journal of Administration Overseas* **8**, 89–96.

Scudder, T. (1973) Summary: resettlement, in Ackermann, W. C., White, G. F. and Worthington, E. F. (eds) *Man Made Lakes: their Problems and Environmental Effects*, American Geophysical Union, Washington, DC, pp. 707–19.

SDD (Scottish Development Department) (1973) *A Measure of Plenty, Water Resources in Scotland: a General Survey*, HMSO, Scotland.

Sears, F. W., Zemansky, M. W. and Young, H. D. (1974) *College Physics Part 1*. Fourth Edition. Addison Wesley, Reading, Massachusetts. 317pp.

Seip, H. M. and Tollan, A. (1985) Acid deposition, in Rodda, J. C. (ed.) *Facets of Hydrology Vol. II*, Wiley, London, pp. 69–98.

Sellars, B. and Newsum, D. (1980) Energy resources – are we planning for the future? – a review, *Energy Research* **4**, 225–33.

Selznick, P. (1949) *T.V.A. and the Grass Roots, a Study in the Sociology of Formal Organisations*, University of California Press, 274pp.

Sewell, W. R. D. (1966) The Columbia river treaty: some lessons and implications, *Canadian Geographer* **10(3)**, 145–56.

Sewell, W. R. D. and Barr, L. R. (1978) Water administration in England and Wales: impacts of reorganisation, *Water Resources Bulletin* **14(2)**, 337–48.

Sewell, W. R. D., Coppock, J. T. and Pitkethly, A. (1985) *Institutional Innovation in Water Management: the Scottish Experience*, Geo Books, Norwich, 160pp.

Seyfried, P. (1980) *A Study of Disease Incidence and Recreational Water Quality in the Great Lakes Phase I*, Report 67–81, Health and Welfare Canada, Ottawa, 161pp.

Shaeffer (1960) *Flood Proofing*, University of Chicago, Department of Geography, Research Paper No. 65.

Shamir, U. (1977) Water research in Israel: achievements and potential, *Kidma* **3(10)**, 11–15.

Shapley, D. (1976) T.V.A. today: former reformers in an era of expensive electricity, *Science* **194**, 814–18.f

Sharman, T. (1984) Taming the Tisza river, *Geographical Magazine* (January), 21–8.

Sharpe, R. G. (1978) Planning and management of river basin resource systems, *Journal of the Institution of Water Engineers and Scientists* **32(5)**, 405–20.

Sharpe, R. G. (1980) The benefits of integrated resource systems, in ICE, *Water Resources a Changing Strategy*, Institution of Civil Engineers, London, pp. 77–84.

Shiklomanov, I. A. (1985) Large scale water transfers, in Rodda, J. C. (ed.) *Facets of Hydrology Vol. II*, Wiley, London, pp. 345–87.

Shoval, P. (1986) Comparison of decision support strategies in expert consultation systems, *International Journal of Man Machine Studies* **24(4)**, 125–39.

Shuval, H. I. (ed.) (1980) *Water Quality Management under Conditions of Scarcity*, Academic Press, London, 352pp.

Shuval, H. I. (1980) General goals of water quality control, in Shuval, H. I. (ed.) *Water Quality Management under Conditions of Scarcity*, Academic Press, London, pp. 1–10.

Shuval, H. I. and Gruener, N. (1972) Epidemiological and toxicological aspects of nitrates and nitrites in the environment, *American Journal of Public Health* **62**, 1045–52.

Skinner, B. J. (1969) *Earth Resources*, Prentice Hall, Englewood Cliffs.

Smith, D. I. and Handmer, J. W. (1983) Health hazards of floods; hospital admissions for Lismore. *Australian Geographical Studies* **21**, 221–30.

Smith, E. D. (1982) Water characteristics: acid rain, *Journal of the Water Pollution Control Federation* (June), 541–3.

Smith, K. (1972) *Water in Britain: a Study in Applied Hydrology and Resource Geography*, Macmillan, London.

Smith, K. and Tobin, G. (1978) *Human Adjustment to the Flood Hazard*, Longmans, London.

Smith, R. J. (1974) Some comments on domestic metering, *Journal of the Institution of Water Engineers and Scientists* **28**, 47–53.

Smith, R. J. (1977) Demand studies in water resources, *Proceedings of the Institution of Civil Engineers* **62(1)**, 331–3.

Snow, J. (1855) *On the Mode of Communication of Cholera*, 2nd edn, J. Churchill, London.

Somlyody, L. and Straten van. G. (eds) (1986) *Modelling and Managing Shallow Lake Eutrophication*, Springer-Verlag, Berlin, 386pp.

SONADER (1977) *Annual Report*, Ministère d'Etat Chargé du Dévelopment Rural, Novakchott, Mauritania.

Stanfield, G. (1982) Disposal of sewage from coastal towns, *Journal of the Royal Society of Health* **2**, 53–8.

Starfield, A. M. and Bleloch, A. L. (1983) Expert systems: an approach to problems in ecological management that are difficult to quantify, *Journal of Environmental Management* **16**, 261–8.

Sterling, M. J. H. and Antcliffe, D. J. (1977) A technique for the prediction of water demand, *Proceedings of the Institution of Civil Engineers* **62(1)**, 331–421.

Stevenson, A. J. (1953) Studies of bathing water quality and health, *Journal of the American Public Health Association* **43**, 529–34.

Stone, B. (1986) China's Chang Jiang Diversion project: an overview of economic and environmental issues, in Goldsmith, E. and Hildyard, N. (eds) *The Social and Environmental Effects of Large Dams. Vol. 2 Case Studies*, Wadebridge Ecological Centre, UK, pp. 314–25.

Stone, B. G. (1978) Suppression of water use by physical methods, *Journal of the American Water Works Association* **70**, 483–6.

Stoner, J. H. (1983) *Acid Precipitation and the Effects on Aquatic Life with Special Reference to Rivers in Wales*, evidence submitted by Welsh Water Authority to the Royal Commission on Environmental Pollution, July, 9pp.

Stoner, J. H. and Gee, A. S. (1985) The effects of forestry on water quality and fisheries in Welsh rivers and lakes, *Journal of the Institution of Water Engineers and Scientists* **39**, 27–46.

Stott, P. F. (1980) Water resources in England and Wales – recent experience and current strategy, in ICE, *Water Resources a Changing Strategy*, Institution of Civil Engineers. London, pp. 3–6.

Street, E. (1981) The role of electricity in the Tennessee Valley Authority, in Saha, S. K. and Barrow, C. J. (eds) *River Basin Planning: Theory and Practice*, Wiley, London, pp. 233–52.

Stumm, W. (1986) Water an integrated ecosystem, *Ambio* **15(4)**, 201–7.

Sultter, V. L., Hurst, V. and Lane, C. M. (1967) Qualification of *Pseudomonas aeruginosa* in faeces of healthy human adults, *Health Laboratory Sciences* **4**, 245–9.

Super, M., Heese, H. V., Mackenzie, D., Dempster, W. S., Plessis, J. and Ferreira, J. J. (1981) An epidemiological study of well water nitrates in a group of South West African/Namibian infants, *Water Research* **15**, 1265–70.

Swainson, N. A. (1979) *Conflict over the Columbia: The Canadian Background to an Historic Treaty*, McGill-Queens University Press, Montreal, 416pp.

Swank, W. T. and Caskey, W. H. (1982) Nitrate depletion in a second order mountain stream, *Journal of Environmental Quality* **11(4)**, 581–4.

Swedish Ministry of Agriculture (1982a) *Acidification Today and Tomorrow*, a Swedish study prepared for the 1982 Stockholm conference on the acidification of the environment, Swedish Ministry of Agriculture, Environment '82 Committee, 231pp.

Swedish Ministry of Agriculture (1982b) Stockholm conference on acidification of the environment, *Proceedings*, Swedish Ministry of Agriculture S-10333, Stockholm, 128pp.

References

Szesztay, K. (1976) Towards water demand management, *Hydrological Sciences Bulletin.* **21**, 491–6.

Szolovitz, P. (1981) *Artificial Intelligence in Medicine*, Westview Press, Boulder.

Tattersall, K. H. (1980) Resource management of an industrial river system, *Journal of the Institute of Water Engineers and Scientists* **34(5)**, 453–73.

Taylor, B. W. (1973) People in a rapidly changing environment; the first six years of lake Volta, in Ackermann, W. C., White, G. F. and Worthington, E. B. (eds) *Man Made Lakes: their Problems and Environmental Effects*, American Geophysical Union, Washington, DC, pp. 99–107.

Teclaff, L. (1976) Harmonising water resource development and use with environmental protection in municipal and international law, *Natural Resources Journal* **16**, 807–58.

Telling, A. E. (1974) *Water Authorities*, Butterworths, London, 152pp.

Thackray, J. E., Cocker, V. and Archibald, G. (1978) The Malvern and Mansfield studies of domestic water usage, *Proceedings of the Institution of Civil Engineers* **64(1)**, 37–61.

Thomas, K., Maurer, D., Fishbein, M., Otway, H. J., Hinkle, R. and Simpson, D. (1980) *A Comparative Study of Public Beliefs about Five Energy Systems*, Report RR-80-15, IIASA, Laxenburg, Austria.

Thomson, H. A. and Wycherley, R. E. (1972) *The Athenian Agora: Results of the Excavation Conducted by the American School of Classical Studies at Athens Vol XIV*, American School of Classical Studies at Athens, Princeton, NJ.

Thornthwaite, C. W. (1962–5) *Average climatic water balance data for the continents.* Part I *Africa* (1962), Part II *Asia* (1963), Part III *U.S.S.R.* (1963), Part IV *Australia* (1963), Part V *Europe* (1964), Part VI *North America (excluding U.S.A.)* (1964), Part VII *United States* (1964), Part VIII *South America* (1965), C. W. Thornthwaite Associates, Centreton, New Jersey.

Thynne, J. (1977) Technology and the environment: water, *Reports for the D.O.I.*, Aspell House, London.

Todorov, A. V. (1985) Sahel: the changing rainfall regime and the 'normals' used for assessment, *Journal of Climate and Applied Meteorology* **24(2)**, 97–107.

Tollan, A. (1981) Effects of acid precipitation on inland waters, *Geojournal* **5(5)**, 409–16.

Tomlinson, T. E. (1970) Trends in nitrate concentrations in English rivers in relation to fertilizer use, *Water Treatment and Examinations* **19**, 277–89.

Toms, R. G., Saunders, C. L. and Hodges, E. (1981) The control of bacterial pollution caused by sea discharges of sewage, *Water Pollution Control* **80(2)**, 204–20.

Tou, J. T. and Cheng, J. M. (1983) *Design of a Knowledge Based Expert System for Applications in Agriculture*, IEEE Computer Society, Gaithersberg, Maryland.

Train, R. E. (1980) *Quality Criteria for Water*, Castle House Publications, London, 256pp.

Tugwell, R. G. and Banfield, E. C. (1950) Grass roots democracy – myth or reality? *Public Administration Review* **10**, 47–55.

TVA (Tennessee Valley Authority) (1972) *Tributary Area Development: Office of Tributary Area Development T.A.D. Organisations*, TVA, Knoxville.

TVA (Tennessee Valley Authority) (1972) *Review of T.V.A. Load Growth/Plant Construction Situation*, TVA 135pp.

TVA (Tennessee Valley Authority) (1981) *Power Programme Summary*, TVA, Knoxville, 56pp.

TVA (Tennessee Valley Authority) (1982) *Growth of the System*, statistics provided by power planning staff dated November 1981, personal communication, September 1982.

UKAWRG (United Kingdom Acid Waters Review Group) (1986) *Acidity in United Kingdom Fresh Waters*, Department of the Environment, London, 46pp.

United Nations (1970) *Integrated River Basin Development: Report of a Panel of Experts*, Department of Economic and Social Affairs, New York.

United Nations (1978a) *Proceedings of the United Nations Water Conference, Mar del Plata, Argentina, Part II*, Paper E/CONF. 70/A.19, *Water Women and Development*,

Pergamon, London, pp. 791–809.

United Nations (1978b) *Proceedings of the United Nations Water Conference, Mar del Plata, Argentina, Part I*, Paper E/CONF. 70/CBP/1, *Resources and Needs: Assessment of the World Water Situation*, Pergamon, London, pp. 1–46.

United Nations (1978c) *Proceedings of the United Nations Water Conference. Mar del Plata, Argentina, Parts I, II, III and IV*, Pergamon, London, 2646pp.

United Nations (1979) The role of the United Nations in water resources development, *GeoJournal* **3(5)**, 471–9.

United Nations (1980) *Register of International Rivers*, Pergamon, London, 55pp.

United Nations (1982) *The World Environment (1972–1982): a Report by the United Nations Environment Programme*, Tycooly International Publishing Ltd, Dublin, 637pp.

Unwin, D. J. and Dawson, J. A. (1985) *Computer Programming for Geographers*, Longman, London, 252pp.

USGS (United States Geological Survey) (1983) *Organic Substances in Water*, USGS Survey Circular 848-C, 19pp.

USDA (United States Department of Agriculture) (1976) *Proceedings of the First International Symposium on Acid Precipitation and the Forest Ecosystem*, USDA Forest Service, Technical Report NE23, 1074pp.

USDA (United States Department of Agriculture) (1981) *The Yearbook of Agriculture*, USDA, Washington, DC.

USSR National Committee for the International Hydrological Decade (1974) *World Water Balance and Water Resources of the Earth*, Leningrad, USSR.

Van Kessel, J. F. (1977) Factors affecting the denitrification rate in two water sediment systems, *Water Research* **11**, 259–67.

Vernadsky, V. I. (1964) *History of minerals in the Earth's Crust Vol. 2. History of Natural Waters*, Moscow.

Volta River Preparatory Commission (1956) *Report of the Preparatory Commission Vol. I and Vol. II*, HMSO, London.

Vriksh, R. (1986) The Narmada valley project: development or destruction? in Goldsmith, E. E. and Hildyard, N. (eds) *The Social and Environmental Effects of Large Dams*, Wadebridge Ecological Centre, UK, pp. 224–44.

Waddy, B. B. (1975) Mosquitoes, malaria and man, in Stanley, N. F. and Alpers, M. P., *Man Made Lakes and Human Health*, Academic Press, London, pp. 7–20.

Walesh, S. G. (1979) Flood insurance program: regional agencies perspective, *American Society of Civil Engineers Journal of the Water Resources Planning and Management Division* **105(WR2)**, 243–57.

Wallace, J. M. and Hobbs, P. V. (1977) *Atmospheric Science: an Introductory Survey*, Academic Press, London, 467pp.

Wallace, J. S., Roberts, J. M. and Roberts, A. M. (1982) *Evaporation from Heather Moorlands in North Yorkshire, England*, Proceedings of the Berne International Symposium on Hydrological Research Basins and Their Use in Water Resources Planning and Management.

Walling, D. E. and Foster, I. D. L. (1978) The 1976 drought and nitrate levels in the river Exe basin, *Journal of the Institute of Water Engineers and Scientists* **32**, 341–52.

Walsh, P. D. (1980) The impacts of catchment afforestation on water supply interests, *Aqua* **4**, 82–5.

Walsh, P. D. (1987) The effects of catchment land use on water yield: a practitioner's perspective, in Kay, D. and McDonald, A. T. (eds) *British Upland Catchment Research*, mimeographed, 156pp.

Ward, B. (1977) *The Economist*.

Ward, R. C. (1978) *Floods: a Geographical Perspective*, Macmillan, London, 244pp.

Water Act (1973) HMSO, London.

Watt, S. B. (1981) Peripheral problems in the Senegal valley, in Saha, S. K. and Barrow, C. J. (eds) *River Basin Planning*, Wiley, London, 357pp.

References

Waxler, N. E. (1985) Infant mortality in Sri Lankan households: a causal model, *Social Science and Medicine* **20(4)**, 381–92.

Webbe, G. (1972) Schistsomiasis, in Miller, M. J. (ed.) *Proceedings of a Symposium on the Future of Schistsomiasis Control*, Tulane University Press, New York.

Weeks, C. R. and McMahon, T. A. (1973) A comparison of urban water use in Australia and the U.S., *Journal of the American Water Works Association* **65**, 231–7.

Weeks, W. F. and Campbell, W. J. (1973) Icebergs as a freshwater source: an appraisal, *Journal of Glaciology* **12(65)**, 207–33.

Welsh Water (1984) *The Twyi Fisheries Scheme*, internal unpublished report, Llanelli Area Laboratory, Furnass, Llanelli, UK.

Welsh Water (1985) *Coastal Sewage Pollution in Wales*, minutes of Evidence to the Commons Welsh Affairs Committee, 5 December 1984, HMSO, London, pp. 18–97.

Welsh Water (1986a) Project reports and minutes, Llyn Brianne project, unpublished, Llanelli Laboratory, Penefai House, Dyfed, UK.

Welsh Water (1986b) *A Survey of Water Quality on Welsh Beaches During the 1985 Bathing Season*, unpublished internal report, Aberaeron Laboratory, Dyfed, UK.

Wemelsfelder, P. J. (1939) Wetmatigheden in het optreden van stormloeden, *Ingenieurs Grav* **44**, 6–13.

Werner, D. (1985) Psycho-social stress and the construction of a flood control dam in Santa Catarina, Brazil, *Human Organisation* **44(2)**, 161–7.

Westing, A. H. (ed.) (1986) *Global Resources and International Conflict*, Oxford University Press, Oxford.

Westmann, N. N. (1985) *Ecology and Environmental Impact Assessment*, Wiley, New York.

Wheater, D. W. F., Mara, D. D. and Oragui, J. (1979) Indicator systems to distinguish sewage from stormwater runoff and human from animal faecal material, in James, A. and Evison, L. (eds) *Biological Indicators of Water Pollution*, Wiley, London, Chapter 21, 27pp.

Wheeler, D. (1986) Water pollution and public health: a time to act, *Environmental Health* **94(8)**, 201–3.

White, G. F. (ed.) (1977) *Environmental Effects of Complex River Developments*, Westview Press, Colorado, 172pp.

White, G. F., Bradley, D. T. and White, A. U. (1972) *Drawers of Water: Domestic Water Use in East Africa*, University of Chicago Press, Chicago, 306pp.

White, W. R. and Godfree, A. F. (1985) Pollution of freshwaters and estuaries, *Journal of Applied Bacteriology Symposium Supplement No. 14*, S67–S80.

White, G. F. and Haas, J. E. (1975) *Assessment of Research on Natural Hazards*, M.I.T. Press, Cambridge, Massachusetts, 487pp.

WHO (World Health Organisation) (1970) *Health Criteria for the Quality of Recreational Water with Special Reference to Coastal Waters and Beaches*, WHO/W.POLL/72.10, 26pp.

WHO (World Health Organisation) (1981) *Drinking Water Sanitation: a Way to Health*, World Health Organisation, Geneva.

WHO (World Health Organisation) (1984) *Guidelines for Drinking Water Quality Vol. I*, World Health Organisation, Geneva, 130pp.

WHO (World Health Organisation) (1986) *World Health Statistics* **39(1)**, 117pp.

Wilkinson, W. B. and Greene, L. A. (1982) The water industry and the nitrogen cycle, *Philosophical Transactions of the Royal Society London* **B296**, 459–75.

Williams, A. (1985) Legal administrative and economic tools for conflict resolution – perspectives on river basin management in industrialized countries, in Lundqvist, J., Lohm, U. and Falkenmark, M. (eds) *Strategies for River Basin Management Environmental Integration of Land and Water in a River Basin*, D. Reidel Publishing Company, Lancaster, pp. 201–8.

Williams, P. (1986) Introduction, in Goldsmith, E. and Hildyard, N. (eds) *The Social and Environmental Effects of Large Dams*, Wadebridge Ecological Centre, Cornwall, UK, pp. 9–16.

Wilson, A. G. (1981) *Geography and the Environment*, John Wiley, Chichester, 297pp.

Wilson, A. G., Clarke, M. E. and McDonald, A. T. (1986) *Networking Systems and Performance Indicators*, a submission to Yorkshire Water in association with Howard Humphries Engineering (mimeographed).

Wisdom, A. S. and Skeet, J. L. G. (1981) *The Law and Management of Water Resources and Supply*, Shaw and Sons, London, 275pp.

WMO (World Meteorological Office) (1973) *Snow Survey from Earth Satellites*, WMO/IHD, Project Report No. 19, 42pp.

WMO (World Meteorological Office) (1974) *Three Centuries of Scientific Hydrology*, UNESCO/WMO, 123pp.

Wolman, A. (1981) Some reflections on river basin management, *Progress in Water Technology* **13(3)**, 1–6.

Wood, L. B. (1982) *Restoration of the Tidal Thames*, Hilgar Press, London.

WRI (World Resources Institute) (1986) *World Resources 1986*, Basic Books, New York.

Wyer, M. D. and Hill, A. R. (1984) Nitrate transformations in Southern Ontario stream sediments, *Water Resources Bulletin* **20(5)**, 729–37.

Xiaozhang, Z., Lin, B., Zengguong, Z. and Naibai, Z. (1982) The experiences of small hydro-power construction in China, in Yuan, S. W. (ed.) *Energy Resources and Environment*, Pergamon, London.

Yegorov, A. N. (1983) Marginal cost estimates of the water resources of the U.S.S.R., *Vodnyye Resursy* **5**, 198–204.

Yorkshire Water (1986) *Annual Report and Accounts*, Yorkshire Water, Leeds, 36pp.

Young, C. P. (1981) The distribution and movement of solutes derived from agricultural land in the principal aquifers of the United Kingdom, with particular reference to nitrate, *Water Science and Technology* **13**, 1137–52.

Youngman, R. E. and Lack, T. (1981) New problems with upland waters, *Water Services* **85**, 13–14.

Zakharov, V. F. (1976) Arctic cooling and the ice cover of Arctic seas [in Russian] *Tr. Arkt. Antarkt. Nauchno-Issled Inst.* **34**, 183–96.

Zon, R. (1927) *Forests and Water in the Light of Scientific Investigation*, Washington DC, US Government Printing Office.

# Index

Index

# Index

Index

# Index

flooding in, 207, *208, 209*
map of, *206*
Seven Mile Project (Canada), 179, *180*
Severn River catchment (UK), 215–16, *215*
  catchment study, 22–5
  nitrate concentrations in, *153*
  supply/demand trends, *216*
Severn Trent Water Authority (UK), *212*
  Dove/Derwent system, 213–15, *214*
  Severn catchment area, 215–16, *215, 216*
sewage treatment, 136
shellfish-growing waters, microbiological
    characteristics of, 140
size (of projects), 224–5
small-scale schemes, 66–86, 225
  integration within, 241–2
societal impact (of projects), 225
soft water, effects of, 137
soil moisture
  as percentage of global resource, *13*
  recycling times for, *19*
solar energy
  cost comparisons for, *172, 174*
  hydro-power as indirect form of, 171
  safety of, *177, 178*
South Africa
  water availability in, *58*
  water use in, *60*
South-east Asia
  sanitation trends in, *83, 88*
  supply trends in, *81, 87*
Soviet . . ., *see* USSR
Spain, wastewater treatment in, *65*
specific heat capacity, water compared with
    other terrestrial compounds, 10, *11*
Stocks Reservoir (UK), catchment study, *21*,
  21–2, *23, 29*
storage systems, small-scale, 75, *77, 78*
storms, effects of, 12
Stour river (UK), nitrate in, *153, 155*
strategies, 230–8
  developed countries, 230–5
  less-developed countries, 235, 237–8
structure (of this book), 5, 7
Sudbury (Canada), nickel smelter at, 161, 162
sulphur oxides, 159
  *see also* acidic precipitation
supply problems
  lessons to be learnt, 107, 109–10
  non-structural approaches to, 103–7
    demand forecasting, 105–6
    demand management, 107
  scale of, 5, 56–65
  structural approaches to, 66–103
    large-scale schemes, 86–103
    small-scale schemes, 66–*86*
Swaziland, water usage survey, 67
Sweden
  wastewater treatment in, *65*
  water availability in, *58*

Switzerland, wastewater treatment in, *65*
Szesztay (water resource development) model,
  103–4, *104*

Tahal (Israeli agency), 47
Tame river (UK), nitrate in, *155*
Tanzania, contamination of water in, *141*
technology
  hydro-power potential affected by, 180
  *see also* appropriate technology
technology transfer, 226
Tennessee Valley Authority (TVA), 193–200
  assessment of, 198, 200
  communications with local groups, 219–20
  context of, 193–4
  environmental impact of, 196, 200
  Force Account system used, 196
  funding of, 196–7
  historical analysis of, 194–8
  power demand growth, 200, *201*
  power-generating capacity, 196, *197*
  social aims of, 194, 195, 197–8, 219
  Tributary Area Development (TAD)
    scheme, 198, *199*, 219
Texas (USA), water rights in, 53
Thames river (UK)
  pollution of, 136, *153, 155*
  restoration/flood control work, 42, 115
Thetford (UK), catchment afforestation study,
  22, 25, *29*
Three Gorges project (China), 185
tidal power, 171–2
  cost comparison for, *172*
Tigris-Euphrates link, 1–2
topography, hydro-power potential affected
  by, 179
training and education, 235, 237
treatment systems, small-scale, 75, *78*
Trent river (UK), *214*
  nitrate in, *153*
trichloroeth[yl]ene, *148*, 156, *159*
trihalomethanes (THMs), *148*, 156, 158, *159*
tubewells, Indian use of, 71–3
Tukiangyen (China), irrigation system, 86, *89,
  90, 91, 92*
Tyne river (UK), nitrate in, *153*

Uganda, contamination of water in, *141*
UK
  acidic precipitation in, *166*, 169–70
  areas of conflict, *30*
  attitude to EEC Bathing Waters Directive,
    143, 145, 146, 170, 240
  attitude to emission control, 164
  bathing waters in, *147*
  beach pollution, clean-up costs, 146
  catchment studies, 20, 21–7
    sites listed, *21, 23*

## Index